Perfect Da

LONDON

Travel with **Insider Tips**

Contents

 TOP 10   4

That London Feeling   6

9

The Magazine
■ In the Flow of Life – On the Thames ■ Pub Life
■ Festive Spirits ■ City of Change
■ Urban Green ■ The Mark of Fame ■ Football Crazy
■ London's Best for Free ■ Live Sounds

33

Finding Your Feet
■ First Two Hours
■ Getting Around
■ Accommodation
■ Food and Drink
■ Shopping
■ Entertainment

47

St James's, Mayfair & Piccadilly
Getting Your Bearings ■ **The Perfect Day**
TOP 10 ■ Buckingham Palace ■ National Gallery
Don't Miss ■ The Mall/Trafalgar Square
At Your Leisure More places to explore
Where to... ■ Eat and Drink ■ Shop ■ Go Out

69

The City
Getting Your Bearings ■ **The Perfect Day**
TOP 10 ■ St Paul's Cathedral ■ Tower Bridge
Don't Miss ■ Tower of London
At Your Leisure More places to explore
Where to... ■ Eat and Drink ■ Shop ■ Go Out

93

Westminster & South Bank
Getting Your Bearings ■ **The Perfect Day**
TOP 10 ■ Westminster Abbey ■ London Eye
Don't Miss ■ Tate Britain ■ Houses of Parliament
■ SEA LIFE London Aquarium ■ Tate Modern
At Your Leisure More places to explore
Where to... ■ Eat and Drink ■ Shop ■ Go Out

119 **Knightsbridge, Kensington & Chelsea**
Getting Your Bearings ■ The Perfect Day
TOP 10 ■ Kensington Palace ■ V&A Museum
Don't Miss ■ Harrods ■ Science Museum
■ Natural History Museum
At Your Leisure More places to explore
Where to... ■ Eat and Drink ■ Shop ■ Go Out

145 **Covent Garden, Bloomsbury & Soho**
Getting Your Bearings ■ The Perfect Day
TOP 10 ■ Covent Garden ■ Madame Tussauds
Don't Miss ■ British Museum ■ British Library
At Your Leisure More places to explore
Where to... ■ Eat and Drink ■ Shop ■ Go Out

169 **Excursions**
■ Kew
■ Windsor

175 **Walks & Tours**
■ 1 Mayfair Squares
■ 2 The City
■ 3 Greenwich
■ 4 Hampstead
■ 5 The No 6 & No15 Bus Trip

Practicalities   195
■ Before You Go ■ When You are There

Street Atlas   201

Street Index   211

Index   219

Credits   213

10 Reasons to Come Back Again   214

For chapters: see inside front cover

TOP 10

Not to be missed!
Our top hits – from the absolute No. 1 to No. 10 –
help you plan your tour of the most important sights.

1 WESTMINSTER ABBEY ➤ 98

The splendour and rich history of this awe-inspiring coronation church right next to Big Ben and the Houses of Parliament makes it our number one place to see in London.

2 BUCKINGHAM PALACE ➤ 52

The Gate, the Palace, the Balcony – and then the view down the Mall: British monarchs have resided in this magnificent setting for over 250 years.

3 LONDON EYE ➤ 101

It is a moving experience in all senses. The Ferris Wheel provides a bird's-eye view of the city and is an ideal way to admire the successful mix of historic buildings and modern architecture.

4 COVENT GARDEN ➤ 150

The former market has developed into a lively venue for street music, theatres, restaurants and shops – a wonderful example of London's colourful street life.

5 ST PAUL'S CATHEDRAL ➤ 74

Walking beneath this awesome dome (left) is an absolutely breathtaking experience. You should not miss Christopher Wren's architectural masterpiece.

6 KENSINGTON PALACE ➤ 124

The royal residence, once home to Princess Diana, looks over Kensington Gardens and Hyde Park and is a lovely place to wander round, both inside and out.

7 NATIONAL GALLERY ➤ 54

Even without the highlights, such as *The Virgin of the Rocks* by Leonardo da Vinci or *Venus and Mars* by Botticelli, this world-class collection of paintings is quite simply amazing.

8 V&A MUSEUM ➤ 126

4000 years of history and exhibitions on design, fashion, photography, sculpture, ceramic art and furniture making, as well as an eclectic art collection: it is impossible not to be impressed.

9 MADAME TUSSAUDS ➤ 152

Feel like it is to be a Bond girl, cuddle up to the Beatles on the sofa or have your photograph taken with the Queen – it's all possible in the wax museum.

10 TOWER BRIDGE ➤ 78

The architectural and technical masterpiece elegantly connecting the Tower of London with the south banks of the Thames is a constant source of fascination.

THAT
LONDON

Find out what makes the city tick, experience its unique flair – just like the Londoners themselves.

PICNIC IN THE PARK

During the week, get yourself something to eat from one of the many sandwich shops, such as **Pret A Manger**, 54 Oxford Street (✚ 205 E2) and stroll to the next park, e. g. **Soho Square** (✚ 205 E2). It does not matter whether you sit on a bench or on the grass, you will experience a taste of real London life: from bank manager to building worker, everyone takes a break here to enjoy the sun or sit in the shade under a tree.

WANDER ALONG THE RIVER

Watch the activities on the river and on the opposite bank while you walk from the **Tate Britain** (➤ 102) south over the **Vauxhall Bridge** (✚ 199 F1). The fortress-like M16 headquarters was in the last James Bond film. On the right of the Thames, head north. Cross Lambeth Bridge towards **Lambeth Palace** (✚ 200 B1), the official residence of the Archbishop of Canterbury.

On the left bank, on the Thames Path (✚ 208 B1), you reach the Houses of Parliament (➤ 104).

TEA TIME WITH STYLE

Enjoy an afternoon treat in London: drinking tea in stylish surroundings. One of the nicest locations is the **Orangery Café** (10–5) in **Kensington Palace** (➤ 124). On dry days, you can sit on the terrace overlooking the garden and sip good English tea from finest porcelain and savour traditional sandwiches and scones with clotted cream.

IN THE WILD EAST

It is young and wild in East London: In **Shoreditch,** off-beat fashion shops have set up, in Spitalfields Market, designers offer their own labels in the "Style Market" (Sat, 11–5, Brushfield Street, ✚ 210 C5) and show that London is open to funky fashion and creative people. Look around you as you continue walking: From the **Fournier Street** (✚ 210 C5) turn left into **Brick Lane** and admire the Street Art in the side streets!

FEELING

Improvised clothes shops, Redchurch Street in Shoreditch

That London Feeling

OASIS OF CALM

An intensive sightseeing tour, for example from Westminster Abbey via Whitehall, Trafalgar Square and to Fleet Street is tiring. There is a small haven from the hustle and bustle of London opposite the Royal Courts of Justice at the entrance to the **Inns of Court** as well as the **Inner Temple** and **Middle Temple** (▶ 87). As soon as you stroll into the narrow cobblestone alleyways, the noise of the traffic fades away and you can hear your own footsteps. Take a rest in front of Temple Church for a while before you continue.

LONDON IN THE COUNTRYSIDE

Rural London? Yes, it exists: take the District Line to **Richmond** (just behind Kew Gardens ▶ 170). Enjoy a summer stroll through this small gentrified district and you will soon forget that you have just come from a teeming metropolis. It is like being on an English country estate. From **Richmond Hill,** you can enjoy the wonderful view of the river and take a boat trip (June–Sept daily, April/May Sat and Sun) on the Thames.

LIKE A GENTLEMAN

St James's is elegant and expensive (✚ 207 D/E5, ✚ 205 D/E1). The windows on St. James's Street show extravagant shaving accessories at **Truefitt and Hill** (71), exclusive leather cases at **Swaine, Adeney, Brigg Ltd** (54), fine wines at **Berry Bros. & Rud** (3) and exqusite cheese at **Paxton & Whitfield** (93, Jermyn St). At the end you can dare a glance into the **Christie's** auction house (8 King St).

MILITARY AND FAMOUS

A visit to the **Royal Hospital** (Mon–Sat 11–noon, 2–4 ✚ 206 A/B1), which has been a home for retired British soldiers since 1692, provides a look at the country's military history, immortalised on the wooden panel in the Great Hall. The garden looks out towards the Thames as do the pensioners clad in red.

The Royal Hospital Road continues south-west to the **Cheyne Walk**. The blue plaques on the houses bear testimony to their famous residents of the past: Mick Jagger, Prime Minister Lloyd George, J. M. W. Turner.

Enjoying a break at the Temple Church

The Magazine

In the Flow of Life – On the Thames 10

Pub Life 12

Festive Spirits 14

City of Change 16

Urban Green 20

The Mark of Fame 24

Football Crazy 28

London's Best for Free 30

Live Sounds 32

In the Flow of Life – on the

THAMES

Ancient and gentle, the River Thames meanders through the city of London. This cappuccino-coloured waterway splits the city into two geographically. Once frequented by trade ships and barges, nowadays trendy houseboats and night cruises have taken over.

Stretching for 215 miles (346km) from Gloucestershire to the estuary, beyond Canvey Island, the Thames is the second-longest river in the UK (after the River Severn). Its tidal route takes it through central London before it winds towards Greenwich.

Liquid History

The Thames has played a major part in the history of London. Neolithic settlements have been unearthed along its length; it suffered an intensive period of attack from the Vikings and enjoyed glorious heydays under the Tudors and Stuarts. In 1929, this colourful past led Parliamentarian John Burns to describe the river as "liquid history".

By the 18th and 19th century, the port of London was flourishing, thanks to the expanding British Empire, and the Thames was the major trade artery into southern England. The 20th-century progression of the rail and road network around Britain and, later, the advent of gigantic container ships needing deep-water ports put paid to the viability of the East London docks and trade along the Thames.

River Sights

Stroll through Chelsea and you will find houseboats near Albert Bridge – probably the best non-city lifestyle London has to offer.

Further east, on either side of Westminster Bridge, are two of the city's most iconic landmarks. The grand Houses of Parliament feature London's famous bell, Big Ben (► 104) in its clock tower. Across the river, there is no mistaking the London Eye Ferris Wheel (► 101), erected to celebrate the Millennium.

Just beyond Greenwich (► 184), the Thames reaches the most important structure along its length. The Thames Barrier was completed in 1982 and serves to protect London from high tides and powerful tidal surges. The threat of rising sea levels, caused by climate change, means that, even with the barrier, the river has never posed a greater potential hazard to London's existence than it does today.

Above: The London skyline with The Shard and The Tower Bridge at dusk
Below: The Thames Barrier was designed to prevent London from flooding

WILD THAMES

The River Thames is now one of the cleanest city waterways in the world. Salmon, Dover sole, sea trout and bass, along with an occasional seal, dolphin or porpoise, can be found swimming in it. Above water, you will likely see black cormorants, herons and swans. As part of the regeneration of the river, two "bubbler" boats ensure the correct oxygen levels in the water.

Pub Life

Pubs have long played a role in London's history, art and literature and they are still part of everyday life. They vary from historic and charming to a practical spot for a quick pint. The best offer a relaxed atmosphere, and the now ubiquitous "gastropubs" serve surprisingly good food.

The Real Thing

The traditional pub is Britain's gift to the world. Beer comes in half pints and pints; wines by the glass. It is also fine to order mineral water and soft drinks, even tea and coffee. Tipping is not expected for drinks.

Olde Worlde

In central London, up an alleyway, is one of London's oldest pubs, the Lamb and Flag (33 Rose Street, WC2. Tube: Covent Garden). Built in 1623, the low door jambs and tiny rooms are a clue to its age, and it oozes authentic charm. The Princess Louise is a classic Victorian pub (208–209 High Holborn, WC1. Tube: Holborn), with beautifully restored wood panelling and etched glass. Surrounded by Soho's trendy advertising, video and music business, The Ship (116 Wardour Street, W1. Tube: Piccadilly Circus) has long been a haunt for musicians. In a Belgravia mews is the Star Tavern (6 Belgrave Mews West, SW1. Tube: Knightsbridge), with its stained-glass windows, fireplaces, plain pine tables and great service. The Antelope is a similarly intimate pub

(22 Eaton Terrace, SW1. Tube: Sloane Square), with a history that dates back to the 17th century.

Some pubs are recreations, using historic premises. Close to the Law Courts, the Old Bank of England (194 Fleet Street, EC4. Tube: Temple) really was a bank before its conversion into an Edwardian-looking tavern, with steel bank doors and a hidden courtyard.

Food, Glorious Food

Britain's first gastropub, The Eagle, opened in 1991 (➤90) revolutionized the British pub scene. Dishes range from sausages with onion gravy and mash to fine dining. Most are located around central London. You should also try the Anchor & Hope (➤117) or The Thomas Cubitt (44 Elizabeth Street. Tube: Victoria station), both gastronomic havens

FESTIVE SPIRITS

Whether you want to celebrate the Chinese New Year, keep those Irish eyes smiling on St Patrick's Day or samba in the streets, London often puts you in party mood. These are the pick of the best and the good news is that they are all free of charge.

Carnaval del Pueblo

This August gathering, formerly in Burgess Park, took place for the first time in the Coronet Theatre (New Kent Road) in 2013. The large Latin American festival offers superb entertainment and live music (www.carnavaldel-pueblo.com) with Brazilian dance groups, salsa rhythms and Bolivian folklore.

The New Year's Day Parade

Since 1987, 10,000 musicians and singers from 20 countries have cheered up London on New Year's Day. The marching bands parade from Piccadilly via Trafalgar Square to Parliament Square. You will need to arrive early to secure a seat on one of the temporary grandstands; 500,000 people attend the parade (www.londonparade.co.uk).

Chinese New Year

Dancing dragons, lions and acrobats combine with Chinese music and fireworks to help London celebrate the Chinese New Year. London's Chinese community is focused on the labyrinth of streets south of Shaftesbury Avenue. Events happen in Leicester Square and Trafalgar Square, along Shaftesbury Avenue and in Chinatown itself (► 162). The date for Chinese New Year varies and each year is named after an animal (lwww.london.gov.uk):

- 2015: 19 Feb (Sheep)
- 2016: 8 Feb (Monkey)
- 2017: 28 Jan (Rooster)
- 2018: 16 Feb (Dog)

Top left: New Year's Day Parade
Right: Notting Hill Carnival

St Patrick's Day

The Irish have long been a significant community in London; they were the powerhouse behind the rapid expansion of the city in the 18th and 19th centuries. On the weekend closest to 17 March, London's St Patrick's Day events include a marching band parade, from Piccadilly to Whitehall, via Trafalgar Square, where a music and dance festival takes place (www.london.gov.uk).

Eid in the Square

Held to celebrate Eid al-Fitr, the end of the Muslim fasting month of Ramadan, Eid in the Square takes place in Trafalgar Square. Live music, traditional food and Asian arts and crafts are on offer throughout the day. Dates for Eid al-Fitr vary (www.eidinthesquare.com); upcoming ones are:

- 2015: 18 July
- 2016: 7 July
- 2017: 26 June
- 2018: 15 June

NOTTING HILL CARNIVAL

This is London's most famous outdoor festival. Exuberant, colourful and, at times, edgy, it is the largest street festival in Europe. With its roots firmly in the Caribbean, the carnival has come a long way from its humble beginnings in 1964; nowadays more than 1 million people attend. The highlights are the spectacular street parades and live music. Dancers and performers of the Mas (short for masquerade) groups swirl to infectious calypso rhythms. The carnival takes place over the August Bank Holiday weekend, with the main parades on Monday (www.nottinghillcarnival.biz).

City of
CHANGE

**London is constantly evolving. War and peace, famine and feast
have all left their mark, but each time the city has emerged
like the phoenix from the ashes. Every facelift has been
marked with significant buildings.**

Take the Roman invasion 2,000 years ago: not only did Emperor Claudius
make the city his capital, but he also built the first London Bridge. Fire
has always been a threat. During the seventh century, most people lived
in thatched cottages, using wood fires and wax candles. If fire broke out,
whole streets burned to the ground in a matter of hours. The first major
stone building, the Tower of London, still stands, built by the Normans
after they invaded in 1066.

Two major events in London's history are always highlighted: the Great
Fire of 1666 and the Blitz, three centuries later. Both left smouldering
ruins, and both changed the face of the city and the way that the survivors
carried on with their daily lives.

London's Burning

On 2 September 1666, the king's bakery in Pudding Lane caught fire:
13,200 houses and 84 churches were destroyed. Officially, only four
died, but 100,000 were made homeless. The disaster inspired new building regulations: all new construction was to be in brick or stone. Streets

had to be wider to enable fire engines to travel more easily. Londoners could not wait for the new construction to be finished and began to build outside the old city walls, just across the river in Southwark, and to the west in Westminster.

Not every church was destroyed in the Great Fire. Gems that survive include St Botolph-without-Bishopsgate, St Ethelburga, St Helen's and, to the west, St Bartholomew the Great. It was the architect Sir Christopher Wren who transformed the City skyline, designing not only the new St Paul's Cathedral, but also 50 new churches.

Cultural Change

It is not just disasters that have changed the face of London. In the early 19th century, as Britain's empire flourished, architect John Nash presented an ambitious urban

Left to right: The Albert Memorial and the Albert Hall; St Bartholomew; the Great Church: St Paul's

renewal scheme with open public spaces, broad streets and attractive terraces of houses. His most obvious legacy is Regent Street (▶67).

Dedicated to industry and culture, the Great Exhibition of 1851 also left Londoners with a homogenous collection of buildings close to South Kensington Tube station: the Victoria & Albert Museum, the Science Museum, the Natural History Museum and the Royal Albert Hall.

Disaster struck again in 1940, when London was bombed for 75 nights by German planes. In a city of 8 million people, a million houses were destroyed and millions more damaged. Slowly, London rose once more from the ashes. Buildings were practical rather than attractive, with chunky office blocks and cheap tower-block housing. In 1951, a century after the Great Exhibition, the Festival of Britain boosted spirits after World War II. The epicentre was the South Bank, where the Royal Festival Hall still anchors the entertainment complex along the river.

Architects rule

The next major change to affect London's skyline came in the years that Margaret Thatcher and the Conservative Party governed (1979–1997). Most of the development by the private sector took place in the City of London, Britain's financial heart, and in Docklands, the former port. With its insides on the outside, Richard Rogers' 1985 Lloyd's

Left to right: Big Ben and the London Eye; the City Hall and the distinctive skyscrapers "The Shard" and "The Gherkin" (right)

Building shocked and excited, while the Canary Wharf, at 771 feet (235m), with its 55 storeys, epitomized the "bigger is better" philosophy of the time. London celebrated the year 2000 with daring new architecture: the Millennium Dome, the Great Court of the British Museum, the London Eye and even the stations along the extension of the Jubilee Line Underground system.

"In 1951, a century after the Great Exhibition, the Festival of Britain boosted spirits after World War II."

The pace has not stopped in the first decade of the millennium. Office blocks in the City such as "The Gherkin" (officially 30 St Mary Axe), the fish-tailed curve of the Willis Building and, next to St Paul's Cathedral, One New Change, a futuristic glass complex with one of the highest public roof terraces in London dominate the skyline.

The Olympic Games held in 2012 generated new sports stadiums, the youngest and tallest buildings in the city are the 944-foot (288m) Pinnacle (22–24 Bishopsgate) and Renzo Piano's 1,003-foot (306m) glass tower. The Shard (▶ 115) was even the tallest building in Europe for a few months.

Urban
GREEN

With eight royal parks covering 5,000 acres (2,000ha), London has long been one of the world's greenest cities. In 1808, Lord Chatham referred to them as "the lungs of London". From meadow-land and lawns to intimate gardens with fountains and ponds, they provide a backdrop for a stroll or a picnic. You can go swimming and horse riding in some, and in summer there are outdoor concerts and theatre.

In summer London's parks fill with people

Hyde Park

Set between Kensington Palace and Park Lane, Hyde Park (left) is perhaps the most iconic of London's parks. Vast and spacious, wonderful walkways circumvent and criss-cross the park, while the Serpentine, a 28-acre (11ha) lake splits it in two. If you feel like cooling off in the heat of summer, the Serpentine Lido offers a chance for a quick dip.

Near to the Lido is the intriguing Diana, Princess of Wales Memorial Fountain. Constructed from Cornish granite, the water flows around the oval bed in two directions before collecting in a peaceful pool. For those wanting to voice an opinion, the legendary Speakers' Corner beckons.

🚇 Hyde Park Corner, Marble Arch, Lancaster Gate

St James's Park

At just over 58 acres (23ha), St James's Park is relatively small compared to London's other green spaces. What it lacks in size though, it makes up for with quality and location. Nestled alongside Buckingham Palace, The Mall, with St James's Palace and Clarence House, runs along its northern edge. Inside, paths fringe the lovely lake, home to the charming, wooded Duck Island. The park was a particular favourite of King Charles II, who used to while away the hours feeding the ducks. Pelicans and many other waterfowl can also be spotted around the island. For great views of Buckingham Palace, take a stroll across the lake on the Blue Bridge.

🚇 St James's Park

UP THE GARDEN PATH

- **Fenton House** (► 189, 183), a 17th-century house with a walled garden containing roses, an orchard and a kitchen garden (Windmill Hill, Hampstead, tel. 020 74 35 34 71, www.nationaltrust.org.uk. Tube: Hampstead).

- **Ham House** (Ham, Richmond, tel: 020 89 40 19 50, www.nationaltrust.org. uk. Tube: Richmond), a 17th-century mansion with formal gardens.

- **Chiswick House** (Chiswick W4 2RP, tel: 020 87 42 39 05, www.chgt.org. uk. Tube: Turnham Green). Surrounding Chiswick House, a grand neo-Palladian villa, are Chiswick House Gardens, created in 1729. Regarded as the birthplace of the English Landscape Movement, and completely restored during a project that finished in 2010, they have inspired countless gardens, including New York's Central Park. The Chiswick camellia collection is thought to be the oldest large collection of its kind in the West. Open daily; free; stylish café.

The Magazine

Insider
Tip

BLOOMING MANIA

- The RHS Chelsea Flower Show, the world's most famous garden event (late May), features new varieties and dozens of specially designed gardens; www.rhs.org.uk
- The National Gardens Scheme organizes access to nearly 200 private gardens all over the capital. These are open between Feb and Oct. Information is available at tourist offices (➤ 37) or check out www.ngs.org.uk

Green Park

Wedged between St James's Park and Hyde Park, this royal park covers 47 acres (19ha). In fine weather, office workers and visitors turn this triangular oasis into a popular lunchtime spot, escaping the traffic along Piccadilly. In spring, 250,000 daffodils bob in the breeze; in summer, you can hire a deck chair. On the east side, stroll down Queen's Walk past some fine old aristocratic homes and you will be walking in the footsteps of Queen Caroline, George II's wife, who loved gardening. Canada Gate, facing Buckingham Palace, is a memorial to Queen Victoria (www.royalparks.org.uk).

🚇 Green Park, Hyde Park Corner, Victoria

Hampstead Heath

The wildest of London's rural areas, Hampstead Heath is a nature lovers' delight. Just 4 miles (6.5km) north of Trafalgar Square, between Hampstead and Highgate, the heath is a favourite place for Londoners to go walking, running and kite flying. It is rumoured that Parliament Hill is so called because Guy Fawkes looked down from here while waiting in vain for his explosives to ignite under Parliament. The hill provides panoramic views over the city, including St Paul's Cathedral and the London Eye. The heath hosts around 30 ponds, woodland, meadows and many ancient trees and hedgerows, which help support a variety of wildlife, including kingfishers, reed warblers and woodpeckers. On the northern side of the heath lies the resplendent Kenwood House (www.cityoflondon.gov.uk)

🚇 Hampstead, Golders Green 🚃 Hampstead Heath

Holland Park

Holland Park is one of the prettiest and most secluded parks. In 54 acres (22ha) of grounds, wilderness and order are juxtaposed. The park attracted a colony of wealthy artists to its fringes in Victorian days. Today, art exhibitions take place at the Ice House or the Orangery Gallery. Families gather at the tea-house, squirrels and peacocks roam in the woods of the northern half, and nannies watch over their charges in

the playground of the formal gardens. The Kyoto Japanese Garden offers a meditative retreat northwest of Holland House (www.rbkc.gov.uk).
🚇 Holland Park

Regent's Park

The most northerly of the royal parks is the work of John Nash, "a thick squat dwarf with round head, snub nose and little eyes" (his own self-appraisal). Appearances aside, this visionary architect came up with the prototype for England's garden suburbs and cities, combining urban and rural to lure the nobility to what was then considered far north of the fashionable West End. The park is edged by the Outer Circle of highly desirable stuccoed residences. Within this lies the Inner Circle of botanical glories, with their diverse and fragrant rose gardens and an open-air theatre, which stages Shakespeare productions in the summer (www.royalparks.org.uk).
🚇 Regent's Park

Greenwich Park

Swooping down the hill that overlooks the River Thames and the National Maritime Museum is Greenwich Park, the oldest of the royal parks and a UNESCO World Heritage Site. In 2012 it hosted two Olympic events: equestrian and modern pentathlon. The park's star attraction is the Royal Observatory, designed by Sir Christopher Wren in 1675, one of the world's most important historic scientific sites (www.royalparks.org.uk).
🚇 North Greenwich 🚉 Greenwich.

Top: The tranquil Kyoto Japanese Garden, Holland Park
Middle: A statue in Queen Mary's Gardens, Regent's Park
Bottom: Spring flowers in bloom in St James's Park

The Mark of
FAME

Writers, artists, politicians or philosophers…, the metropolis bristles with blue plaques posted on the former residences of its illustrious inhabitants. The plaque scheme, now run by English Heritage, started in 1867.

Creative Londoners

London has inspired thousands of writers over the centuries. Long established as popular areas for the city's literati are the northern districts of Hampstead, Camden Town and Islington. Some houses have even been home to more than one famous inhabitant, as at 23 Fitzroy Road, Primrose Hill (Tube: Chalk Farm), once occupied by the Irish poet W. B. Yeats and later by the American poet Sylvia Plath. Plath was drawn to Yeats' blue plaque as she passed by and visited the agent soon afterwards to negotiate the lease for the top-floor apartment.

George Orwell (1903–50), in keeping with his socio-political concerns, lived closer to the pulse of less erudite streets, gravitating between

From left to right: Plaque to George Frideric Handel; Charles Dickens; Karl Marx; plaque to Jimi Hendrix

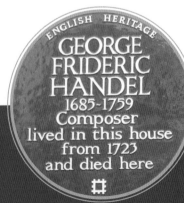

Camden Town and rent-free rooms above a bookshop in South End Green where he worked. He later moved to 27b Canonbury Square in Islington (Tube: Highbury and Islington), at the time a far from gentrified address. Another socially concerned writer, H. G. Wells (1866–1946), meanwhile lived in style overlooking Regent's Park from 13 Hanover Terrace (Tube: Baker Street). When negotiating the lease he said, "I'm looking for a house to die in". This he did 10 years later, having survived the world war that he had so grimly predicted.

Drawn to Chelsea

Exoticism and scandal always went hand in hand here, but Chelsea's notoriety really took off in Victorian times when custom-built artists' studios became the rage. At this time, Oscar Wilde (1854–1900) penned plays at 34 Tite Street (Tube: Sloane Square). Though Wilde's wife and children lived here, he was partying madly with his boyfriend "Bosie", a double life perfectly reflected in his novel *The Picture of Dorian Gray*.

The Magazine

Left: Sir Winston Churchill in RAF uniform in 1948
Right: Irish wit and dramatist Oscar Wilde, photographed *c*.1882

Notorious

Beatles fans flock to Marylebone to see the blue plaque unveiled by Yoko Ono in 2010. The basement flat at 34 Montagu Square, W1 (Tube: Marble Arch) has a colourful history. Bought by Ringo Starr in 1965, it was later rented out to both Paul McCartney and Jimi Hendrix. In 1968, John Lennon moved in with Yoko Ono. Here, in the couple's first London home, the sensational nude photo was taken for the *Two Virgins* album, the first of their three albums with experimental music. Lennon also worked on The Beatles' only double album, the *White Album*. In October of that year, John Lennon and Yoko Ono were arrested for possession of cannabis resin; Lennon appeared at nearby Marylebone Magistrates' Court, where he was fined £150. Few properties in London encapsulate the events of the Swinging Sixties better.

Political Exiles

With democracy stamped on the nation's soul and tolerance on its psyche, it is hardly surprising that numerous politicos on the run made London their base. Napoleon III (1808–1873), Bonaparte's nephew, found himself exiled in London twice over and in 1848 lived at 1 King Street, in the

---

THE BLOOMSBURY GROUP

London's most famous 20th-century literary coterie was the Bloomsbury Group. Members included writers Virginia Woolf, E. M. Forster and the economist John Maynard Keynes. Virginia and her husband, Leonard, marked the group's heyday in 1924 when they moved the Hogarth Press from Richmond to Tavistock Square in Bloomsbury. Among members who lived in nearby Fitzroy Square (Tube: Warren Street) were Roger Fry (at 33) and Virginia Woolf (blue plaque, at 29).

---

gentlemanly heart of St James's (Tube: Green Park). He became so inspired by the parks of the English capital that on his coronation as emperor he ordered his city architect to set about copying them in Paris. Nearly a century later, another Gallic exile, General Charles de Gaulle (1890–1970), was notoriously less of an anglophile, despite an equally salubrious address at 4 Carlton Gardens (Tube: Charing Cross). This was his base for organizing the Free French forces while broadcasting to resistance fighters before a triumphal return at Liberation.

Communist Writers

At the other end of the political spectrum was Karl Marx (1818–1883) who, after expulsion from Germany, settled in London to pursue a rocky, often impecunious existence. From 1851 to 1856 he lived in what was then a seedy Soho, at 28 Dean Street (Tube: Tottenham Court Road), later writing much of *Capital* in the British Museum's Reading

"The basement flat at 34 Montagu Square … has a colourful history."

Room. He was buried in Highgate Cemetery beneath a gigantic bust bearing the words "Workers of the World Unite".

Marx's wealthier compatriot, supporter and fellow thinker, Friedrich Engels (1820–1895), was also buried in Highgate Cemetery after spending much of his life in London. From 1870 to 1892 he lived at 121 Regent's Park Road, a desirable address overlooking the park (Tube: Camden Town). And no less than Vladimir Ilyich Lenin (1870–1924), who in 1905 lived at 16 Percy Circus (now the Royal Scot Hotel. Tube: King's Cross), near the London Patriotic Society where he worked. This 1737 building now houses the Marx Memorial Library (37a Clerkenwell Green. Tube: Farringdon).

Football
CRAZY

Fast, flowing and often dramatic, football is England's favourite brainchild. London introduced the organization and rules that transformed a rough-and-ready pastime into the professional game that swept around the world.

A New Code

In 2013, the Football Association celebrated its 150th anniversary, making it the world's oldest football organization. Although the earliest written references to football in London appear in the 14th century, it was in 1863 that the modern game was born. Back then, different clubs played to different rules. It was not until a governing body, the Football Association, was founded that standard rules were introduced. The first meetings of the Association were held at what is now the Freemason's Arms, in Covent Garden (81–82 Long Acre, WC2. Tube: Covent Garden). Today, the FA (Football Association) headquarters are at Wembley Stadium.

London Clubs

About a dozen professional clubs play in the capital; each has its own history, from Chelsea, with its millionaire players, to the less glamorous

LONDON'S PREMIER LEAGUE TEAMS (FOOTBALL SEASON 2014/2015)

FC Arsenal Emirates Stadium, N5, www.arsenal.com

FC Chelsea Stamford Bridge, SW6, www.chelseafc.com

Crystal Palace FC Selhurst Park, SE25, www.cpfc.co.uk

Queens Park Rangers South Africa Road, London W12, www.qpr.co.uk

Tottenham Hotspur White Hart Lane, N17, www.tottenham hotspur.com

West Ham United FC Boleyn Ground, E13 (moving to the Olympic Stadium in 2016), www.whufc.com

Left: Wembley Stadium Arch; Bottom left: A London derby, such as Chelsea v Arsenal, is guaranteed to pull in the crowds, at the stadiums and in the pubs

Brentford and Leyton Orient. The city's first professional club is Arsenal, founded in 1886 by workers at Woolwich Arsenal, an ammunition factory in southeast London. When they moved to north London in 1913, they kept Arsenal as their name and "the Gunners" as their nickname. Founded in 1882, Tottenham Hotspur is named after Sir Henry Percy, known as Harry Hotspur.

Wembley Stadium

Wembley Stadium is probably the world's best-known football ground, staging everything from major sports events to rock concerts. Owned by the Football Association, the stadium has been home to the FA Cup Final since 1923. Small boys (and grown men) fantasize about "lifting the Cup at Wembley". In 1966, it was in this stadium that the World Cup Final between England and West Germany took place and where the host team scored one of the most famous goals in history to win the World Cup 4:2 after extra time. The old stadium was demolished in 2000; the new stadium provided the venue for the 2012 Olympic Games.

London's Best
for Free

It may be one of the world's most expensive cities, but London has a surprisingly rich array of enthralling things you can enjoy for free, from music and art galleries to markets or simply great views.

Music

London's free concerts are still relatively undiscovered. Many churches hold lunchtime concerts where you can recharge your spiritual batteries. Good examples are St Martin-in-the-Fields on Trafalgar Square (► 58) and St James's, Piccadilly (► 176, 179).

The Southbank Centre (► 112) hosts a wide range of free events, from jazz and classical recitals to poetry readings and art. Pubs and clubs with free live music include The Lock Tavern (35 Chalk Farm Road, NW1. Tube: Camden Town), Ain't Nothin but Blues Bar (20 Kingly Street, W1. Free Sun to Thu; free before 8:30 Fri–Sat. Tube: Piccadilly Circus), and Nottinghillartsclub (► 144).

The Magazine

Galleries and Museums

Some 70 museums and galleries offer free entry. These include the National Gallery (➤ 54), Tate Modern (➤ 108), Tate Britain (➤ 102), the British Museum (➤ 154) or the V&A Museum (➤ 126), as well as suburban attractions, such as the museums in Greenwich (➤ 184). Don't miss the free lectures at galleries for an expert in-depth analysis of a painting or an artist, and grab a gold bar at the Bank of England Museum (➤ 86).

Markets

There are some superb markets to peruse. Bermondsey Market (SE1, ✚ 202 B1) glitters with silverware, paintings, odd furniture and obsolete objects. Open from Thursday to Sunday, Camden Markets (➤ 160) is for anyone hankering after street fashions, crafts, jewellery or furniture. On Saturday, you should visit Portobello Road Market (➤ 139) for every-thing from antiques to fruit and vegetables, and bric-a-brac, or Spitalfields Market (➤ 92), known for its young designer creations. And for delicious, fresh produce, head to Borough Market (➤ 114).

Something Different

Visitors are amazed at the treasures in the London Silver Vaults (53–64 Chancery Lane. Tube: Chancery Lane). Line up outside the Cromwell Green visitor entrance to see a debate in the Houses of Parliament (➤ 104),

usually Mon to Thu. A wait of an hour is common. In the British Library (➤ 158), you can see Magna Carta, the Gutenberg Bible, Leonardo da Vinci's note-books and original lyrics by The Beatles.

Above: Tate Britain
Left: Borough Market
Opposite: The Victoria and Albert Museum

LIVE SOUNDS

Rock, indie, jazz, soul, blues, country, samba; no matter what your tastes, it is possible to attend live concerts most nights of the week.

Jazz It Up

If jazz is your thing, then you really are spoiled for choice. One of the most glamorous venues to get your fix is at Ronnie Scott's Jazz Club (47 Frith Street, W1) in Soho. Opened over 50 years ago by the late saxophonists Scott and Pete King, it has hosted some of the jazz greats. For something more intimate, the atmospheric 606 Club (90 Lots Road, SW10) in Chelsea is popular with aficionados.

Mix It Up

For an eclectic mix of styles in an intimate, but somewhat downbeat, setting head to the famous 12 Bar Club (22 Denmark Street, WC2) near Tottenham Court Road. It features four acts every night of the week and it is not unknown for big names to turn up and play secret gigs. Another great place to catch a variety of sounds is Barfly (49 Chalk Farm Road, NW1) in Camden. Over the years, it has secured an impressive reputation for featuring upcoming bands, with Coldplay, the Kaiser Chiefs and Oasis playing there early in their careers. Also in Camden, The Dublin Castle pub (94 Parkway, NW1) is another cool venue for catching up-and-coming acts.

Big Bands

One of London's most respected larger venues is the Roundhouse (Chalk Farm Road, NW1). Originally a steam engine turning shed, this concert hall has featured Jimi Hendrix, Pink Floyd and the Rolling Stones, and can hold more than 3,000 people. For more venues, ▶45.

Live band in Dover Street Restaurant and Bar

Finding Your Feet

First Two Hours   34
Getting Around   35
Accommodation   37
Food and Drink   41
Shopping   44
Entertainment   45

First Two Hours

London has five airports. Heathrow, Gatwick and Stansted are the principal ones; Luton and London City are smaller, but also busy and provide easy access.

From Heathrow

Heathrow (code LHR) lies 15 miles (24km) west of central London and is served by good road and rail connections. All the services below go from all five terminals and are well signposted.

- The **London Underground** (tel: 0343 2 22 12 34, www.tfl.gov.uk), Piccadilly line, serves Heathrow from Mon–Sat 5:15am to 11:40pm and Sun 5:15am to 11:30pm. The journey to central London takes about an hour and can get very crowded in the rush hour, but is the most convenient, best-value option.
- The **Heathrow Express** (tel: 0845 6 00 15 15; www.heathrowexpress.com) is a high-speed train to Paddington station. It runs from Mon–Sat 5:05am to 11:45pm, Sun from 6:15, and the journey takes around 15 minutes. The Heathrow Connect to Paddington is cheaper and takes 25 minutes www.heathrowconnect.com).
- **National Express** coaches (www.nationalexpress.com) run to Victoria coach station in about an hour.
- You can pick up a black metered **taxi** outside any terminal. Expect around an hour's journey time and pay £55 to £65 to central London.

From Gatwick

Gatwick (code LGW) is 27 miles (43km) south of central London.

- **Gatwick Express** (tel: 084 58 50 15 30; www.gatwickexpress.com) train service runs to Victoria station in central London. It runs every 15 minutes most of the day and hourly most of the night with the last train at 1:35am and service resuming at 4:35am; journey time is 30 minutes. Slower trains include First Capital Connect to London Bridge and St Pancras International (tel: 084 50 26 47 00; www.firstcapitalconnect.co.uk), and Southern to Victoria (tel: 084 51 27 29 20; www.southernrailway.com).
- **National Express** coaches (www.nationalexpress.com) run to Victoria coach station in about two hours. Low-cost easyBus.co.uk (www.easybus.co.uk) goes to London's Earl's court/West Brompton.
- **Taxis** Checker Cars, the airport's official partner, charge around £145; journey time is approximately 1 hour to London (tel: 012 93 56 77 00; www.checkercars.com).

From Stansted

Stansted (code STN) lies 35 miles (56km) northeast of central London.

- **Stansted Express** (tel: 084 58 50 01 50; www.stanstedexpress.com) train service runs to Liverpool Street station, every 15 to 30 minutes, from 5:30am to 1:30am (0:30am on Sat). Journey time 45 minutes; trains stop at Tottenham Hale Tube station for connection to the Victoria line.
- Buses to Central London include **National Express** (www.nationalexpress.com), **Terravision** (www.terravision.eu) and **easyBus.co.uk** (www.easybus.co.uk). Journey time is about 2 hours.
- **Taxis** Checker Cars, the airport's official partner, charge around £200; journey time is approximately 1 hour to London (tel: 01279 66 11 11; www.checkercars.com).

From London City Airport

London City Airport (code LCY) is the most central of the capital's airports, lying just 9 miles (15km) east of central London.

■ The quickest option is the **Docklands Light Railway** (DLR) from London City Airport (www.tfl.gov.uk). Trains leave every 8 to 15 minutes, with a journey time of 22 minutes to Bank Underground station on the Central line.

■ Black metered **taxis** wait outside the terminal and the journey time is about 30 minutes into Liverpool Street. The cost is around £30, but expect to pay around £40 for journeys to central London, depending on the traffic conditions.

Train Arrivals

International train services (Eurostar, www.eurostar.com) from France (Lille and Paris) and Belgium (Brussels) arrive at St Pancras International Terminal where you connect with the Underground system.

Getting Around

Visitors to London soon familiarize themselves with what was the world's first public transport system. Although there are bus routes, the London Underground or Tube (www.tfl.gov.uk/tube) is easiest to use. This subway system goes to all the main sites, and everywhere in between.

Tickets

Save time and money with the "pay-as-you-go" Oyster card, a "smart card" ticket the size of a credit card with a chip in it. Visitors to London can buy a Visitor Oyster Card ahead of time, then use it as soon as they arrive. Get one online at www.visitbritainshop.com. Pre-load it with, say, £10, then "top up" at any Tube station. The card does not expire.

■ Alternatively, you can buy **Oyster cards, regular tickets and Travelcards** in Tube stations. London is divided into nine zones, with most attractions in the central area, Zones 1 and 2. Travelcards allow you to make as many journeys as you like within specified zones. Buy a 1-day card daily; for stays of 4 days or more, save money by buying a 7-day card.

■ The **Oyster card** is valid on all Tube trains, buses, trams and some regular train services. To get through the Tube gates or board a bus, "touch in" on the disc-shaped yellow electronic reader. You will hear a bleep. On exiting "touch out", so that the card records the completion of your journey.

■ **Children aged 10 years and under** travel free at any time, as long as they are accompanied by an adult with a valid ticket/Visitor Oyster Card.

The Tube

The Tube system operates on 12 lines, which are colour-coded.

■ **Lines have names** that relate to their routes: the Circle (yellow) encloses the centre of the city; the District (green) goes deep into the suburbs. Look at the platform signs to see the destination of the next train.

■ Many Tube stations have **long escalators**, but there are some with lifts (elevators).

Finding Your Feet

Buses

London has an extensive bus network, with special night buses. On most central London routes you need a valid ticket before boarding.

- If you do not have an Oyster or Travelcard, **buy a ticket** from a machine at the stop. These do not give change!
- When you board, **"touch in"** next to the driver; unlike the Tube there is no need to touch out at the end of the trip.

Docklands Light Railway (DLR)

East of central London, the Docklands Light Railway is an above-ground train system operating from Bank Tube station to Stratford and the Olympic area in the north and to Lewisham, via Greenwich (➤ 184), in the south. Both offer good views of London en route.

Taxis

Black cabs (also in a variety of other colours) are available from outside stations and hotels, but you can also hail them from the roadside.

- Cabs **available for hire** will have the yellow "For Hire" sign lit.
- All taxis **are metered** and the fare will depend on journey time; there are surcharges after 10pm. Drivers expect a 10 per cent tip.
- To ring for a taxi: **Radio Taxis** (tel: 020 72 72 02 72) and **Dial-a-Cab** (tel: 020 72 35 50 00) are both 24-hour services.
- **Black Taxi Tours of London** (tel: 020 79 35 93 63; www.blacktaxitours. co.uk) offer 2-hour, tailor-made sightseeing tours.

Sightseeing Buses

Several companies operate private bus routes that cover the top tourist sights. The tour is usually in open-topped buses with a commentary in several languages. It's a hop-on, hop-off service. For more information contact:

- **Big Bus Company** (tel: 020 72 33 95 33; www.bigbustours.com)
- **The Original London Sightseeing Tour** (tel: 020 88 77 17 22; www.theoriginaltour.com)

Car Hire

Only rent a car if you plan making your own excursion. Companies include **Avis** (tel: 08445 81 01 47; www.avis.co.uk), **Europcar** (tel: 08713 84 99 00; www.europcar.co.uk) and **Hertz** (tel: 0870 8 44 88 44; www.hertz.co.uk).

Bicycles

Another way to explore is with the Barclays Cycle Hire bike scheme: £1 for one hour. It's self-service: pay with a credit or debit card. Take a silver-and-blue bike from a docking station; when you are finished leave it at any convenient docking station. Details available on www.tfl.gov.uk.

Driving

In the United Kingdom, you need a full driving licence or an International Driver's Permit (available from motoring organizations in your own country).

- Traffic in the United Kingdom drives on the **left**.
- It is obligatory to wear **seat belts**.
- The **speed limit** in built-up areas is 30mph (48kph); 60mph (97kph) on single carriageways; and 70mph (113kph) on dual carriageways (divided highways) and motorways (expressways).
- There are stringent laws against **drinking and driving**.
- Private cars are banned from **bus lanes**.

Congestion Charging

To reduce traffic, a congestion charge dissuades private-car owners from entering central London between 7am and 6pm, Monday–Friday. Weekends and official holidays are free. The charge is £10 per day. Parking inside the zone is very expensive. Pay online (www.cclondon. com), by phone (tel: 0845 9 00 12 34), at petrol stations and shops, or self-service machines at car parks inside the zone.

Tourist Office

Get official tourist information from the **London Tourist Board** (www.visit london.com); the **Britain & London Visitor Centre** (open daily), 1 Lower Regent Street, SW1 (🚇 Piccadilly Circus); **City of London Information Centre** (open daily, next to St Paul's Cathedral. 🚇 St Paul's), airports and railway stations.

Visitor Passes

All-inclusive passes, such as the **London Pass** (www.londonpass.com) include free entrance to most of London's major attractions.

Accommodation

Although London is expensive, there are alternatives to grand hotels: newer, trendier budget hotels, bed and breakfasts, apartments and even student rooms.

Hotels

The hotels listed on pages 38–40 are mainly in the medium price range, offering service, character and well-maintained rooms. More hotel and B&B listings can be found by going to the Hotels and B&B link on the AA website: www.theAA.com/travel.

Grand Hotels

London is known for its grand hotels, with eye-watering prices, well over the highest price category. Check out the refurbished Savoy (www.fairmont. com), with its art deco Beaufort Bar, The Dorchester (www.thedorchester. com), The Ritz London (www.theritzlondon.com) and Claridge's (www. claridges.co.uk). New luxury hotels include the Four Seasons Hotel (www. fourseasons.com/london), W London (www.wlondon.co.uk), the St Pancras Renaissance London Hotel (www.marriott.com) and the Shangri-La at the Shard (www.shangri-la.com).

Bed & Breakfasts

Bed and breakfasts can be a less expensive alternative to hotels. At their simplest, they offer a bedroom in a private house with a shared bathroom, but further up the scale are rooms with private bathrooms in beautiful old houses.

Budget Accommodation

The wide range of budget places for backpackers has grown.

Hostels run by the Youth Hostel Association (www.yha.org.uk) include the YHA London Central, with seven floors of modern rooms (104 Bolsover

Finding Your Feet

Street, W1, tel: 0845 3 71 91 54). Also central are Piccadilly Backpackers (www.piccadillyhotel.net) and Generator Hostels (www.generatorhostels. com). During the student summer vacations, you can stay in central London in university halls of residence: London School of Economics (www.lsevacations.co.uk), University College London (www.ucl.ac.uk/ residences), King's College (www.kcl.ac.uk), Imperial College (www. imperial.ac.uk/summeraccommodation).

■ **Inexpensive hotel chains** include five easy hotels (www.easyhotel.com), a dozen or more Travelodges (www.travelodge.co.uk) and Premier Inns (www.premierinn.com).

■ It is worth considering renting a **flat (apartment)** if you are staying for a few days. You save on meal costs among other things. Book through Coach House London Vacation Rentals (www.rentals.chslondon.com) or SACO Apartments (london.sacoapartments.co.uk). The Citadines group (www.citadines.com) has six apartotels in London.

Seasonal Discounts

London is always busy, but July, August and September are high season, as are the Easter and pre-Christmas periods. In winter, rooms may be discounted. It's always worth asking about special deals.

Accommodation Prices
Prices are per night for a double room:
£ under £75   **££** £75–£150   **£££** £151–£250   **££££** over £250

Central

The Academy £££
Part of the Eton Collection of elegant boutique hotels, this is cosy, light and close to the British Museum. In this combination of five Georgian town houses, the 49 luxurious bedrooms are perfect for a romantic break. Breakfast is extra but lavish. The private garden is a bonus.
✚ 205 E4 ✉ 21 Gower Street, WC1 ☎ 020 76 31 41 15; www.theacademyhotel.co.uk
Ⓔ Goodge Street

Arosfa Hotel ££/£££
In a 200-year-old house that was once the home of artist John Millais is this family-owned bed and breakfast with small but practical rooms, free high-speed WiFi and English breakfast. It's opposite one of London's most famous bookstores.
✚ 205 E4 ✉ 83 Gower Street, WC1
☎ 020 76 36 21 15; www.arosfalondon.com
Ⓔ Russell Square

Charlotte Street Hotel ££££
One of London's six stylish design hotels is in a buzzy area just north of Soho, close to theatres, restaurants and bars. Expect all the latest high-tech equipment in the 52 rooms, as well as original modern artwork. This is also a fine spot for a tourist-free traditional English high tea.
✚ 205 E3 ✉ 15–17 Charlotte Street, W1
☎ 0800 37 46 83 57; www.designhotels.com
Ⓔ Tottenham Court Road

The Fielding £££
This no-frills hotel, offering good value in the heart of London, is in a pedestrian area, steps from Covent Garden Tube station, theatres and Seven Dials' trendy shops. In the early 19th-century building, rooms are on the small side for some visitors, but the cheerful welcome always compensates. No breakfast served, but plenty of nearby cafés.

🏠 208 A4　✉ 4 Broad Court, Bow Street, WC2
☎ 020 78 36 83 05; www.thefieldinghotel.co.uk
Ⓜ Covent Garden

Hart House Hotel ££/£££

Owned and run by the Bowden
family for 35 years, this popular
16-room hotel is in a Georgian
terrace just off Oxford Street, close
to many major attractions. Much
of the late 18th-century charm
survives, alongside practical modern bathrooms. Rates include a
traditional English breakfast.

🏠 204 A3　✉ 51 Gloucester Place, W1
☎ 020 79 35 22 88; www.harthouse.co.uk
Ⓜ Baker Street

Hazlitt's Hotel £££

This 30-room hotel, with its panelling, old oil paintings and rugs, is like
stepping back 300 years, but with
all contemporary comforts and cour-
teous service. Long-established as
a hideaway for celebrities, expect
attentive service right in the heart
of Soho. Breakfast can be taken in
your room or in the library.

🏠 205 E2　✉ 6 Frith Street, W1
☎ 020 74 34 17 71; www.hazlittshotel.com
Ⓜ Tottenham Court Road

Montagu Place ££/££££

Elegant, yet close to museums and
shops, this boutique hotel looks
Georgian on the outside, yet is totally
contemporary inside. The 16 rooms
are graded as Comfy, Fancy and
Swanky; breakfast is buffet style.

🏠 204 A3　✉ 2 Montagu Place, W1
☎ 020 74 67 27 77; www.montagu-place.co.uk
Ⓜ Baker Street, Marble Arch

The Sumner Hotel £££

With 19 rooms, this small, award-
winning hotel is just steps from
Oxford Street, Mayfair, Hyde Park
and the Tube. The interior design is
discreetly tasteful. Included in the
price are internet access, a buffet
breakfast and an honesty bar.

🏠 204 A2　✉ 54 Upper Berkeley Street, W1
☎ 020 77 23 22 44; www.thesumner.com
Ⓜ Marble Arch

Thanet Hotel ££

This family-run 16-bedroom hotel
in Bloomsbury makes an ideal base
for the British Museum, West End
theatres and Covent Garden. Rooms
are bright and practical, with
showers. A generous English
breakfast is included in the price.

🏠 208 A5　✉ 8 Bedford Place, WC1
☎ 020 76 36 28 69; www.thanethotel.co.uk
Ⓜ Russell Square

West London

No 90 ££

Insider Tip

No 90 is an upmarket version of
a bed and breakfast with just three
luxurious bedrooms in a private
house in Chelsea. Think of it as
an experience, rather than a hotel.
Owner Nina St Charles knows all
the in-places in the area. There's
also a nice garden. Minimum
2-night stay.

🏠 off 206 A1　✉ 90 Old Church Street, SW3
☎ 07 83 68 91 67; www.chelseabedbreakfast.
com　Ⓜ South Kensington

Abbey Court Hotel ££

Just steps away from the Tube
station and Notting Hill, this award-
winning, elegant, town-house hotel
is on a quiet side street. The 22 bedrooms range from singles to family
rooms; some even have antique
four-poster beds. Breakfast is included; discounts available on
advance bookings.

🏠 202 A4　✉ 20 Pembridge Gardens,
Kensington, W2　☎ 020 72 21 75 18; www.
abbeycourthotel.co.uk　Ⓜ Notting Hill Gate

Gate Hotel ££

Flowers offer a cheerful welcome to
this 19th-century town house that
faces one of London's best-known
streets, thanks to its large market
(► 139). The seven small bedrooms
have modern comforts. Continental
breakfast is served in your room
between 8 and 10.

🏠 202 A4　✉ 6 Portobello Road, W11
☎ 020 72 21 07 07; www.gatehotel.co.uk
Ⓜ Notting Hill Gate

Finding Your Feet

myhotel Chelsea £££

This former police station is now a fun boutique hotel, with 45 bright, edgy, designer bedrooms on five floors. The contemporary restaurant serves lunch, dinner and buffet breakfasts.

➕ off 206 A1 ✉ 35 Ixworth Place, SW3
☎ 020 72 25 75 00; www.myhotels.com
🚇 South Kensington

Number Sixteen ££££

A boutique hotel long before the term was invented, this row of Victorian houses was combined to provide 42 bedrooms that are now fresh and contemporary. In summer, traditional afternoon tea in the garden is a highlight. Museums, Harrods and Knightsbridge are in walking distance.

➕ off 206 A2 ✉ 16 Sumner Place, SW7
☎ 020 75 89 52 32; www.firmdale.com
🚇 South Kensington

Insider Tip

The Rockwell ££/£££

All the latest luxury gadgets and trendiest fabrics have been put into the 40 chic rooms in this designer hotel in West London. Free broadband and gym membership.

➕ 202 B1 ✉ 181 Cromwell Road, SW5
☎ 020 72 44 20 00; www.therockwell.com
🚇 Gloucester Road

Twenty Nevern Square ££

Thanks to a much-needed upgrade, this is once again a value-for-money destination in West London. The rooms in this Victorian town house on a quiet square have individuality and a hearty British breakfast in the Café Twenty is included in the price.

➕ off 202 A1 ✉ 20 Nevern Square, SW5
☎ 020 75 65 95 55; www.twentynevernsquare.co.uk 🚇 Earl's Court

City and East

The Hoxton ££

This ground-breaking hip hotel has taken London by storm with everything from its contemporary design to its reservation policy: book early

for low prices, book late and pay more. Expect high standards of comfort in the 205 rooms.

➕ off 210 B5 ✉ 81 Great Eastern Street, Hoxton, EC2 ☎ 020 75 50 10 00; www.hoxtonhotels.com 🚇 Old Street

Malmaison ££££

In a converted nurses' home, the London Malmaison is part of this trendy UK group of hotels, with 97 rooms that are designer-led. The bar and brasserie are just as hip.

➕ off 209 E5 ✉ 18–21 Charterhouse House Square, EC1 ☎ 020 70 12 37 00; www.malmaison.com 🚇 Barbican, Farringdon

South

Bermondsey Square Hotel ££

The trendy Hotel is close to the South Bank and just a step from Tower Bridge. The 60 rooms are all contemporary, with the latest gadgetry. Gegg's Bar & Grill is part of the hotel. Free wireless broadband.

➕ 210 B1 ✉ Bermondsey Square, SE1
☎ 081 9 43 03 50; www.bermondseysquare hotel.co.uk 🚇 London Bridge

London Bridge Hotel ££/£££

Opposite London Bridge is this 138-room, unashamedly bright and modern hotel. Some rooms have views over the rooftops, others over the Thames. Close to Shakespeare's Globe Theatre, Borough Market, Tate Modern. Children under 12 stay free when sharing their parents' room.

➕ 210 A2 ✉ 8–18 London Bridge Street, SE1
☎ 020 78 55 22 00; www.londonbridgehotel.com
🚇 London Bridge

Mad Hatter Hotel ££

Stay above a pub, close to Shakespeare's Globe, Tate Modern and the trendy South Bank. The 30 plain but comfortable rooms are in a tastefully renovated hat factory – hence the name. The restaurant below serves hearty British dishes.

➕ 209 D3 ✉ 3–7 Stamford Street, SE1
☎ 020 74 01 92 22; www.fullershotels.com
🚇 Waterloo

Food and Drink

London is regarded as one of the restaurant capitals of the world, offering dozens of styles and types of cuisine prepared by chefs from every corner of the globe. The days of dull dining and boiled vegetables are a thing of the past. If you do decide to go somewhere well-known, book well in advance.

Trends

With new restaurants opening every week, the choice of where to eat is one of the most difficult decisions to make in London. There is modern cooking from all over the world, however, for most visitors, the revelation is the quality and variety of British cuisines, using fresh, often organic produce from Ireland, Wales and Scotland, as well as England.

When to Eat

In general, lunch is served between noon and 3pm; dinner from 7:30pm till 11pm, but London is so much more flexible nowadays, with brasseries, bistros and even pubs that are open from breakfast till midnight.

London's office workers usually flood pubs and fast-food outlets, cafés and restaurants during the lunch hour between 1 and 2pm. Go earlier or later to avoid the rush. Look for the good value "dish of the day", or two courses for a set price.

Many restaurants close to theatres in the West End offer pre-theatre menus of two or three courses at a set price, served from 5 or 5:30pm. After the theatre, don't expect to linger over a meal after midnight unless you are in the heart of Soho and the West End.

What to Tip

In Britain, the rule of thumb is to tip 10 to 12.5 per cent, but many restaurants now automatically add 12.5 per cent to the bill. It may be termed an "optional" gratuity. Be sure to check the menu and the bill; ask if unsure. It is easy to add a second and unnecessary tip.

The Chains

Many British chains offer consistent quality and value for money. These include sandwiches, soups, salads and sushi at **Pret A Manger** and **EAT**; you can eat in the shop or take the food away. **Marks & Spencer** also has a similarly wide range of fresh, ready-to-eat food for you to take with you. If you prefer to sit down, try the Italian-style pizza and pasta at branches of **Pizza Express**, **Prezzo**, **Strada** and **ASK**. Bistro- and brasserie-like chains include **Chez Gérard** (French) and **All Bar One** (part bar, part restaurant). Coffee houses include **Caffè Nero** and **Costa**, while **Carluccio's** upmarket restaurant/cafés also have an Italian food shop.

London's quietest culinary revolution is in its museums, galleries and cathedrals. When you fancy a snack or a meal, the chances are that there is not just a good café, but a gourmet restaurant on the premises. Find well-prepared dishes using fresh British produce in places such as the crypt of **St Martin-in-the-Fields** (►64), the restaurant on top of the **National Portrait Gallery** (►65), at the **British Museum**'s restaurant overlooking the Great Court (►165), and even **St Paul's Cathedral**, with its afternoon teas (►91).

Insider Tip

Finding Your Feet

Pubs and Gastropubs

Most pubs still serve traditional "pub grub": soup, sandwiches, sausages. Although much is made of the gastropub phenomenon, there are few examples in central London (➤ 12).

Bars

London has a lively bar scene, ranging from traditional wine bars such as century-old **Gordon's** (➤ 117) to cocktail specialists, like **Mark's Bar at Hix** (➤ 166), and, with stunning views from the eighth floor of the OXO Tower, the **OXO Bar** (➤ 117).

Modern British

Forget the traditional and somewhat stodgy steak and kidney pie, fish and chips, bangers and mash, roast beef and Yorkshire pudding. The best of today's British cuisine is lighter, full of flavour and prepared with the freshest local ingredients. At the same time, chefs have reinvented traditional dishes, so that batter on the fish is crisp, the bangers (sausages) might be pork with apple or venison and chilli, not forgetting traditional British desserts, from pies and puddings to crumbles and fools.

World Cuisine

Ethnic restaurants are everywhere. Soho was long known for Italian food, but now you can eat your way around the world here. As well as the mundane, Chinatown has an array of authentic and often spicy Chinese restaurants, representing every province and style of cooking. On Edgware Road, just north of Marble Arch, are many Middle Eastern restaurants; around Brick Lane, in the East End of London, South Asian restaurants abound.

Afternoon Tea

As well as a wide choice of Indian and China teas, expect a selection of small, savoury sandwiches (smoked salmon, cucumber, cheese and so on), dainty cakes and British scones, served with strawberry jam and clotted cream. The setting is formal, with men wearing jacket and tie. These teas are really more like a meal, with hotels now serving from late morning onwards, offering several sittings. Reservations are always essential, often weeks in advance for a preferred time. Expect to pay between £50 and £70 for two, though smart West End restaurants and smaller hotels are now also serving more affordable traditional afternoon teas.

Restaurant Prices

Expect to pay per person for a meal, excluding drinks and service:
£ under £25   **££** £25–£50   **£££** over £50

The Berkeley ££

In the Caramel Room, enjoy the Prêt-à-Porter, where fashion-inspired cakes and "fancies" are named after designers.

➕ 206 B4 ✉ Wilton Place, SW1
☎ 020 71 07 88 66; www.the-berkeley.co.uk
⊙ Daily 1–5:30pm Ⓢ Knightsbridge

Brown's Hotel ££

Visit the English Tea Room, which contrasts the original wood panelling, fireplaces and plaster ceiling with modern fabrics and lighting.

➕ 205 D1 ✉ 33–34 Albemarle Street, W1
☎ 020 75 18 41 55; www.brownshotel.com
⊙ Mon–Fri 3–6, Sat–Sun 1–6 Ⓢ Green Park

The Bulgari ££

The modern design of this tea lounge makes it very inviting. The choice of teas to choose from your afternoon tea range is as wonderful as the exquisite cakes macaroons, fruit and savoury tartlets.

+ 206 A4 ⊠ 171 Knightsbridge SW7
☎ 020 71 51 10 34; www.bulgarihotels.com
🕘 daily 1–5 🚇 Knightsbridge

The Dorchester ££

Afternoon tea is served in The Promenade, the heart of the hotel, with huge displays of flowers, thick carpets and deep armchairs. Alternatively, settle in the elegant surrounds of the "Spatisserie", where you can enjoy the same sandwiches, cakes and pastries.

+ 206 B5 ⊠ 54 Park Lane, W1
☎ 020 76 29 88 88; www.dorchesterhotel.com
🕘 5 daily sittings; 1:15, 2:30, 3:15, 4:45 and 5:15
🚇 Hyde Park Corner

The Ritz ££

The cream and gold of the Palm Court, with its opulent Louis XVI decor, is one of the most famous and popular afternoon tea spots in London. Reservations are required.

+ 207 D5 ⊠ Piccadilly, W1
☎ 020 73 00 23 45; www.theritzlondon.com
🕘 11:30–7:30 every two hours
🚇 Green Park

The Savoy ££

With its new winter garden, the century-old Thames Foyer is a most elegant spot for tea, with the tinkling accompaniment of a piano. You can buy Savoy teas and jams, and watch pastry chefs and chocolatiers at work at the Savoy Tea, a shop in the hotel.

+ 208 B3 ⊠ The Strand, WC2
☎ 020 78 36 43 43; www.fairmont.com
🕘 Daily 1:30–5:45pm, for 1 hour 45 min
🚇 Charing Cross, Embankment

Fish & Chips

What hamburgers are to Americans, fish & chips are to the British: hot, relatively cheap, filling and best eaten with your fingers. However, several top-quality "chippies" are really restaurants, where you sit down and eat off a plate. Expect to pay about £9–12.

Fish Central £

Regarded by many as *the* best place to eat fish & chips. The bustling restaurant also serves all kinds of deliciously prepared seafood.

+ 209 E5 ⊠ 149 Central St, King Square, EC1
☎ 020 72 53 49 70; www.fishcentral.co.uk
🕘 Mon–Sat 11:30am–2:30pm, Mon–Thu 5pm–10:30pm, Fri–Sat 5pm–11pm
🚇 Angel, Old Street

North Sea Fish Restaurant £

Very popular with London taxi drivers who tend to sit at the back of the restaurant, while the rest of the customers sit in the front on pink velvet beneath the fish trophies.

+ 205 F5 ⊠ 7–8 Leigh Street, WC1
☎ 020 73 87 58 92; www.northseafishrestaurant.co.uk 🕘 Mon–Sat 12–2:30, 5:30–11
🚇 Russell Square

Rock and Sole Plaice £

Popular with theatre-goers, and with a history stretching back to 1871, this Covent Garden chippie claims to be the oldest *chippie* in London. Reservations necessary.

+ 208 A4 ⊠ 47 Endell Street, WC2
☎ 020 78 36 37 85 🕘 Mon–Sat 11:30–10:30, Sun 12–9:30 🚇 Covent Garden

Sea Shell £

Choose between the refurbished restaurant (reservations recommended) and the take-away for top-class fish and seafood dishes. A children's menu is available. Excellent brochettes and crab cakes.

Insider Tip

+ 204 A3 ⊠ 49–51 Lisson Grove, NW1
☎ 020 72 24 90 00; www.seashellrestaurant.co.uk 🕘 Mon–Fri 12–2:30, 5–10:30, Sat 12–10:30 🚇 Marylebone

Shopping

When it comes to shopping, London has it all. The top end includes centuries-old businesses, which are fun for window-shopping and browsing, even if the prices are out of your range. Brits want good value for money, so there is a huge choice in the middle range. As for those on a tight budget, there are inexpensive stores and markets, though these tend to be away from the main shopping areas. In general, retailers are open seven days a week, usually from 10am, with "late-night shopping" for an extra hour or two, perhaps Wednesday or Thursday. Sunday is often a busy day, though the hours are shorter, usually 11am/noon until 5–6pm. The City, the financial district, is quiet at weekends.

Fashion

Ever since the Swinging Sixties, London has been known for edgy designers and quirky street fashion. The capital caters for all tastes, ages and pockets: designer labels and expensive bespoke (made-to-measure), British and international chains, classic as well as young and fun.

■ British "high-street fashion" means familiar chain stores selling good quality clothes in the mid-price range. **Regent Street** (➤ 67), **Oxford Street** (➤ 67), **Covent Garden** (➤ 167) and **Kensington High Street** (➤ 143) have the widest choice. Marks & Spencer has branches across the city, but the flagship store is at 458 Oxford Street.

■ To find everything under one roof, look in fashion-orientated department stores: **Harrods** (➤ 130), **Harvey Nichols** (➤ 142), **Liberty** (➤ 67) and **Selfridges** (➤ 67).

■ For boutiques, try **Chelsea** and **Kensington** (➤ 142); designer names are on **Bond Street** (➤ 68) and **Sloane Street** (➤ 142) and in the department stores below.

■ Classic British names **Aquascutum** and **Burberry** have flagship stores on Regent Street (➤ 67). For upmarket traditional menswear, walk down Jermyn Street; Savile Row is a byword for made-to-measure tailoring.

■ For young alternative fashions, retro, second-hand and vintage clothing, try **Portobello Road Market** (➤ 139) and **Camden Markets** (➤ 160).

■ For a one-stop base, with 275 shops in both high-street and designer categories, visit the **Westfield centre** (Tube: Shepherds Bush, Wood Lane) in West London.

Department Stores

■ For general gift ideas, household goods and clothes, check out: **Debenhams** and **John Lewis** (both on Oxford Street; ➤ 67) and **Peter Jones** on Sloane Square (➤ 143).

Art and Antiques

A thriving commercial art scene has both antiques and art from a bygone age, as well as pictures so fresh the paint is still drying. Many art galleries have small exhibitions, so even if you aren't buying, you can still go in to look.

■ If antiques are your passion, the auction houses of **Sotheby's** (34–35 New Bond Street, W1, www.sothebys.com) and **Bonham's** (101 New Bond Street, W1, www.bonhams.com. Tube: Bond Street), plus **Christie's** in South Kensington (85 Old Brompton Road, SW7, www.christies.com. Tube: South Kensington) provide the best hunting grounds. Viewing days before auctions are free and open to the public. Or, walk up Kensington Church Street (➤ 143), known for its antiques shops and art galleries.

■ The **galleries of Mayfair**, primarily Cork Street and Bond Street, show established names and sure-fire investments, with plenty of late 20th-century work.

■ Less intimidating (and less expensive) are the galleries in trendy **Hoxton** (Tube: Old Street). Here up-and-coming artists show their work.

Markets

■ **Portobello Road Market** (➤ 139) is one of London's best for antiques on Saturday; shops on the street are also worth a visit on weekdays.

■ **Borough Market** (➤ 114) is a cornucopia of delicious things to eat, from cheeses and hams to fruit and vegetables.

■ **Camden Markets** (➤ 160) offer the biggest and most eclectic range of stalls in London: clothing, antiques, food and crafts.

■ You can find young designer fashion in Spitalfields Market (➤ 92).

Entertainment

From theatre to musicals, clubbing to ballet, classical music to blues, the list of what to see and enjoy in London is endless. You can find entertainment at all levels and all prices: grand concert halls and theatres, experimental theatre and cramped clubs. London also boasts one of the world's most popular music venues, the 23,000-seat O2 Arena that sells over two million tickets a year. For listings of what's on and where, on every day and night of the week, buy a copy of *Time Out*, the weekly magazine.

Music

When it comes to variety, few cities can match London's year-round array of music, from rock and classical to jazz and world music. In summer, look out for open-air concerts in parks and in the grounds of grand mansions. Take a picnic and choose a fine day.

There are dozens of live gigs every night in London. Major concert venues include **The O2** (www.theo2.co.uk. Tube: North Greenwich), **HMV Hammersmith Apollo** (www.hammersmithapollo.com. Tube: Hammersmith), **Brixton Academy** (www.o2academybrixton.co.uk. Tube: Brixton), the **Roundhouse** (www.roundhouse.org.uk. Tube: Chalk Farm), **Shepherd's Bush Empire** (www.o2shepherdsbushempire.co.uk. Tube: Shepherd's Bush) and **Wembley Arena** (www.wembleyarena.co.uk. Tube: Wembley Park), as well as the **Barbican Centre** (➤ 92), **Queen Elizabeth Hall**, **Royal Festival Hall** (➤ 118) and **Royal Albert Hall** (➤ 144). Book ahead. Smaller venues include Ronnie Scott's, the famous jazz club. More of a nightclub is the Barfly, while the Dublin Castle pub features up-and-coming bands (➤ 32 and 168).

Clubbing

If you know the difference between hip hop, house, electro, techno and breaks, then London is the place for you. Favourite clubs include **Cargo**, **Proud**, **Fabric**, **nottinghillartsclub**, **Scala** and **Pacha**. Popular on the gay and lesbian scene are **Heaven** (www.heaven-live.co.uk. Tube: Charing Cross) and **Madame Jojo's** in Soho (➤ 168).

Finding Your Feet

Cinema

Film lovers should head for Leicester Square where there are several multi-screen cinemas, including **The Odeon**, showing the latest blockbusters. If you want to enjoy retro or arthouse films, try the **Prince Charles Theatre**, just off Leicester Square.

Classical Music & Opera

London has five orchestras: London Symphony Orchestra, London Philharmonic, Philharmonia, Royal Philharmonic and the BBC Symphony Orchestra.

- In summer, don't miss the **Proms**, an annual festival at the Royal Albert Hall, held from mid-July to mid-September (➤ 144).
- For opera, choose between the prestigious **Royal Opera House** (➤ 150) and the **English National Opera** (➤ 168), where works are sung in English.

Theatre

London is the world capital of live theatre and its 50 or so theatres attract some 14 million theatregoers each year.

- The **"West End"**, the area around Piccadilly Circus and Covent Garden, is synonymous with theatre.
- Central, but outside the West End are the **Royal National Theatre** (➤ 118) at the South Bank Centre, the **Barbican Centre** (➤ 92) and **Shakespeare's Globe** at Bankside (➤ 114). The **Royal Court** (➤ 144) and the **Old Vic** (➤ 118) are known for promoting the works of young unknowns, as well as major new plays by avant-garde writers.
- For buzzy "Off-West End" and fringe theatre, check out the **Almeida** (Almeida Street; www.almeida.co.uk).

Dress

Londoners rarely dress up for the theatre, opera, ballet (or even restaurants) any more, unless they are going out for a special celebration. "Smart casual" is the norm, but even well-cut jeans and trainers won't look out of place for a standard show.

Buying Tickets

- Go to the theatre box office **in person**. These are usually open from 10am to just before the evening performance; often there is no booking fee.
- Queue up at the **"tkts" ticket booth** in Leicester Square, WC2 (Mon–Sat 9–7, Sun 11–4). This sells reduced-price seats on the day, as well as up to a week in advance. The reductions tend to be for expensive seats, so these are value for money, rather than "cheap". Small booking fee.
- Buy tickets and find "special offers" on the **Society of London Theatre website** (www.officiallondontheatre.co.uk). Small booking fee.
- Use a ticket agency. There are many shops and agencies selling theatre tickets; the best and most reliable are members of the Society of Ticket Agents & Retailers, listed at **www.star.org.uk**.
- **Never buy tickets from anyone in the street**.
- The **cheapest tickets** are farthest from the stage, usually in the top tier, nicknamed the "gods", where you may need binoculars.
- **Matinees** (afternoon performances) can be cheaper than evening shows and it is usually easier to get tickets for them.
- Some theatres offer **restricted-view seats** (with a pillar in the way or off to one side) at a reduced rate.

St James's, Mayfair & Piccadilly

Getting Your Bearings   48
The Perfect Day   50
TOP 10   52
Don't Miss   58
At Your Leisure   60
Where to …   64

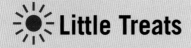 **Little Treats**

Feel Like the Queen
Take a Sunday stroll from Trafalgar Square through the Admiralty Arch and over **The Mall** (➤ 58).

Penthouse-style Dining
Enjoy a gourmet meal and a splendid at the **Portrait Restaurant** (➤ 65) in the National Portrait Gallery.

A Shop with the Flair of a Theatre
At **Liberty** (➤ 67), you not only shop in style, you can watch what's going on below from the antique wooden balustrade.

Getting Your Bearings

With royal palaces and fabulous art collections, historic churches and shops, as well as verdant parks, this area is quintessential London. If you have only one day in the city, consider spending it here.

A district of considerable wealth and architectural grandeur, this area contains the leafy squares and prestigious residential buildings of Mayfair, the exclusive gentlemen's clubs of St James's, and the long-established shops and hotels of Piccadilly, one of London's great thoroughfares. The heart of the empire beats at Buckingham Palace, the monarch's official residence, which since 1993 has thrown open its doors, in part at least, to the general public during August and most of September. At the eastern end is Trafalgar Square, with the National Gallery, home to the country's premier art collection.

Horse Guards on parade in Whitehall

The area owes its original development to St James's Palace, built by Henry VIII in the 1530s and subsequently the home of several later sovereigns, including Elizabeth I and Charles I. Charles, the current Prince of Wales, lived here, though he now resides in the adjacent Clarence House. Even though Buckingham Palace has been the main royal residence since 1837, ambassadors from foreign countries are still accredited to "the Court of St James".

The influence of royalty can be seen throughout this district. In the 17th century, King Charles II opened beautiful St James's Park to the public for the first time. By the 18th century, members of the aristocracy, wishing to be close to court, had built fine mansions within a short carriage drive. Today, Mayfair and St James's still exude the atmosphere of days gone by, with bespoke (made to measure) tailors, galleries selling Old Masters, designer boutiques and some of London's finest hotels, but there are also cosy pubs and shops selling antiques, and even a regular craft fair in a church, St James's Piccadilly. Do as Londoners do: take a walk in Green Park or St James's Park, and in fine weather, enjoy a simple picnic lunch on the grass. History and art, shopping and fun – you can have it all in this part of London.

Insider Tip

TOP 10
⭐ Buckingham Palace ➤ 52
⭐ National Gallery ➤ 54

Don't Miss
⓫ The Mall/
   Trafalgar Square

At Your Leisure
⓬ Churchill War Rooms ➤ 60
⓭ Royal Academy of Arts ➤ 60
⓮ Piccadilly & Regent Street ➤ 60
⓯ Piccadilly Circus ➤ 61
⓰ National Portrait Gallery ➤ 62
⓱ Banqueting House ➤ 62
⓲ Whitehall ➤ 63

Perfect Days in...

The Perfect Day

If you're not quite sure where to begin your travels, this itinerary recommends a practical and enjoyable day out in St James's, Mayfair and Piccadilly, taking in some of the best places to see. For more information see the main entries (52–63).

⏱ 10:00am

Start at ⭐**Buckingham Palace** (below, ➤ 52) and walk around to the left (south) side, Buckingham Gate. Visit the Queen's Gallery, which has changing exhibitions from the Royal Collection. The pavilion-style building is in the form of an Ionic temple and was designed by John Nash.

⏱ 11:00am

Be in front of the palace to watch the Changing of the Guard, one of London's most famous ceremonies (➤ see box below).

⏱ 12:15pm

The Changing of the Guard over, stroll through St James's Park; at the end, turn up to the tree-lined ➊ **Mall** (➤ 58).

Continue through Admiralty Arch; built a century ago, the gated central arch is opened only for the monarch. Since 2003, the revamped Trafalgar Square has become a focal point of the city. Now, Nelson looks down from his column at concerts, demonstrations and visitors photographing the lions.

CHANGING OF THE GUARD AT BUCKINGHAM PALACE

With their scarlet tunics and bearskins, the Queen's Guard is one of London's best-known sights. It is divided into two detachments: the Buckingham Palace Detachment and the St James's Palace Detachment. The idea of the ceremony is simple: the replacement of the current guard by a new one. From May to July, it takes place daily at 11:30; for the rest of the year, it's on alternate days. Be in place by 11, to see the arrival of the replacement troops, accompanied by a band with plenty of brass and drums. As well as military marches, they play popular melodies, like tunes from musicals. Note: there's no ceremony on very rainy days (www.royal.gov.uk).

✪ 1:00pm

Time for lunch. St Martin-in-the-Fields, at the top right (northeast) side of Trafalgar Square, has an inexpensive café in its Crypt, or try the Café or Espresso Bar at the National Gallery.

✪ 2:00pm

While away the afternoon viewing the superlative art collection at the ★ **National Gallery** (ill. below, ➤ 54). Rent one of the audio guides or join the free tour at 2:30; it lasts an hour and takes in half-a-dozen paintings.

Piccadilly & Regent Street **14**
Piccadilly Circus **15**
National Portrait Gallery **16**
al Academy of Arts **13**
National Gallery ★
The Mall/ Trafalgar Square **11**
Banqueting House **17**
Whitehall **18**
Buckingham Palace **2** ★
Churchill War Rooms **12**

✪ 4:00pm

Drop into the **16** National Portrait Gallery (➤ 62) for a quick look at its fascinating collection of portraits of famous Brits. Stop for a snack in the café at the top, which has a terrific view over London. Alternatively, leave Trafalgar Square for Pall Mall. After Lower Regent Street, take any right turn up into the area known as St James's. Jermyn Street is lined with historic shops selling perfume, menswear and cheese. Duke Street and King Street have art galleries.

⭐ Buckingham Palace

Buckingham Palace, one of London's most famous sights, so familiar to millions from newsreels and postcards, was built in the early 1700s by the Duke of Buckingham as Buckingham House. It was transformed into a palace by George IV in the 1820s, and has been the sovereign's home since Queen Victoria and Prince Albert moved here in 1837. The exterior doesn't look terribly impressive – more plain, solid and dependable rather than an exuberant celebration of majesty in stone.

Inside, however, the palace is absolutely sumptuous, and visitors can see the pomp for themselves during its six-week opening in late summer. Of the 775 rooms, the tour includes 19. These are the **State Rooms**, where the real work of royalty goes on, from state entertaining and investitures to receptions and official banquets.

Plush red carpet leads up the marble Grand Staircase, where the portraits remain as Queen Victoria placed

The white marble Queen Victoria Memorial in front of the palace

them. Everything is historic and opulent: glittering chandeliers, precious tapestries, priceless porcelain and fine furniture. In the Picture Gallery are masterpieces by Canaletto, Rembrandt and Rubens. At the end of the Throne Room, two "chairs of state" stand under a canopy; the State Dining Room is all scarlet and gilt, while the White Drawing Room dazzles. The glimpse of palace life

is fascinating; but don't expect to meet any of the Royal Family – they move elsewhere when the public come to call.

TAKING A BREAK

Along Buckingham Palace Road, opposite the Royal Mews, is the Rubens Hotel (tel: 020 78 34 66 00), where the **Cavalry Bar and Palace Lounge** serves sandwiches, salads and hot dishes.

Insider Tip

The Scots Guards head to Wellington Barracks after the Changing of the Guard parade

➕ 207 D4 ✉ SW1A 1AA
☎ Enquiries and credit card bookings: 020 77 66 73 00. Royal Mews: 020 77 66 73 02. Queen's Gallery: 020 77 66 73 01; www.royalcollection.org.uk
🕔 State Rooms: Aug–late Sept daily 9:30–6:30 (last admission 3:45). Royal Mews: late Mar–Oct daily 10–5; rest of year 10–4 (last admission 45 min before closing. Closed during state visits and some other days).
Queen's Gallery: 10–5:30; last admission 4:30. Closed some days
🚇 Green Park, Hyde Park, St James's Park, Victoria 🚌 Piccadilly 9, 14, 19, 22; Victoria Street 11, 211; Grosvenor Place 2. 16, 36, 38, 52, 73, 82
🎫 State Mews: £19 Mews, Queen's Gallery: £16.25 (combination ticket)

INSIDER INFO

- **Reserve tickets in advance** by credit card and collect them on the day. This is essential for the State Rooms (only a few are available on the day) and useful for the Queen's Gallery and Royal Mews (see below). Although tickets can be sent out by mail, you need to allow two weeks for United Kingdom and at least three weeks for overseas addresses.
- An **audio guide** (available in six languages) is included in the ticket price.
- The **Changing of the Guard** ceremony is very popular, so arrive early to get a good position in front (➤ 50).
- **Special tickets** offering a discount include a Royal Day Out (State Rooms, Gallery and Mews) and a Combined Visit (Gallery and Mews).

What is more:

- Unlike the State Rooms, you can visit the **Royal Mews** all year round to see the state carriages and coaches together with their horses. The collection's gem is the Gold State Coach.
- The **Queen's Gallery**, one of the finest private collections of art in the world, can be visited almost all year round.

☆ National Gallery

The National Gallery has one of the world's greatest collections of paintings. Covering the period from around 1250 to 1900, the cream of the nation's art collection includes some 2,300 significant works of European art. Behind the grand 1838 facade that dominates Trafalgar Square, virtually every famous western European artist is represented.

It is good to have a plan, rather than wandering around aimlessly. Choose a favourite period, a favourite painter, join a tour, or rent a themed audio tour. The gallery itself is free, so you can also see a little at a time. With four interconnected wings, the new Sainsbury Wing, the East, West and North Wings, the Gallery has three entrances. Start at the right-hand Getty entrance: you can pick up information, buy a gallery plan (£1), get your bags checked and leave your coats. From here you go up to the next floor.

West Wing

Just inside the Portico entrance, the West Wing is to the left. In Room 2, devoted to **Leonardo da Vinci and Northern Italy** are paintings by Correggio and Parmigianino. Room 4 is known for Hans Holbein the Younger's *The Ambassadors* (1533), with almost life-size portraits. The picture is crammed with symbol and allusion, mostly aimed at underlining the fleeting nature of earthly life. In the foreground is a clever trompe l'oeil of what appears be simply a white disc. The picture originally hung on a ceiling. Step to the right side of the painting and you can see that the disc is actually a 3D painting of a human skull. Devoted to Venice 1530–1600, Room 9 is filled with giant canvases by some of the giants of art: Tintoretto, Veronese and Titian. Tintoretto's fresh, dashing technique was quite revolutionary for its time.

Sainsbury Wing

Cross from the West Wing to the Sainsbury Wing through a series of archways that frame a Renaissance altarpiece by Cima da Conegliano at the far end. Highlights in this wing include the small but delicate *Wilton Diptych* (Room 53), a late 14th-century altarpiece commissioned by Richard II for his private prayers. Here, you will also find

An allegory of motherhood – the celebrated Leonardo da Vinci cartoon (*c*.1499) in the National Gallery depicts the Madonna and Child with a young John the Baptist an St Anne, the mother of the Virgin Mary

The National Gallery was designed as the architectural focus of Trafalgar Square

two world-famous works by Leonardo da Vinci his exquisite charcoal and chalk drawing of *The Virgin and Child with St Anne and St John the Baptist* (*c*.1499) in Room 51 and *The Virgin of the Rocks* (1508) in Room 57. Nearby are more star attractions: the *Battle of San Romano* (1438) by Paolo Uccello that dominates Room 54; Van Eyck's *Arnolfini Portrait* with its Latin inscription above the mirror saying "van Eyck was here" (Room 56); and Giovanni Bellini's *Doge Leonardo Loredan* among an identity parade of 15th-century VIPs in Room 62.

North Wing

Painters who challenged the primacy of the Italians during the **16th and 17th centuries** are the stars of the North Wing – Rubens, Rembrandt, Van Dyck, Velázquez, Vermeer and Claude. In Room 30, **Velázquez's *The Toilet of Venus*** (also known as *The Rokeby Venus* after Rokeby Hall in England where it once hung) is fascinating. Finished in 1651, when the Spanish Inquisition was in full swing, the nude figure was considered shocking. Also, look at the mirror: the goddess seems to be looking at you, rather than herself.

THE WINGS

The gallery is divided into four wings. Despite all its signage, it is hard to find your way around. The excellent staff are always happy to help.

- **West Wing** 16th century, Rooms 2–14
- **Sainsbury Wing** 13th–15th century, Rooms 51–66
- **North Wing** 17th century, Rooms 15–32
- **East Wing** 18th–early 20th century, Rooms 33–46

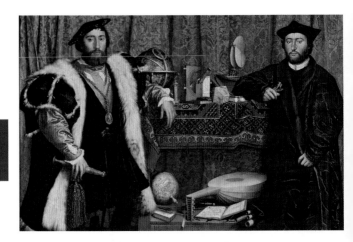

East Wing

With works by popular **British and modern French artists**, this is the busiest area. Rooms 34–36 feature 18th- and 19th-century Brits: portraits by Gainsborough and Reynolds, racehorses by Stubbs, plus **John Constable's *The Hay Wain*** (Room 34). First exhibited in 1821, the painting's unfinished nature took critics by surprise. More works by Constable are on display in Tate Britain (► 102) and the V&A Museum (► 126). In the same room, you can see how J. M. W Turner, a contemporary of Constable, developed a radically different style. Two of his finest pictures, *The Fighting Téméraire* (1838) and *Rain, Steam and Speed* (1844), display the almost hallucinatory effects of light on air and water, characteristic of the painter (Room 34). More of the same can be seen in Tate Britain (► 102).

In Room 35 are a **series of six paintings by Hogarth**: *Marriage A-la-Mode* (1743), a moral tale about the rise and fall of a family. Nearby, his *Shrimp Girl* looks as fresh as the day he painted it 250 years ago.

Rooms 43 to 46 are full of **Impressionist and post-Impressionist masterpieces**. Instantly recognizable paintings include one of Monet's seductive water lily paintings (Room 43), Seurat's *Bathers at Asnières* (1884) in Room 44, Van Gogh's *Sunflowers* (1889) in Room 45, and *Miss La La at the Cirque Fernando* (1879) by Degas, in Room 46.

▋TAKING A BREAK

Try the **National Dining Rooms** (Sainsbury Wing), **National Café** (Getty Entrance) or **Espresso Bar** (Getty Entrance).

The Ambassadors by Hans Holbein is among the best known of the National Gallery's many impressing masterpieces

Right: The splendid interior of the National Gallery provides a suitably grand setting for one of the greatest collections of paintings in Europe

---

✚ 205 F1 ✉ Trafalgar Square, WC2
☎ 020 77 47 28 85; www.nationalgallery. org.uk 🕐 Sat–Thu 10–6 (Fri till 9)
🍽 Restaurant and Café Ⓜ Charing Cross, Leicester Square 🚌 3, 6, 9, 11, 12, 13, 15, 23, 24, 29, 88, 91, 139, 159, 176, 453 🎟 free, special exhibitions, *c.* £7

INSIDER INFO

- The **audio guides** are excellent. Available in 12 languages, the one-hour tour is a fine introduction to the collection's major treasures. There are also themed audio tours, such as *Manet to Picasso* and the *Sounds of the Gallery*, with music. The cost is £3.50.
- The three children's  guides include the popular *Art Detectives* tour. With an audio guide, the younger generations follow two detectives on their search for clues through the museum and learn something about the paintings at the same time. Afterwards, they paint a picture. (under 12s go free with a paying adult).
- **ArtStart**, a multimedia touch-screen guide, has information on every painting and artist in the collection. The 14 computers in the Espresso Bar area near the Portico entrance are the busiest. The ArtStart area in the Sainsbury Wing is quieter, but has no coffee.
- Arguably, the best way to explore is on **a free tour**. One-hour tours take place daily at 11:30 and 2:30 (also Friday at 7pm). Meet at the Sainsbury Wing information desk. On weekdays, the 10-minute talk at 4pm focuses on an individual painting.
- There are **three shops** that are known for the quality of their merchandise, from books and prints to postcards and unusual souvenirs and gifts.
- **Friday Lates** features performances by students from the Royal College of Music on Friday evenings, when the gallery, café and bar are open till 9pm.

⓫ The Mall/ Trafalgar Square

The Mall is the grand, tree-lined processional avenue between Buckingham Palace and Trafalgar Square, a thoroughfare that comes into its own on ceremonial occasions such as the State Opening of Parliament in November and Trooping the Colour in June. Near the Mall are two royal parks: Green Park, which is at its best in spring when the daffodils are in flower, and St James's Park, which is a delight at any time of year.

The Mall

The Mall is a busy thoroughfare for most of the week. On state occasions, lined by enormous flags, it looks grand and dignified. On Sundays and holidays, however, it is closed to traffic, so people stroll, cycle and run along its red paving. Back in the 17th century, this was where King James I played a French game known as *palle-maille* (anglicized to pell mell), a mallet-and-ball game like croquet. The game has long gone out of fashion, but it is remembered in the names of the Mall and nearby Pall Mall.

Looking down the Mall on the left you can see 19th-century **Clarence House**, named after its first resident, the Duke of Clarence, who became King William IV in 1830. In 1953, when Queen Elizabeth II acceded to the throne, it became the London home of the late Queen Mother. After her death in 2002, Prince Charles, current heir to the throne, moved here. Behind Clarence House rise the red-brick Tudor turrets of **St James's Palace**, built in the 1530s by Henry VIII (who died here).

Outside Buckingham Palace is the white marble memorial to Queen Victoria, who died in 1901. As well as the monarch's statue, there are figures representing Courage, Constancy and Victory. From the palace, head off to explore **St James's Park**. Walk past the lake to the far end. In front of you is **Horse Guards Parade**, the huge open area. In June, it

The sweeping facade of Admiralty Arch

provides the stage for the ceremony, Trooping the Colour, to mark the Queen's birthday. A tradition of over 200 years, this pageant combines marching bands, troops and mounted cavalry. Throughout the year, the changing of the **Horse Guard** takes place here (➤ Tip below).

On to Trafalgar Square

To the north, facing the Mall is the elegant Carlton House Terrace, whose early 19th-century white stucco facade was the work of architect John Nash. To the right, through Admiralty Arch, is another

Nelson's Column dominates Trafalgar Square

Nash design, **Trafalgar Square**, laid out between 1829 and 1841. It commemorates British naval hero Admiral Horatio Nelson, whose statue, three times life-size, stands atop the 169-foot (51.5m) column. In 2006, during cleaning, the column was re-measured from the top of Nelson's hat to the ground and found to be much shorter than had been reported for 150 years: a full 14 feet (4.4m). Reliefs at its base depict four of his greatest naval victories; the most famous is the Battle of Trafalgar against the French in 1805 – where Nelson died. Since 2005, an eclectic succession of sculptures has topped the Fourth Plinth, on the plaza's northwest side. Dominating the northern flank is the **National Gallery** (➤ 54); to its right rises the spire of **St Martin-in-the-Fields**, a lovely church known for its concerts, first-rate café and brass-rubbing centre (➤ Tip below).

TAKING A BREAK

With its freshly prepared food, the self-service **Café in the Crypt** beneath St Martin-in-the-Fields church (➤ 64) is a popular spot at any time of day. You can enjoy a coffee, a glass of wine, a full meal or treat yourself to afternoon tea.

Insider Tip

🗐 207 D4–F5

At Your Leisure

12 Churchill War Rooms

You can almost feel Churchill's presence and smell his cigar smoke and, thanks to the free audio guides, you can hear his rasping voice for real as the bombs drop and the air-raid sirens sound outside. This underground warren provided secure accommodation for the War Cabinet and their military advisers during World War II and was used on more than 100 occasions. Today it is a time capsule, with the clocks stopped at 16:58 on 15 October 1940. You can visit the Map Rooms, the Transatlantic Telephone Room, the Cabinet Room, Churchill's bedroom and a museum devoted specifically to the great British leader.

➕ 207 F4
✉ Clive Steps, King Charles Street, SW1
☎ 020 79 30 69 61; http://cwr.iwm.org.uk
🕐 Daily 9:30–6 (last admission 5)
Ⓠ Westminster, St James's Park
🚌 3,11,12, 24, 53, 88, 148, 159, 211
🎫 £17

13 Royal Academy of Arts

Burlington House is one of the few remaining 18th-century Piccadilly mansions. Today it houses one of London's most illustrious art galleries, the Royal Academy, which stages a variety of high-profile exhibitions. June to August sees its annual Summer Exhibition, for which every aspiring artist in the country hopes to have a piece selected.

The Royal Academy is *the* artistic establishment; when it was founded in 1768, the association consisted of artists and architects – and Academicians, as members are called, are still chosen from these fields. They include David Hockney, Sir Anthony Caro and, from the younger generation, Tracey Emin. Spot up-and-coming talent at exhibitions of work by students at the Royal Academy School.

➕ 205 D1
✉ Burlington House, Piccadilly, W1
☎ 020 73 00 80 00; www.royalacademy.org.uk
🕐 Sat–Thu 10–6, Fri 10–10
🍽 Café and restaurant
Ⓠ Piccadilly Circus, Green Park
🚌 9, 14, 22, 38 🎫 £8–14

14 Piccadilly & Regent Street shopping

If you need a change from sightseeing and culture, visit some of London's most traditional stores along and around Piccadilly, St James's and Regent Street (➤ 67). The best of the Piccadilly shops are the old-fashioned bookstore, **Hatchards**, the high-class grocery, **Fortnum & Mason** (➤ 67), and the covered arcades of prestigious shops that lead off to left and right.

Don't miss **Burlington Arcade**, where the choice of cashmere knitwear and antique jewellery is particularly good. Piccadilly itself was named in honour of a 17th-century tailor who made his fortune from stiff collars called "picadils" and built a house, Piccadilly Hall – at least, that is one of the theories. The tradition of tailoring continues, but nowadays, the top names are in **Savile Row** and **Jermyn Street** (► 67). Looking like something out of a costume drama, Jermyn Street is lined with shops, many dating back two centuries.

In Regent Street, near Oxford Circus, is **Liberty**. Since its opening in 1875, when it promoted art nouveau and the Arts and Crafts Movement, it has been known for fabrics and design. Also on Regent Street are **Jaeger**, **Burberry** and **Aquascutum**, offering classic British styling. For children of all ages, the main attraction here is **Hamleys**, with seven floors full of toys.

➕ 205 E1
☎ www.regentstreetonline.com

🖪 Piccadilly Circus

While Piccadilly Circus features large in the minds of visitors to the city (a photograph in front of the statue at its heart is almost obligatory), most Londoners dismiss it as a tacky melee of tourists, traffic and noise.

Back in 1819, it was part of architect John Nash's ambitious

Elegant Burlington Arcade

design for this part of London, and was a real circus, or circle of buildings. The Eros statue, which represents the Angel of Christian Charity not the Greek god of love, was erected in 1893 in honour of Lord Shaftesbury (1801–1885). This campaigner for workers, the poor and the mentally ill is also commemorated by Shaftesbury Avenue; with six theatres, it is one of the main venues of London's theatreland.

The neon advertisements were introduced in the early 20th century, and have become something of a London icon – come after dark for the best effects.

➕ 205 E1

🔟 National Portrait Gallery

The gallery houses what is, arguably, the world's largest collection of portraits, paintings, sculptures and photographs of eminent Britons past and present. The material dates from the early 16th century to the modern era, and includes many of the country's most famous faces.

The monarchs represented here include Richard III, Henry VII,

Henry VIII, Elizabeth I and many members of the present Royal Family. However, it is the portraits of non-royals that are most memorable: the familiar image of Shakespeare, a drawing of Jane Austen by her sister, a painting of the Brontë sisters by their brother Patrick and striking photographs of Oscar Wilde, Virginia Woolf and Alfred, Lord Tennyson. Among recent literary stars are Salman Rushdie and Dame Iris Murdoch.

Politicians and figures from the arts, sciences, sport and media are also well represented. Look for the portraits of British prime ministers Margaret Thatcher and Tony Blair, scientist Stephen Hawking, film director Alfred Hitchcock and football player David Beckham. As well as the pemanent collection, there are special themed exhibitions, plus free lectures and workshops. At the top, the Portrait Restaurant has grand views over London (▶ 65).

➕ 205 F1 ✉ St Martin's Place, WC2
☎ 020 73 06 00 55; www.npg.org.uk
🕐 Daily 10–6 (also Thu–Fri 6–9)
Ⓔ Charing Cross, Leicester Square
🍴 Café and restaurant 🚌 3, 6, 9, 11, 12, 13, 15, 23, 24, 29, 53, 88, 91, 139, 159, 176
💷 free (some exhibitions £6.50–£13)

🔟 Banqueting House

The Banqueting House is the only remaining part of the old Palace of Whitehall, formerly the monarch's official home, which was destroyed by fire in 1698. It was built by the great architect Inigo Jones in the

The Contemporary Room at the National Portrait Gallery

Whitehall's elaborately decorated
Banqueting House

blocked off by a large gate, is where
the British prime minister has his (or
her) official residence. Traditionally
this is at No 10, while No 11 plays
host to the Chancellor of the
Exchequer. The only real patch of
colour is provided by the mounted
soldiers at Horse Guards.

At the centre of Whitehall is
the **Cenotaph**, a memorial to the
war dead and the solemn focus
of the annual Remembrance Day
Ceremony in November.

🕂 208 A2

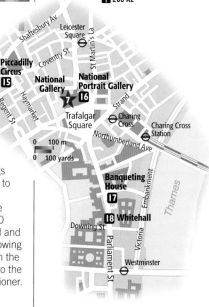

early 17th century, and
includes a painted ceiling
by Flemish artist
Peter Paul Rubens
as its decorative
centrepiece.
Installed in 1636,
the ceiling was com-
missioned by the
king, Charles I, who
paid the artist £3,000, an
astronomical sum at that
time. This, and other paintings
were all conceived as paeans to
Charles's father, James I.

It was from a window of the
Banqueting House that, on 30
January 1649, Charles I, tried and
convicted of high treason following
the defeat of Royalist forces in the
English Civil War, stepped onto the
scaffold and faced his executioner.

🕂 208 A2 ✉ Whitehall, SW1
☎ 0844 4 82 77 77; www.hrp.org.uk
🕐 Mon–Sun 10–5; closed public holidays and
for functions 🚇 Westminster, Embankment
🚌 3, 11, 12, 24, 53, 87, 88, 159
💷 £5; audio guide included

🔞 Whitehall

This busy but undistinguished
street lined by the bland facades
of government offices takes you
south from Trafalgar Square through
the heart of British Government.
Downing Street, a side turning

🎮 PLAYFUL PASTIMES

If the Changing of the Guard is not
sufficient to keep the youngsters
happy, you can offer them game fun
in the Hamleys, one of the world's
largest toy shops, Regent Street
(► 67), in the Disney Store, Oxford
Street (► 68), or at Funland, in the
Trocadero entertainment complex,
Piccadilly/Coventry St (► 67).

Where to...
Eat and Drink

Prices
The quoted prices are per person for a meal and do not include drinks or service.
£ under £ 25   ££ £25–50   £££ over £50

1707 Wine Bar, Fortnum & Mason £
The idea that a store's restaurant is more than somewhere to rest your feet is still somewhat novel, but the dishes served here are modern and innovative: ballotine of duck with walnuts and onion sauce, English brie and red pepper tart. Or just enjoy a glass of wine at the bar. Named for the date of Fortnum's founding, this cool, designer wine bar has added benefits: you can order any wine from the next door Wine Department and pay reasonable corkage. Ideal for pre-theatre meals.
✚ 205 D1 ✉ 181 Piccadilly, W1
☎ 084 56 02 56 94; www.fortnumandmason.com
🕐 Mon–Sat 12–9, Sun 12–6
Ⓠ Piccadilly Circus, Green Park

Al Duca ££
Tucked away on a side street in the posh St James's area, this cheerful, busy, stylish and very Italian oasis serves breakfast as well as lunch and dinner. Authentic dishes on the well-priced set menu might include roasted pork belly with lentils and black truffle, calf's liver in a Marsala sauce with pine nuts and raisins, or hazelnut parfait with warm chocolate sauce. The unfamiliar Italian wines offer good quality and good value.
✚ 205 E1 ✉ 4–5 Duke of York Street, SW1
☎ 020 78 39 30 90; www.alduca-restaurant.co.uk 🕐 Mon–Fri 8–11pm, Sat 12:30–11
Ⓠ Piccadilly Circus

Café in the Crypt £
There is no more unusual setting for a restaurant than the 18th-century crypt under St Martin-in-the-Fields.

This is, arguably, the best self-service restaurant around; the emphasis is on British dishes, prepared freshly from locally sourced ingredients. Ever popular are the traditional roast lunch on Sundays, fish & chips on Fridays, and apple crumble with custard. It also serves cream teas. The profits go to church projects.
✚ 208 A3 ✉ St Martin-in-the-Fields, Trafalgar Square, WC2 ☎ 020 77 66 11 58; www.stmartin-in-the-fields.org 🕐 Mon–Tue 8–8, Wed 8am–10:30pm, Thu–Sat 8am–9pm, Sun 11–6 Ⓠ Charing Cross, Leicester Square

Davy's at St James £
In an expensive part of town, this cellar-like restaurant, hidden away down a narrow alleyway, is affordable. Davy's is known as a wine merchant, so the food is more pub grub than fine dining: well-aged steaks, herb-crusted rack of lamb, Cumberland sausages for the bangers and mash, and bread-and-butter pudding with chocolate sauce for dessert. The evening two- or three-course set menu is good value.
✚ 207 E5 ✉ Crown Passage, off Pall Mall, SW1 ☎ 020 78 39 88 31; www.davy.co.uk
🕐 Mon–Fri 11–11 Ⓠ Green Park

Inn the Park £/££
The lovely setting in the heart of Royal St James's Park, overlooking the lake, makes this stylish restaurant and self-service café a popular spot to hang out. The approach is good, simple, British seasonal fare, from tasty breakfasts and mouth-watering cakes, to sandwiches, traditional pies and Sunday roasts.

In summer the place is buzzing, and there is a rooftop bar and alfresco dining area to take advantage of during milder weather.

➕ 207 E5 ✉ St James's Park, SW1
☎ 020 74 51 99 99; www.innthepark.com
🕐 Mon–Fri 8–4:30, Sat, Sun 9–5; dinner May–Sep daily 6–8:30 🚇 St James's Park, Green Park, Charing Cross

National Dining Rooms £/££

Climb the wide, stone staircase of the National Gallery's Sainsbury Wing, take a sharp left turn, and enter this quintessentially British restaurant. The bright, modern dining room is divided into a bakery-cum-café and a lunch-only restaurant, and the menu created by the head chef provides classic, regional dishes. Large picture windows give fine views over Trafalgar Square.

➕ 205 F1 ✉ The National Gallery, WC2
☎ 020 77 47 25 25 🕐 Daily 10–5 (Fri until 8:30) 🚇 Charing Cross

Portrait Restaurant ££

The contemporary Portrait Restaurant, at the top of the National Portrait Gallery, 92 feet (30m) above Trafalgar Square, is one of the hot spots to eat in London. What's more, the food actually matches the view over the Houses of Parliament and the London Eye: seared cured salmon, pumpkin, sweet potato and aubergine curry, venison, forest berry and sloe gin stew, apple, pear and blackberry crumble. Menus follow the seasons, so on a winter's day, look for traditional shepherd's pie or guinea fowl with mustard mash. Theatregoers enjoy the pre-theatre menu (Thu–Sat 5:30–6:30).

➕ 205 F1 ✉ St Martin's Place, WC2
☎ 020 73 12 24 90; www.npg.org.uk 🕐 Daily 10–11, 11:45–2:45, 3:30–5; dinner Thu–Sat 5:30–8:15 🚇 Leicester Square, Charing Cross

Sotheby's Café ££

One of Bond Street's best-kept secrets is tucked away in the lobby of Sotheby's auction house. Join the café's cosmopolitan clientele for stylish lunches and afternoon tea.

➕ 204 C2 ✉ 34–35 New Bond Street, W1
☎ 020 72 93 50 77 🕐 Mon–Fri 9:30–11:30, 12–4:45 🚇 Bond Street

Terroirs £/££

This French-style bistro has been an instant hit. Choose between a quiet or buzzy area, then enjoy a wide range of charcuterie (hams, terrines, *jambon persillé*) and cheeses, or hot dishes such as braised duck pie and slow-cooked pork belly with beans. There are also trendy small plates, or large tapas: smoked duck salad, potted shrimps, piperade Basquaise. Desserts include cherry clafoutis, Agen prune and Armagnac tart, and there's a grand selection of well-priced wines.

➕ 208 A3 ✉ 5 William IV Street, WC2
☎ 020 70 36 06 60; www.terroirswinebar.com
🕐 Mon–Sat 12–11 🚇 Charing Cross

Tibits £

Insider Tip

Connected with Europe's oldest vegetarian restaurant (Hiltl in Zurich), this is modern and hip. In a quiet pedestrian courtyard, so you can eat outside in fine weather, tibits is all about fresh produce: freshly squeezed juices, 35 inventive home-made salads and ever-changing hot dishes. Serve yourself, pay by the weight of what you choose. The cocktail bar is busy before dinner.

➕ 205 D1 ✉ 12–14 Heddon Street, off Regent Street, W1 ☎ 020 77 58 41 10; www.tibits.co.uk
🕐 Mon–Wed 9am–10:30pm, Thu–Sat 9am–midnight, Sun 11:30–10:30 🚇 Oxford Circus

Truc Vert £/££

A little bit of France in London, Truc Vert is a casual deli, *traiteur*, café and restaurant all in one. It's open all day, and the ambience changes in the evening for romantic dinners. The menu is more modern European than French: duck terrine with grilled brioche, roast fig, home-made pasta, grilled meats, sticky toffee pudding with vanilla ice cream, and vanilla honey panna-cotta with lemon syrup. Choose your wine in the store; many are from smaller, selected vineyards.

🚇 204 B2 ✉ 42 North Audley Street, W1
☎ 020 74 91 99 88; www.trucvert.co.uk
🕐 Mon–Fri 7:30–11:30, 12–10 Sat–Sun 9–4
Ⓜ Marble Arch, Bond Street

The Wolseley ££/£££

The award-winning Wolseley is housed in an opulent art deco building resplendent with chandeliers and marble pillars. Despite its grandeur it is friendly, serves excellent Modern British café-style food throughout the day and is perfect for breakfast or afternoon tea. Try one of the tempting old-fashioned ice cream sundaes.

🚇 207 D5 ✉ 160 Piccadilly, W1
☎ 020 74 99 69 96; www.thewolseley.com
🕐 Mon–Fri 7am–midnight, Sat 8am–midnight, Sun 8am–11pm Ⓜ Green Park

BARS & PUBS

Albannach £–££

A wee corner of Scotland, where the A Lounge has one of the best collections of single malt whiskies in London. In the vaults beneath Trafalgar Square, Albannach also serves signature whisky cocktails, and there are DJs at weekends. The Mezzanine restaurant offers authentic Scottish dishes, including haggis with neeps and tatties (turnips and potatoes) year round.

🚇 205 F1 ✉ 66 Trafalgar Square, WC2
☎ 020 79 30 00 66; www.albannach.co.uk
🕐 Restaurant: Mon–Sat 12–11, Sun 12–5;
A Lounge: Thu–Sat 7pm–1am (free), Fri–Sat 7pm–3am (charge) Ⓜ Piccadilly Circus, Charing Cross

The Clarence £

Steps away from the most powerful government offices, The Clarence is a traditional pub with lots of mock Tudor, from leather benches to beams and sturdy tables. One of the draws is the above-average

menu in the upstairs dining room: roast lamb, poached salmon salad, even ham hock hash, with a fried duck egg and brown sauce. The all-day breakfast is a useful fallback.

🚇 208 A3 ✉ 53 Whitehall, SW1
☎ 020 79 30 48 08; www.geronimo-inns.co.uk
🕐 Mon–Sat 12–9, Sun 12–10:30
Ⓜ Charing Cross, Embankment

Connaught Bar £££

This elegant bar, whose stylish interior is rather reminiscent of a luxury liner, is located in the Swiss Connaught Hotel. The cocktail prices match the refined surroundings – you should try a martini though, which is stylishly served in an extra trolley. The Coburg Bar is a bit more discreet. If you are hungry, the Espelette Restaurant service exquisite dishes. Both are in the same building.

🚇 204 C1 ✉ Carlos Place, W1K
☎ 020 73 14 34 19; www.the-connaught.co.uk
🕐 Mon–Sat 4–1, closed Sun Ⓜ Bond Street

Dover Street Restaurant & Bar ££/£££

For those who enjoy a cocktail, followed by dinner and dancing, this Dover Street favourite provides all three. The food is French/Mediterranean and the live bands play a variety of jazz, from funk and swing to blues and soul.

🚇 205 D1 ✉ 8–10 Dover Street, W1
☎ 020 74 91 75 09; www.doverst.co.uk
🕐 Mon–Thu 6pm–2am, Fri–Sat 7pm–2am
Ⓜ Green Park, Piccadilly Circus

The Only Running Footman £/££

Inside Tip

It is nice to find a real pub, just steps away from elegant Berkeley Square. As well as seriously gourmet sandwiches, such as seared scallops, butternut puree, pancetta crisps and sage butter, favourites include beer-battered fish and chips with real mushy peas.

🚇 204 C1 ✉ 5 Charles Street, W1 ☎ 020 74 99 29 88; www.therunningfootmanmayfair.com
🕐 Daily Mon–Fri 7:30am–11pm, Sat/Sun 9:30am–11pm Ⓜ Green Park

Where to ...
Shop

SAVILE ROW & JERMYN STREET

Both of these streets are known for top-quality menswear (🚇 Piccadilly Circus). Savile Row is synonymous with made-to-order tailoring. **Henry Poole** (at 15, www.henrypoole. com) was founded in 1806; almost 200 years later, **Richard Anderson** opened its doors (at 13, www. richardandersonltd.com).

Jermyn Street has the monopoly on men's shirt makers, with **Turnbull & Asser** (at 71–72, www.turn bullandasser.com) a well-known name. Many, such as **Hilditch & Key** (at 73, www.hilditchandkey. co.uk), now cater for women as well. Even if these don't suit your interest or price range, check out the other shops: **Floris**, per-fumers since 1730 (at 89, www. florislondon.com) and **Paxton & Whitfield**, offering 150 types of cheese (at 93, www.paxtonand whitfield.co.uk).

REGENT STREET

Regent Street (🚇 Piccadilly Circus, Oxford Circus) is a mix of old and new, home-grown and foreign names. Along Regent Street, stores range from **Aquascutum** (since 1851, at 100, www.aquascutum. com), purveyors of raincoats and tailored tweedy jackets since 1851, to **Apple** (at 235, www.apple.com), with the latest technology. From its mock-Tudor facade to the fash-ion and fabrics inside, **Liberty** (at 210–220, www.liberty.co.uk) is all about distinctive and beautiful design. **Hamleys** (at 188–196, www.hamleys.com) is one of the world's largest toy stores. On its seven floors, children or the young at heart can watch magic tricks and demonstrations – such as the pirate party!

Just off Regent Street, to the east, are other streets, such as the famous **Carnaby Street**, with an eclectic choice of shops (➤ 167).

PICCADILLY

On Piccadilly, **Fortnum & Mason** is a London institution (at 181, www. fortnumandmason.com), famous for its food emporium ranging from hams to single-estate-bean choco-late bars. The bookstore **Hatchards** (at 187; www.hatchards.co.uk) and **Waterstones** (at 203–206, www. waterstones.com) offer a wide selection of reading material. **The Trocadero** (near Piccadilly Circus, 7–14 Coventry Street, www.london trocadero.com) provides enter-taining games in its Gamerbase. (🚇 Green Park, Piccadilly Circus.)

OXFORD STREET

Britain's most famous shopping street is busy seven days a week. Right in the middle is Oxford Circus: in general, less expensive stores are to the east near Tottenham Court Road; to the west are de-partment stores (🚇 Oxford Circus, Bond Street, Marble Arch).

Topshop is always crowded, always up-to-the-minute and touts itself as the world's largest high-street fashion store (at 216, www. topshop.com). Right on Oxford Circus is **Niketown**, with everything for the sporty (at 236, http://Store. Nike.com/UK).

Heading west, the first depart-ment store is **John Lewis** (at 300, www.johnlewis.com). Known for quality and good prices, it sells everything from fashion to com-puters. The **Disney Store** satisfies fans of its films (at 350, www.disney store.co.uk), while **Selfridges** depart-ment store (at 400, www.selfridges.

com) is a must for cosmetics and fashions. Next door is **Marks & Spencer** (at 458, www.marksand spencer.com), one of Britain's best-known places to buy well-made, well-priced clothes for men, women and children. For inexpensive fashion, try the very popular **Primark** (at 499, www.primark.co.uk).

OFF OXFORD STREET

The South Molton Street is home to the somewhat smaller **Browns** and its sister boutique, **Browns Labels for Less** (at 24–27 and 50, www.brownsfashion.com). Steps away is **Gray's** (58 Davies Street and 1–7 Davies Mews, www.graysantiques.com), with 200 antique dealers in two adjacent locations. On the north side, the tiny **Gees Court** leads to **St Christopher's Place** (www.stchristophersplace.com); both are good for stylish boutiques.

BOND STREET

Glamorous and expensive: that is Bond Street (🚇 Bond Street, Piccadilly Circus, Green Park, Oxford Street). From Piccadilly, it flows north to Oxford Street past international legends: **Chanel**, **Dolce & Gabbana**, **Donna Karan New York**, **Yves St Laurent**. For British names, stop on Old Bond Street at **Joseph** (at 23, www.joseph.co.uk), which has an effortlessly stylish look.

On New Bond Street is **Nicole Farhi** (at 158, www.nicolefarhi.com), whose designs are as chic as her French background. Nearby is **Asprey** promises glamour with silver, jewellery, leather goods, china and glass (at 167, www.asprey.com). Further up is **Fenwick** (at 63, www.fenwick.co.uk), which has a good choice of fashion under one roof. Finally, as you walk along, pop into the side streets, such as Conduit Street, which also have upmarket boutiques.

Where to...
Go Out

NIGHTLIFE

Chinawhite (4 Winsley Street London W1, tel: 020 72 90 05 80, www.chinawhite.com) is exclusive and expensive. This Oriental-style celebrity haunt has loud music and bright lights (Wed–Sat 8pm–3am). **Babble** (Lansdowne House, 59 Berkeley Square, W1, tel: 020 77 58 82 55, www.babble-bar.co.uk) has a DJ every night. Open till 3am.

COMEDY

The **Comedy Store** is known for its hard-hitting, stand-up comedy (1a Oxendon Street, W1, tel: 084 48 71 76 99. 🚇 Piccadilly Circus). Food and drinks are served; over-18s only. Arrive at 6:30pm for a table; shows start 8pm (Tue–Sun).

MUSIC

An icon in rock 'n' roll's history, the **100 Club** (100 Oxford Street, W1, tel: 020 76 36 09 33; www.the100club.co.uk. 🚇 Oxford Circus) has featured everyone from the Rolling Stones and Kinks to Sir Paul McCartney in 2010. It features jazz, blues, comedy and more.

CINEMA

For unusual art-house films, check out the **Curzon Mayfair** (38 Curzon Street, W1, tel: 0330 5 00 13 31. Tube: Green Park); the **ICA** (The Mall, W1, tel: 020 79 30 36 47. Tube: Charing Cross) and the **Prince Charles** (7 Leicester Place, WC2, tel: 020 74 94 36 54. Tube: Leicester Square, Piccadilly Circus).

The City

Getting Your Bearings   70
The Perfect Day   72
TOP 10   74
Don't Miss   82
At Your Leisure   86
Where to ...   90

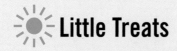 **Little Treats**

Building of the Future from the 1970s
Sit on a bench at the **Barbican** (➤ 71) mull over the impressions of this labyrinth of culture as you stare at the fountains.

Concealed, dark, quaint
Go on a trip back through time to the **Ye Olde Cheshire Cheese pub** (➤ 91) – admittedly not that easy to find.

Green lawyers
If you wander through **Lincoln's Inn** (➤ 87), the lawyer's park, you can appreciate the love of the English for a well-kept garden.

Getting Your Bearings

The City of London, the commercial heart of the capital, is one of the busiest financial centres in the world, with banks, corporate headquarters and insurance companies occupying dramatic showcases of modern architecture. Yet alongside the glass-and-steel office buildings, you find beautiful 17th-century churches, cobbled alleyways, historic markets and even fragments of the original Roman city wall.

The modern City stands on the site of the Roman settlement of Londinium, and has long been a centre of finance and government. Historically, it had an identity separate to that of the rest of the capital. When Edward the Confessor moved his palace from the City of London to Westminster in 1042, the area retained some of its ancient privileges, and later in the 14th century secured charters granting it the right to elect its own mayor and council. Even the sovereign could not enter the City without formal permission. Today, the legacy of these privileges still survives. The Corporation of London, the successor to the original council, which is overseen by the Lord Mayor, administers the City through council meetings held in the Guildhall.

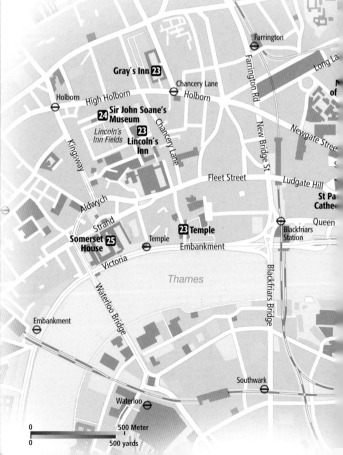

Getting Your Bearings

Much of the medieval City was destroyed by the Great Fire of 1666 (►16), although the Tower of London survived. In the construction boom that followed, architect Sir Christopher Wren was commissioned to build more than 50 churches, the most prominent and well-known of which is St Paul's Cathedral.

The City is also home to the modern Barbican Centre, a performing arts complex. There are also a number of notable museums in the city, i. a. the acclaimed Museum of London; the Museum of the Bank of England; the Sir John Soane's Museum, a 19th-century time capsule with the most diverse exhibits; and the Courtauld Gallery with a breathtaking collection of Impressionist and Post-Impressionist paintings. Just on the outskirts of the city lie the historic Inns of Court, the heart of legal London.

TOP 10

⭐ St Paul's Cathedral ►74
🔟 Tower Bridge ►78

Don't Miss

⑲ Tower of London ►82

At Your Leisure

⑳ Leadenhall Market ►86
㉑ Bank of England Museum ►86
㉒ Museum of London ►86
㉓ Inns of Court ►87
㉔ Sir John Soane's Museum ►88
㉕ Somerset House ►89

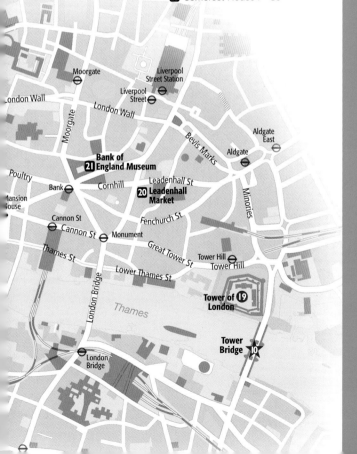

The Perfect Day

If you're not quite sure where to begin your travels, this itinerary recommends a practical and enjoyable day out in the City, taking in some of the best places to see. For more information see the main entries (➤ 74–89).

🕘 9:00am

Try to be at the **⑲ Tower of London** (left, ➤ 82) as it opens (at 10am on Sunday and Monday) to beat the worst of the crowds, even if this means you may get caught up in the morning rush hour. The rewards are the Crown Jewels, ravens, Beefeaters and an insight into the long and often bloody history of London from the perspective of its famous fortress. You can buy entrance tickets in advance online at www.hrp.org.uk.

🕚 11:30am

Walk up on to nearby **⑩ Tower Bridge** (below, ➤ 78) and visit the Tower Bridge Exhibition for an excellent history of the structure. Stunning views of the River Thames make the climb to the top worthwhile.

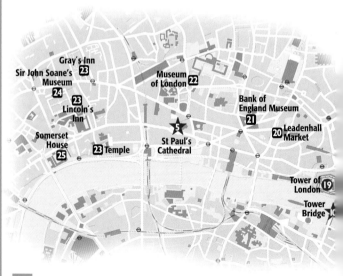

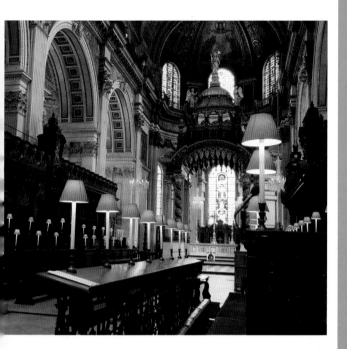

🕐 1:00pm

Take a break for refreshment with a hearty pub lunch at the atmospheric Hung Drawn & Quartered (➤ 91), a few steps from the Tower of London.

🕑 2:15pm

Walk back across the bridge and catch the No 15 bus from Tower Hill, the main road to the north of the Tower, which will deliver you outside St Paul's Cathedral.

🕒 3:00pm

Go up to the galleries at the top of the dome of ⭐**St Paul's Cathedral** (above, ➤ 74) for magnificent views of the city. Stop for a coffee in the café in the crypt, then soak up the magnificence of the architecture and artefacts around you.

🕔 5:00pm

Stroll down Ludgate Hill to Fleet Street. Beat the office workers' rush to one of London's most famous pubs: up an alleyway, **Ye Olde Cheshire Cheese** (➤ 91) has hosted writers such as Dr Samuel Johnson, Mark Twain and Sir Arthur Conan Doyle in its day. Catch the No 15 bus back to Trafalgar Square.

⭐5 St Paul's Cathedral

The towering dome of St Paul's Cathedral has stood sentinel over London for around 300 years, a lasting testament to the revolutionary genius of its architect, Sir Christopher Wren. Innovative and controversial, the cathedral rose from the ashes of the Great Fire of London in the 17th century, making it a positive youngster when compared with the medieval cathedrals of most European countries. Centuries later it became a symbol of London's unbeatable spirit, standing proud throughout the wartime Blitz of 1940–41. Later again it was the scene of national events, such as the wedding of Prince Charles to the late Diana, Princess of Wales (then Lady Diana Spencer) in 1981.

On first entering the cathedral take a few moments to just soak up the building's grandeur. Soaring arches lead the

VITAL STATISTICS

- The cathedral's, and Britain's, largest bell, Great Paul, which weighs 16.5 tons (15,000kg), is rung at 1pm every day for 5 minutes.
- The distance from ground level to the very top of the cross on the cathedral's roof measures just short of 365 feet (111.3m).
- The clock, Big Tom, on the right-hand tower on the cathedral's West Front is almost as big as the one in Big Ben. It is 16 feet (5m) in diameter and the minute hand 10 feet (3m) in length.

St Paul's Cathedral

eye towards the huge space below the main dome, and on to a series of smaller, decorated domes that rise above the choir and distant high altar.

Move to the centre of the nave, marked by an intricate black-and-white compass pattern. Looking up into the **dome** from here you can admire the Whispering Gallery (► below), the monochrome frescoes by 18th-century architectural painter Sir James Thornhill (1716–1719) of the life of St Paul, and the windows in the upper lantern. The ceiling's shimmering mosaics, completed in the 1890s, are made from around 30 million pieces of glass.

Then take in the area around the **altar**, a part of the cathedral filled with exquisite works of art. Master wood-carver Grinling Gibbons designed the limewood choir stalls, and Jean Tijou, a Huguenot refugee, created the intricate ironwork gates (both were completed in 1720). The canopy, based on a bronze canopy in St Peter's, Rome, is made of English oak and dates from 1958.

The Galleries and Crypt

You children will enjoy a visit to the top of the dome. Part way up, after 257 steps, is the 🔢 **Whispering Gallery**: whisper on one side and you can be heard on the other. For breath-taking views over London, climb the full 528 steps to the **Golden Gallery** (279 feet/85m). By contrast, beneath the cathedral, is Western Europe's largest crypt. This is a peaceful spot, with its tombs of great painters and poets, as well as two legendary British war heroes: Admiral Nelson and the Duke of Wellington. Wellington's ornate funeral car was made from guns captured at Waterloo and needed 12 horses to pull it. Read the Latin inscription on a wall plaque near the plain stone that marks the grave of the architect Christopher Wren. Translated, it is one of Britain's best-known epitaphs: "If you seek a memorial, look around you."

Looking up at the dome of St Paul's Cathedral

TAKING A BREAK

Visit the **Café** for cakes, the Barrow in the Crypt for cheeses and breads, and the Restaurant for lunch (►91).

✚ 209 E4 ☎ 020 72 36 41 28; www.stpauls.co.uk ✉ Ludgate Hill, EC4
🕙 Mon–Sat 8:30–4:30 (last admission 4) 🍴 Café and restaurant
Ⓡ St Paul's 🚌 4, 11, 15, 23, 25, 26, 100, 242 💷 £16; free for Sun service

Wren's legacy

The second largest church dome in the world after St Peter's Basilica in Rome came into being "thanks" to a catastrophe. After the Great Fire of 1666, it was necessary to replace the Old St Paul's which had burnt down. The new cathedral is the architectural legacy of Sir Christopher Wren.

❶ Towers: The bell towers are 154 feet (47m) high. There are twelve bells in the left tower, and the right tower contains Great Paul. Cast in 1882, it remains England's largest and heaviest bell, weighing 16.5 tons (15,000kg).

❷ Nave: The entire building is 557 feet (170m) long, and the nave is 246 feet (75m) wide. Stand in the centre and look up into the dome: it is a breathtaking sight!

❸ Dome: Measured from the base to the crucifix, the dome has a height of 364 feet (111m). Two galleries, the Stone Gallery and the Golden Gallery provide beautiful views down into the church.

❹ Crypt: There are many famous Britons entombed in the crypt: Wellington, Nelson, Lawrence of Arabia and naturally Christopher Wren.

❺ Gable decoration: Francis Bird created the statue of St Paul, which stands atop the West Front flanked by the apostles St John and St Peter.

❻ Whispering Gallery: 108 feet (33 m) above the ground, the Whispering Gallery offers not only a wonderful view of the dome's murals but also an amusing phenomenon due to the construction: you can hear every word whispered on the opposite side.

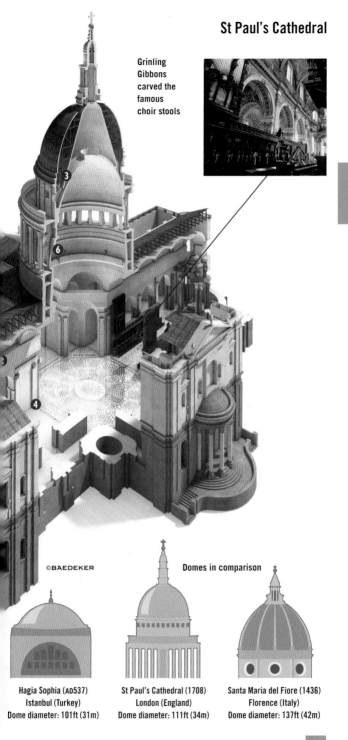

Grinling Gibbons carved the famous choir stools

3

6

4

©BAEDEKER

Domes in comparison

Hagia Sophia (AD537)
Istanbul (Turkey)
Dome diameter: 101ft (31m)

St Paul's Cathedral (1708)
London (England)
Dome diameter: 111ft (34m)

Santa Maria del Fiore (1436)
Florence (Italy)
Dome diameter: 137ft (42m)

⭐ 10 Tower Bridge

Tower Bridge is one of London's most familiar landmarks and the views from its upper walkway are some of the city's best, yet it has occupied its prominent place on the capital's skyline for only a little over 100 years.

By the late 1800s, crossing the River Thames had become a major problem. London Bridge was then the city's most easterly crossing, but more than a third of the population lived even further east. Building a new bridge, however, posed a dilemma for architects and planners. Any construction had to allow tall-masted ships to reach the Upper Pool, one of the busiest stretches of river in the world, handling ships and goods from all corners of the British Empire. It also needed to be strong and adaptable enough to allow for the passage of motor and horse-drawn vehicles. Though

Opened in 1894, Tower Bridge is one of the most recognizable bridges in the world

INSIDER INFO

Anyone travelling with children should try to see the 🚩 **bridge lifting**. It does not open every day, so phone: 020 79 40 39 84 or visit the website www.towerbridge.org.uk for times. Equally exciting is the view from the top and in the Victorian engine room which houses the drive system used to raise the bridge. The noises and smells are like a step back in time.

designs had been submitted to Parliament since the 1850s (more than 50 were rejected), it wasn't until 1886 that one was finally approved. The plan for a remarkable lifting roadway (known as a "bascule" bridge after the French word for see-saw), was the brainchild of architect Horace Jones and engineer John Wolfe Barry.

Access to the bridge's towers and walkways is via the **Tower Bridge Exhibition**, a display of film, artefacts and photographs explaining the history, construction and operation

of the bridge. You also get to visit the original Victorian engine rooms, which were used to power the bridge right up until 1976.

The highlight of your visit, however, is the view from the upper walkway, where there are also some fascinating archive photographs, as well as interactive computers which offer more detail on Tower Bridge and the surrounding area.

TAKING A BREAK

For a treat, have lunch on the south bank of the river at **Cantina del Ponte** (➤ 116): Italian food, great views of the bridge.

✚ 210 C3 ☎ 020 74 03 37 61, www.towerbridge.org.uk
🕓 April–Sep daily 10–6; Oct–Mar 9:30–5:30. Last entry 30 min before closing time 🚇 Tower Hill, London Bridge
🚌 40, 42, 47, 78, 100, RV1 J£8

VITAL STATISTICS
■ The bridge took eight years to build and involved 5 contractors and the labour of 432 constructions workers.
■ Its structure is brick and steel, but it is clad in Portland stone and granite to complement the nearby Tower of London.
■ The bridge is 801 feet (244m) long, the central span is 200 feet (61m) long and the towers are 213 feet (65m) high.
■ Each moving bascule weighs *c.* 1,200 tons.
■ The height from the road to the upper walkways is 108 feet (33m).

Masterpiece of Engineering

Tower Bridge competes with Big Ben for the position of London's most famous landmark. You can count yourself lucky if you see the bridge open, an experience you can ensure you have by looking up the times and names of the ships passing underneath at www.towerbridge.org.uk.

These days, the bridge opens on average only 20 times a week

St Paul's Cathedral

❶ North Tower: Like its opposite half, the North Tower is 213 feet (65m) high and stands on a pier containing *c.* 71,000 tons of concrete – which was, at the time of construction, the heaviest in the world. Today, this is the entrance to the bridge exhibition.

❷ Upper walkway: is 108 feet (33m) above the road and 139 feet (42.4m) above the annual mean high tide. In 1912, Frank McClean flew a biplane between the upper and lower spans of the bridge.

❸ South Tower: In the South Tower, there is an exhibition depicting the everyday life of the people who built the bridge.

❹ Steel skeleton: Each tower has a steel framework clad in stone. The bridge contains a total of over 11,000 tons of iron and steel as well as over 37,000 tons of concrete, 29,000 tons of bricks and 30,000 tons of natural stone.

❺ Bascules: Each of the two bascules weighs *c.* 1,200 tons. They function like a rocker and take about a minute to lift to their maximum angle of 86 degrees. They are operated using a modern electro-hydraulic drive system. The original pumping engines can be viewed in the old engine room under the south side of the bridge.

❻ Passage: When the bascules are open, ships of up to 10,000 BRT can pass through the wide passage (200 feet/ 61m). In 1952, a crowded double-decker bus had to leap over the gap – the bridge attendant had given the driver incorrect information.

©BAEDEKER

🄆 Tower of London

The Tower of London, begun by William the Conqueror shortly after the 1066 conquest, has survived for more than 900 years as a palace, prison, place of execution, arsenal, royal mint and jewel house. Throughout this time it has remained woven into the fabric of London and its history, while maintaining its essential character as a fortress and self-contained world within the defensive walls.

The Tower of London was begun in 1066, its position affording clear views of any enemy forces that might approach up the Thames

The Crown Jewels

Begin at the Jewel House. In 2012, Britain celebrated Queen Elizabeth II's Diamond Jubilee. To mark her 60-year reign, a special exhibition featured the Crown Jewels, one of the world's richest collections of regalia (ceremonial objects). What distinguishes the English regalia from most European royal treasures is that it is still in regular use. Archive footage of the Queen's coronation in 1953 shows off the most important piece on display: the St Edward's Crown, used since 1661 to crown a new sovereign. The most dazzling has to be the **Imperial State Crown**, worn by the monarch at the State Opening of Parliament (in October or November), encrusted with 2,868 diamonds, 273 pearls, 17 sapphires, 11 emeralds and 5 rubies. Other treasures include the **Sovereign's Sceptre**, which contains the world's largest cut diamond, Cullinan I. Equally magnificent is the crown of Elizabeth, the late Queen Mother, with its fabled Koh-i-Noor diamond. Believed to bring bad

Historical weapons in the White Tower

Tower of London

luck to men, this is only ever used in a woman's crown. Move on to the Salt Tower, where the walls have graffiti carved by prisoners.

Tower Green

This benign-looking spot was the place of execution of seven high-ranking prisoners, the most notable of whom were Anne Boleyn and Catherine Howard, Henry VIII's second and fifth wives (both beheaded following charges of adultery and treason). Execution here was an option reserved for the illustrious – less socially elevated prisoners met a much slower, more painful end on nearby Tower Hill. The executioner's axe and block are on display in the White Tower.

The White Tower

The Tower's oldest and most striking feature is the White Tower, begun around 1078, its basic form having remained unchanged for more than 900 years. Today its highlight is a superlative collection of armour, a display that manages to be awe-inspiring and strangely beautiful at the same time. Henry VIII's personal armour is the main attraction, but smaller pieces, such as the suits crafted for young boys, are equally interesting. Be sure to see the evocative and still used, Chapel of St John's, one of England's earliest remaining church interiors, and also take a peep into some of the tower's "garderobes" – 11th-century lavatories.

The Bloody Tower

Not all prisoners in the Tower lived – and died – in terrible conditions. Some passed their time in more humane lodgings. One such prisoner was Sir Walter Raleigh, explorer, philosopher and scientist, who was held in the Bloody Tower from 1603 to 1616, accused of plotting against James I. The Tower's most notorious incumbents, partly the reason for its name, were the "Princes in the Tower". Following the death of King

THE TOWER RAVENS

Ravens have been associated with the Tower throughout its history. Legend tells how King Charles II wanted to get rid of the birds, but was told that if they ever left the White Tower the kingdom would fall and disaster would strike. No chances are taken these days – one wing of each raven is clipped. Royal ravens have to behave though. Raven George was sacked, for example, when he developed a taste for television aerials.

Edward IV in 1483, the princes – the King's sons Edward (the heir to the throne) and his younger brother Richard – were put in the Tower under the "protection" of their uncle, Richard, Duke of Gloucester. However, the boys mysteriously vanished and, in their absence, their uncle was crowned King Richard III. The skeletons of two boys, presumed to be those of the princes, were found hidden in the White Tower 200 years later. Richard's involvement, or otherwise, in the boys' death has been much debated since, but never proved one way or the other.

The Medieval Palace

The entrance to the Medieval Palace lies just beside the infamous **Traitors' Gate**, the river entrance to the Tower through which many prisoners arrived for their execution. The palace is laid out as it would have been

Above: The Tower seen across the River Thames

Right: Traitor's Gate was the entrance to the Tower from the river

Below: The forbidding walls of the Tower

Tower of London

BEEFEATERS

The tower's guards, or Yeoman Warders, are commonly known as Beefeaters – believed to be due to them being able to eat as much beef as they liked from the King's table. About 35 in number, they all have a military background, and perform ceremonial duties around the Tower – they'll also answer your questions and give you directions. On state occasions, the Beefeaters change into a red and gold uniform.

in Edward I's reign (1272–1307), and staffed by costumed guides. From the palace you should stroll along the Wall Walk on the Tower's south side, a route that offers fine views of Tower Bridge (▶78). This route also takes you through the Wakefield Tower, in whose upper chamber Edward I's throne room has been dramatically reconstructed.

TAKING A BREAK

Choose between the New Armouries Restaurant in the Tower, snacks from Raven's kiosk or the Apostrophe Café. Or order sandwiches for a picnic on the grass.

✚ 210 C3 ✉ Tower Hill, EC3
☎ 0844 4 82 77 99; www.hrp.org.uk
🕑 Mar–Oct Tue–Sat 9–5:30, Sun–Mon 10–5:30;
Nov–Feb Tue–Sat 9–4:30, Sun–Mon 10–4:30.
Last admission 30 min before closing
🍴 Café and restaurant
🚇 Tower Hill 🚌 15, 42, 78, 100, RV1
💷 £19.50

INSIDER INFO

- Come **early** in the morning to avoid the crowds.
- **Buy admission tickets in advance online** at www.hrp.org.uk to **avoid a long wait** at the main ticket office.
- On arrival, head straight for the Jewel House and visit the **Crown Jewels** – this is the Tower's most popular attraction and soon becomes crowded.
- 👫 Children can discover the palace secrets by taking the Knights and Princesses Trail through the tower. A pencil and a map are available in the Welcome Centre.
- If you have time, the Yeoman Warders (▶Beefeaters, above) lead free, hour-long **guided tours**, departing every 30 minutes (until 3:30 in summer, 2:30 in winter), throughout the day. Most of the guides are great characters and bring the history of the Tower wonderfully alive.

Insider
Tip

At Your Leisure

20 Leadenhall Market

This iron-and-glass Victorian food hall, built on the site of an ancient medieval market. The huge glass roof and finely renovated and painted ironwork, plus the bustle of the crowds, make this one of the best places in the City to browse, grab a snack or linger over lunch.

Insider Tip

➕ 210 B4
✉ Whittington Avenue, EC3
🕐 Mon–Fri 7–4
🚇 Monument 🚌 25, 40

21 🏛 Bank of England Museum

With a history going back to 1694, the Bank of England set the pattern for modern banking. All this is explained on the excellent audio guide, but it is the hands-on exhibits that are so popular. Children interested in history can learn about how banks worked in earlier times or about inflation. The interactive exhibits are entertaining, especially the genuine gold bar that you can actually pick up! Learn how bank notes are printed and the complex security devices used to beat counterfeiters. If you fancy yourself as a financial whizz-kid, there are interactive computer programs that allow you to simulate trading on the foreign exchange markets.

➕ 210 A4
✉ Bartholomew Lane, EC2
☎ 020 76 01 55 45; www.bankofengland.co.uk
🕐 Mon–Fri 10–5 🚇 Bank
🚌 8, 11, 23, 25, 26, 47, 48, 133, 141, 149, 242
✋ Free

22 🏛 Museum of London

Long one of London's most fascinating museums, this is now even better thanks to the five new Galleries of Modern London. There is a particularly evocative portrayal of the turbulent 17th century, which is also fun for children. How were people treated during the Great Plague? How did they experience the Great Fire of 1666? Wearing a fireman's helmet, you enter a multimedia environment that brings the catastrophe to life. In the garden, historical costumes and window displays conjure up the Victorian period. The exhibition is chronologically arranged and begins with the "London before London" exhibition, highlighting the ever-important River Thames. Featuring 300 objects dredged from the Thames, the "River Wall" displays iron and bronze swords. Hundreds of historic objects, and dozens of hi-tech interactive displays ensure that layer upon layer of London's history comes

Kids find London's "Galleries of Modern London" interesting as well

to life, from the reconstruction of a Roman kitchen and a Stuart dining room to a grim cell from Newgate prison and a 1920s shop interior.

🔳 209 E5
✉ London Wall, EC2 ☎ 020 70 01 98 44; www.museumoflondon.org.uk
🕐 Daily 10–6; last admission 5:30
🍴 Café 🚇 St Paul's, Barbican
🚌 4, 8, 25, 56, 100, 172, 242, 521 🎫 Free

🔢 Inns of Court

Entered through narrow, easy-to-miss gateways, the four Inns of Court are a world away from the busy city outside. Their ancient buildings, well-kept gardens and hushed atmosphere create an aura of quiet industry. Home to London's legal profession, the Inns began life in the 14th century as hostels where lawyers stayed. Until the 19th century, the only way to obtain legal qualifications was to serve an apprenticeship at the Inns, and even today barristers must be members of an Inn.

While most of the buildings are private, some are open to the public; even if you don't see inside any of the august institutions it is enough simply to wander the small lanes and cobbled alleyways, where you often stumble upon unexpected courtyards and gardens.

Inner and Middle Temple

Fans of *The Da Vinci Code* flock to **Temple Church** to see the effigies

of 10 knights who were part of the riddle. Dating from 1185, this round church had links with the Knights Templar, soldier monks, who protected pilgrims travelling to the Holy Land. That probably explains why its design resembles Jerusalem's Church of the Holy Sepulchre. Thanks to Shakespeare's *Henry VI, Part I*, the legend grew that the 15th-century Wars of the Roses were triggered in Temple Gardens, when rival knights plucked a red and a white rose. Still in use, the 450-year-old **Middle Temple Hall** has hosted Queen Elizabeth I and Sir Walter Raleigh. A table is made from the hatch of *The Golden Hind*. And in 1602, Shakespeare's *Twelfth Night* was first performed here.

🔳 208 C4
✉ Access from Fleet Street, just opposite end of Chancery Lane, EC4 🕐 Middle Temple Hall: usually Mon–Fri 10–12, but it can be closed if there is a function taking place 🚇 Temple

Lincoln's Inn

Still used by lawyers are the medieval Hall, the late 17th-century New Square in the centre, and the fine Victorian Gothic Great Hall and Library beside Lincoln's Inn Fields. As well as educating 15 British Prime Ministers, from Pitt to Tony

ST OLAVE'S CHURCH RECITALS *Insider Tip*

This tiny, medieval church had a lucky escape when it was spared the ravages of the Great Fire of London in 1666 (▶ 16) by a sudden change of wind direction. The church was restored after wartime bombing. It is the burial place of famed diary-keeper Samuel Pepys, who used to worship at the church. Every Wednesday and Thursday lunchtime (except August) at 1:05pm there are free classical music recitals, a tradition of more than 50 years. A donation is welcomed though.
🔳 210 B3 ✉ Hart Street, EC3 🕐 Sept–July Mon–Fri 10–5 🚇 Aldgate, Tower Hill

The City

Blair, the Inn's halls are lined with reminders of illustrious former students, such as the poet John Donne and William Penn, the founder of Pennsylvania. Designed by Inigo Jones in the early 17th-century, the chapel is atmospheric, with four fine stained-glass windows by Dutch masters Abraham and Bernard Van Linge.

✚ 208 C5
✉ Entrances off Chancery Lane and Lincoln's Inn Fields, WC2
🕐 Chapel: Mon–Fri 12–2:30 🚇 Holborn

Gray's Inn

Entrance from High Holborn, Gray's Inn Road and Theobald's Road. This Inn dates from the 14th century, but was much restored after damage during World War II. Famous names to have passed through its portals include the writer Charles Dickens, who was a clerk here between 1827 and 1828. Its highlights are the extensive gardens or "Walks" as they are commonly known (Mon–Fri 12–2:30), once the setting for some infamous duels and where diarist Samuel Pepys used to admire the ladies promenading. The chapel is also open to the public (Mon–Fri 12–6), but lacks the charm of its Lincoln's Inn equivalent (►87).

✚ 208 C5
🚇 High Holborn, WC1
🕐 Chapel: daily
🚇 Holborn

24 Sir John Soane's Museum Inside Tip

When 19th-century gentleman, architect and art collector Sir John Soane died in 1837, he left his home and its contents to the nation. The only condition of his bequest, the terms of which were enshrined in a special Act of Parliament, was that nothing in his home be altered. The resulting museum, a charming artistic and social showcase, has remained unchanged for 175 years.

Soane was i. a. the architect of the Bank of England and rich enough to pursue his passion for collecting; a passion that seems to have been more or less unchecked or unguided – he simply bought whatever caught his eye. As a result, the house is packed with a miscellany of beautiful but eclectic objects, with ceramics, books, paintings, statues and even a skeleton jostling for space. One of the collection's highlights is hidden behind shutters, so ask a warden to show you the eight paintings that make up William Hogarth's *A Rake's Progress*. Painted in 1733, this series is like a moral cartoon, describing the rapid downfall of Tom Rakewell, a young man

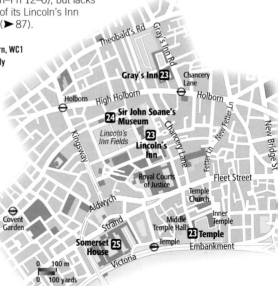

who inherits a fortune from his father, then loses it through self-indulgence. Other treasures include the death mask of actress Sarah Siddons (1755–1831).

The museum is undergoing an exciting expansion programme, "Opening up the Soane", due to finish in 2015. Restoration includes Soane's private apartments: bedroom, bathroom, Mrs Soane's Morning Room and the Model Room.

➕ 208 B5
✉ 13 Lincoln's Inn Fields, WC2
☎ 020 74 05 21 07; www.soane.org
🕐 Tue–Sat 10–5 (also first Tue of month 6–9pm with some rooms candlelit). **No advance booking; get there early**
Ⓜ Holborn
🚌 1, 8, 25, 68, 91, 168, 171, 188, 243, 521
💷 Free (donation appreciated)

🄬 Somerset House

Built to house government offices some 200 years ago, this handsome neoclassical building, with its court-yard overlooking the Thames, is now home to a range of visual arts, including the Courtauld Institute of Art's superb Courtauld Gallery.

Outside, the courtyard has danc-ing fountains in summer, as well as opera, pop concerts and late-night film shows; in winter, there is a popular open-air ice rink. Year-round the major draw is one of the world's finest collections of Impressionist

The Courtauld Gallery in Somerset House holds many treasures, including paintings and ceramics

and post-Impressionist paintings. Outstanding and familiar works include Paul Cézanne's famous paintings of peasant card players, a version of Manet's *Déjeuner sur l'Herbe*, as well as his supreme and final work, *Bar at the Folies-Bergère*, alongside Degas' ballet dancers and Vincent Van Gogh's 1889 work, *Self-Portrait with a Bandaged Ear*. One seminal work is Renoir's *La Loge*, shown in the first-ever Impressionist exhibition in Paris in 1874.

Don't miss important works from earlier periods, such as *Adam and Eve* by Lucas Cranach the Elder (1526) and 29 paintings by Rubens, including portraits, such as one of his friend Jan Brueghel the Elder, and *Landscape by Moonlight* (1635–1640). Twentieth-century masterpieces include works by the Fauves and German Expressionists.

➕ 208 B4　✉ Strand WC2
☎ 020 78 45 46 00 (recorded information); www.somersethouse.org.uk
🕐 Daily 10–6　🍴 Café, restaurants
Ⓜ Temple (closed Sun), Embankment or Covent Garden
🚌 6, 9, 11, 13, 15, 23, 87, 91, 139, 176
💷 Courtauld Institute Gallery: £6; free to students and under 18s; free Mon 10–2

Where to...
Eat and Drink

Prices
The quoted prices are per person for a meal and do not include drinks or service.
£ under £ 25   ££ £25–50   £££ over £50

Alba £

This smart, modern Italian restaurant, just a short walk from the
Barbican Centre, provides excellent
value for money and is deservedly
popular. It is filled with business
people at lunchtime and theatregoers in the evening. The menu is
short, encouraging some serious
cooking. Dishes such as fried sea
bass or lamb rump with pumpkin
purée, and classics like *risotto
primavera* are prepared with first-
rate ingredients. The annotated
wine list gives an impressive selection of wines from the best Italian
vineyards.

✚ 209 F5 ✉ 107 Whitecross Street, EC1
☎ 020 75 88 17 98; www.albarestaurant.com
◷ Mon–Sat 12–3, 6–11; closed 10 days
Christmas, bank holidays Ⓠ Barbican

Le Comptoir Gascon £/££

The little brother of the Michelin-
starred Club Gascon, this bistro
could be in France, with its duck
rillettes, platters of Toulouse
sausage, cassoulet and barbecued
shoulder of lamb. It is the chips
that are almost a thing of legend:
real French fries, hand-cut, thick,
crunchy and cooked twice in
duck fat, then scattered with sea
salt. The wines are from regions
of France that rarely appear on
British lists. The stripped down,
bare-brick look is contemporary
yet cosy, some might even say
romantic.

✚ 209 E5 ✉ 63 Charterhouse Street, EC1
☎ 020 76 08 08 51; www.comptoirgascon.com
◷ Tue–Sat 12–2, 7–10 (Thu–Fri till 11pm)
Ⓠ Farringdon, Barbican

The Eagle £

The Eagle was one of the pioneers
of converted pubs specializing in
very good food and still leads the
field. Choose from a short, but
mouth-watering selection of Asian
and Mediterranean-influenced
dishes; all are great value for money.
Reservations are not taken and you
need to arrive early to secure a
table and have the best choice from
the blackboard. You order and pay
for your food and drink at the bar.

✚ 209 D5 ✉ 159 Farringdon Road, EC1
☎ 020 78 37 13 53 ◷ Daily 12–11
Ⓠ Farringdon

Medcalf £/££

Housed in a former butcher's shop
in buzzing Exmouth Market in
trendy Clerkenwell, Medcalf serves
the best of Modern British cooking
into the early evening and is a popular bar later on, with DJs on Friday
and Saturday nights. The cooking
draws from a seasonal and often
organic menu, featuring classic
British dishes such as oxtail,
scallops and oysters, but the chic
young crowd that is drawn here is
anything but traditional.

✚ 209 D5 ✉ 40 Exmouth Market, EC1
☎ 020 78 33 35 33 ◷ Lunch: Mon–Sat 12–3,
Sun 12–4. Dinner: Mon–Thu 6–10; Bar: Mon–
Sat 12–11 (Fri to midnight), Sun 12–4
Ⓠ Farringdon

Northbank ££

Tucked under the Millennium
Bridge, this bar/restaurant has
great views over the Thames, and
serves the best of Modern British
food, beautifully presented: beef

from Devon, roast loin of pork from East Anglia, fish and handcrafted cheeses from the West of England.

🌐 209 E4 ✉ Millennium Bridge, 1 Paul's Walk, EC4 ☎ 020 73 29 92 99; www.northbankrestaurant.com ⏰ Mon–Sat 12–11 Ⓣ St Paul's, Mansion House

St John Bar & Restaurant £/££

Gourmets enthuse about the menus featuring old English recipes using offal (organ meats). An affordable way to enjoy the atmosphere in this former smokehouse near Smithfield is to have a drink and a hearty, calorie-rich snack at the bar: cold roast beef on dripping toast, Welsh rarebit (cheese on toast) or grilled sardines, followed by Eccles cake with Lancashire cheese or a slice of chocolate cake.

🌐 209 E5 ✉ 26 St John Street, EC1 ☎ 020 72 51 08 48; www.stjohnrestaurant.com ⏰ Lunch: Mon–Fri 12–3. Dinner: Mon–Sat 6–11, Sun 1–4 Ⓣ Farringdon

St Paul's Café and Restaurant £/££

Even St Paul's Cathedral has embraced the "best of British" philosophy. Head for the café in the crypt for Chelsea buns, lemon drizzle cake and real shortbread; pick up a hot pie from the oven or a ploughman's lunch of British cheese and pickle on artisan breads; enjoy a fixed-price lunch in the restaurant, or afternoon tea with cucumber sandwiches, scones with clotted cream and cakes.

🌐 209 E4 ✉ St Paul's Cathedral, EC4 ☎ 020 72 48 24 69; www.restaurantstpauls.co.uk ⏰ Lunch: Mon–Fri, Sun 12–3; Café: Mon–Sat 9–5, Sun 10–4; Teas: Mon–Sat 2:30–5 Ⓣ St Paul's

Sweetings £/££

An institution dating back to 1889 exuding the charm of days gone by. At midday, the dishes are exclusively hearty traditional fish courses, such as scallops, prawn cocktail, smoked eel, fish filet or the exquisite fish pie. Anyone who

can manage a dessert after the generous main course has a choice between apple pie or bread and butter pudding.

🌐 209 F4 ✉ 39 Queen Victoria Street ☎ 020 72 48 30 62 ⏰ Mon–Fri 11:30am–3pm, reservations not possible Ⓣ Mansion House

BARS & PUBS

Cicada £

At this stylish bar/restaurant, drinkers outnumber those eating in the evening. The young clientele creates a lively atmosphere. The food, should you wish to eat here, is oriental in style, backed up by excellent, inexpensive wines from a list that includes chilled sake.

🌐 209 E5 ✉ 132–136 St John Street, EC1 ☎ 020 76 08 15 50; www.rickerrestaurants.com ⏰ Mon–Fri 12–11, Sat from 6pm Ⓣ Farringdon

Hung Drawn & Quartered £

Forget the name that is a gruesome reminder of execution methods at the nearby Tower of London and ignore the noose behind the bar. Instead, enjoy local beers and wines by the glass, as well as hearty pies and burgers, salads and sandwiches. Office workers flock to this historic red-brick building, where oil paintings of British monarchs line the walls. It's always busy, with cheerful bar service, and is open at weekends.

🌐 210 B3 ✉ 26–27 Great Tower Street, EC3 ☎ 020 76 26 61 23; www.fullers.co.uk ⏰ Mon–Fri 11–11, Sat/Sun 12–6 Ⓣ Tower Hill

Ye Olde Cheshire Cheese £

This 350-year-old institution is one of those "straight out of Harry Potter" pubs: low ceilings, sawdust on the floor, vaulted cellars, narrow stairs. There's even a century-old stuffed parrot called Polly. Food is traditional British, such as steak and kidney pudding and roast beef.

🌐 209 D4 ✉ Wine Office Court, 145 Fleet Street, EC4 ☎ 020 73 53 61 70 ⏰ Mon–Fri 11–11, Sat 12–11 Ⓣ Temple

Where to ...
Shop

An indication of how much the City of London is trying to change into a seven-day shopping and leisure destination is **One New Change** (www.onenewchange.com), just east of St Paul's Cathedral. London's first building designed by award-winning French architect Jean Nouvel, this urban mall has some 60 familiar British and international stores, restaurants and bars. Among the quintessentially British shops are **L.K. Bennett** (women's fashions), **T.M. Lewin** (men's shirts) and **Hotel Chocolat**, who not only make luxury chocolates, but also have their own cocoa estate. The sixth-floor Roof Terrace has close-up views of St Paul's.

Insider Tip

The City has also retained some historic markets. Visit **Columbia Road Flower Market** (Columbia Road, E2, open Sun 8–3. Tube: Old Street) for the funky boutiques, as well as plants and flowers. It's worth a visit even if you don't buy anything. Also buzzing on a Sunday from 9–2 is **Petticoat Lane Market** (Middlesex Street and beyond, E1. Tube: Aldgate), where the draw is cheap clothing, often obtained by haggling over prices.

The giant Victorian covered **Spitalfields Market** (Commercial Street, between Lamb Street and Brushfield Street, E1. Tube: Liverpool Street) is a throwback to medieval markets, with its range of stalls devoted to clothes, food and jewellery. Although Sunday is always the busiest day, stalls operate daily (Mon–Fri 10–4, Sun 9–5). Thursdays are devoted to antiques and bric-a-brac. The treasure trove of items range from William Morris prints to vintage fashion.

Where to ...
Go Out

The City is quiet at night, but during the day there is plenty going on. Most obvious are the lunchtime concerts (1pm) in churches, such as St Michael Cornhill, St Sepulchre without Newgate, St Olave Hart Street and St Stephen Walbrook.

An annual highlight is the **City of London Festival** (www.colf.org), one of the UK's best arts events. Over three weeks in June and July (with some events in August), the performances are held in historic buildings, such as Mansion House and St Paul's Cathedral. Alongside films, walks and talks, world-class artists perform music for all tastes. About 50 performances are ticketed, while around 100 outdoor events are free.

On the second weekend in September, the **Mayor's Thames Festival** is London's largest free outdoor arts festival (www.thamesfestival.org). Enjoy music, markets and more between Westminster Bridge and Tower Bridge. If you like dance, check out the **Peacock Theatre**, a branch of Sadler's Wells (Portugal Street, WC2; www.peacocktheatre.com. Tube: Holborn).

Year-round, the **Barbican Centre** (Silk Street, EC2; www.barbican.org.uk. Tube: Barbican and Moorgate) offers everything from art, music and theatre to dance and film. Here, in Europe's largest multi-arts venue, the crown jewels are the **London Symphony Orchestra** (principal conductor Valery Gergiev) and the Associate Orchestra, the **BBC Symphony Orchestra** (Chief Conductor, the Finn Sakari Oramo, who is married to the Finnish soprano Anu Komsi)

Westminster & The South Bank

Getting Your Bearings	94
The Perfect Day	96
TOP 10	98
Don't Miss	102
At Your Leisure	110
Where to…	116

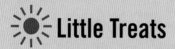 **Little Treats**

Foodies will love it

Connoisseurs know it well enough: Britain produces some very fine cheese! Find out for yourself at the **Borough Market** (➤ 114).

An Evening on the Bridge

What could be more romantic than watching the sun go down on a warm summer evening on **Waterloo Bridge** (➤ 111)?

Coffee With a View

Drink an espresso as you gaze across the Thames at St Paul's Cathedral and then enjoy modern art at the **Tate Modern** (➤ 108).

Getting Your Bearings

Stand on one of the bridges or embankments and as you gaze at the slowly flowing River Thames you can't help but notice the contrast between the water's stately progress and the noise and drama of the surrounding city.

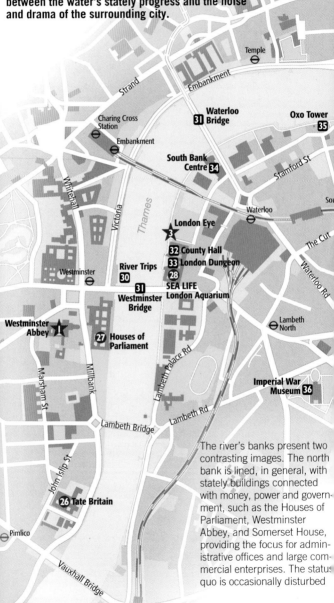

The river's banks present two contrasting images. The north bank is lined, in general, with stately buildings connected with money, power and government, such as the Houses of Parliament, Westminster Abbey, and Somerset House, providing the focus for administrative offices and large commercial enterprises. The status quo is occasionally disturbed by new buildings – Charing Cross railway station is a notable example – but generally the river's north side is stable and established, retaining the political, historical and religious significance it has enjoyed for centuries.

The South Bank has a very different flavour. In Shakespeare's time it was the place to which actors, considered a bad influence, were banished and where early theatre flourished. The reborn Globe is turning the clock

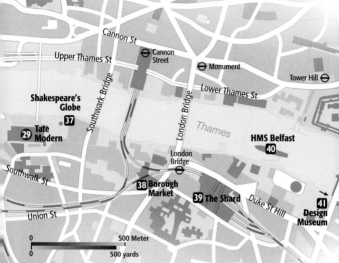

back 400 years. By the early 20th century the area was a mixture of wasteland and heavy industry, but after World War II, the Southbank Centre, and the Royal Festival Hall in particular, marked the start of a makeover. Continuing the shift, as London entered the new millennium, the old Bankside Power Station was transformed from industrial behemoth to cultural superstar in the shape of the Tate Modern gallery. Yet even Tate Modern has been eclipsed in popularity and profile by the surprise success of the London Eye.

TOP 10

★ Westminster Abbey ➤ 98
★ London Eye ➤ 101

Don't Miss

26 Tate Britain ➤ 102
27 Houses of Parliament ➤ 104
28 SEA LIFE London Aquarium ➤ 105
29 Tate Modern ➤ 108

At Your Leisure

30 River Trips ➤ 110
31 Westminster & Waterloo Bridges ➤ 111
32 County Hall ➤ 111
33 London Dungeon ➤ 112
34 South Bank Centre ➤ 112
35 Oxo Tower ➤ 112
36 Imperial War Museum ➤ 113
37 Shakespeare's Globe ➤ 114
38 Borough Market ➤ 114
39 The Shard ➤ 115
40 HMS *Belfast* ➤ 115
41 Design Museum ➤ 115

Perfect Days in...

The Perfect Day

If you're not quite sure where to begin your travels, this itinerary recommends a practical and enjoyable day out exploring Westminster and the South Bank, taking in some of the best places to see. For more information see the main entries (➤ 98–115).

◑ 9:00am
Allow 2 hours to enjoy the grandeur of ★**Westminster Abbey** (➤ 98), seeking out the numerous memorials to royal and literary figures among breathtaking architecture, particularly the Royal Chapels.

◑ 11:30am
Admire the **㉗ Houses of Parliament** and **Big Ben** (above, ➤ 104), cross **㉛ Westminster Bridge** (➤ 111) and turn left, towards the landmark ★**London Eye** (opposite, ➤ 101). Here you are spoiled for choice, with the Eye, the **㉘ SEA LIFE London Aquarium** (➤ 105) and the attractions of **㉜ County Hall** (➤ 111). Note: trips on the London Eye should be reserved in advance.

⊕ 1:30pm

Stroll along the river to the
35 Oxo Tower (➤ 112),
take a lift (elevator) to the
top for a wonderful view
over the Thames, and have
lunch in their brasserie
(➤ 117).

⊕ 2:30pm

After lunch, browse in the
tower's designer work-
shops, then make your
way to **29 Tate Modern**
(right, ➤ 108), London's
striking modern art gallery,
set in the former Bankside
Power Station. Close by is
37 Shakespeare's Globe
(➤ 114), an accurate
reconstruction of the
17th-century Globe
Theatre, which is open
for tours. Visit the gourmet
food stalls at **38 Borough
Market** (➤ 114) or one
of the nearby pubs and
restaurants.

★ Westminster Abbey

Britain's greatest religious building is a church, a national shrine, the setting for coronations and a burial place for some of the most celebrated figures from almost a thousand years of British history. Most of the country's sovereigns, from William the Conqueror in 1066 to Queen Elizabeth II in 1953, have been crowned at Westminster, while in 2011 Prince William married Kate Middleton here. The building has ancient roots, but construction of the present structure, a masterpiece of medieval architecture, began in the 13th century. Since then, the building has grown and evolved, a process that continues to the present day as ever more modern memorials are erected.

Westminster Abbey is a top tourist destination, drawing huge crowds. It's impossible to appreciate all the abbey's riches in one visit, so concentrate on the highlights below.

The Visitors Route

Visitors follow a set route around the abbey. From the entrance through the North Door you turn left along the ambulatory, the passageway leading to the far end of the abbey. At the top of the steps, the chapel on the left contains the **tomb of Elizabeth I** (1533–1603) and her older half-sister, **Mary Tudor** (1516–1558), daughters of the much-married Henry VIII. Although they lie close in death, there was little love lost beween them in life – Mary was a Catholic, Elizabeth a Protestant at a time when religious beliefs divided the country and religious persecution was rife.

Next comes the sublime **Henry VII Chapel**, built in 1512, possibly to ease Henry's troubled conscience: his route to the throne was a violent one. The abbey's most gorgeous chapel, it was described by one commentator as *orbis miraculum,* or a wonder of the world. The brilliantly detailed and gilded fan vaulting of the roof is particularly fine, as are the vivid banners of the Knights of the Order of the Bath (an order of chivalry bestowed by the monarch) above the oak choir stalls. Behind the altar are the magnificent tombs and gilded effigies of Henry VII and his wife, Elizabeth, created to a design by Henry himself.

As you leave this area, a side chapel holds the tomb of Mary, Queen of Scots (1542–1587). Mary, a rival to Elizabeth I's throne, was imprisoned for 19 years before finally being executed in 1587. Mary's son, James VI of Scotland, became James I of England when the unmarried, childless Elizabeth died. He had his mother's body exhumed and brought to the

POETS' CORNER

Notables buried here:

- Alfred, Lord Tennyson
- Robert Browning
- John Masefield
- Charles Dickens
- Thomas Hardy
- Rudyard Kipling
- Dr Samuel Johnson
- R. B. Sheridan

abbey 25 years after her death and erected the monuments to both Elizabeth I and Mary – but his mother's is much the grander.

Next comes **Poets' Corner** (▶ left), packed with the graves and memorials of literary superstars. You'll spot Geoffrey Chaucer, author of *The Canterbury Tales*; Shakespeare, commemorated by a memorial (he is buried in Stratford-upon-Avon); and Charles Dickens, buried here against his wishes on the orders of Queen Victoria. Thomas Hardy's ashes are here, but his heart was buried in Dorset, the setting for many of his novels.

From Poets' Corner, walk towards the centre of the abbey and the highly decorated altar and choir stalls. One of the loveliest views in the abbey opens up from the steps leading to the altar, looking along the length of the nave to the window above the West Door. For a restful interlude head into the 13th-century cloisters, a covered passageway around a small garden once used for reflection by monks. Contemplation is also the effect created by the simple black slab memorial at the western end of the abbey – the grave

The stunning view along the choir stalls towards the altar

of the Unknown Warrior, a memorial to the dead of World War I. As you leave the abbey don't miss **St George's Chapel** to see the unassuming coronation chair (**King Edward's Chair**), which has been used at the coronation of most British monarchs since 1308 and has been in the Chapel since its detailed restoration.

The *Battle of Britain* window contains the badges of the 65 fighter squadrons that withstood the 1940 German air campaign against Britain

TAKING A BREAK

From Mon–Sat, the **Cellarium Café** (20 Dean's Yard, SW1) breakfast, lunch and afternoon tea menus offer everything to satisfy the hunger of the cathedral visitor, such as French toast, steak-ciabatta, brownies and cream tea.

✚ 207 F4
✉ Broad Sanctuary, SW1 ☎ 020 72 22 51 52; www.westminster-abbey.org
🕐 Thu–Tue 9:30–4:30, Wed till 7. Last admission 1 hour before closing. Sun open for worship only. College Garden: Apr–Sep Tue–Thu 10–6; Oct–Mar 10–4. Chapter House daily 10:30–4 (natural light permitting). Abbey Museum and Pyx Chamber: Mon–Sat 10:30–4 🍴 Coffee counter in cloisters and Broad Sanctuary
🚇 Westminster, St James's Park 🚌 3, 11, 24, 53, 159, 211 🎫 £18

INSIDER INFO

- Attend a **choral service** to see the abbey at its best. Evensong is at 5pm on weekdays (3pm Sunday). Times of other services are displayed, otherwise ring for details.
- **Guided tours** led by abbey vergers leave several times daily (90 min, additional charge £3). Book at the information desk. There is also an **audio guide** (included in the admission charge), available in several languages, which provides good additional background (60 min).
- You can also visit free-of-charge the beautiful 13th-century **Chapter House**, the Abbey Museum with its fascinating wax effigies of royalty, and – in summer – the College Gardens.

③ London Eye

Just as the Eiffel Tower shocked Paris in 1889, the London Eye took Londoners by surprise in 2000. Both were modern structures; both are now considered part of the skyline. At 443 feet (135m) in diameter, this is the biggest Ferris wheel in Europe. Fixed on the outside, rather than hung from it, the 32 glass capsules offer 360-degree views over the city.

The  EDF Energy London Eye is in constant motion, rotating 10in (26cm) per second at the hub of the wheel, which is slow enough for both young and old to enjoy the all-round view. Each capsule represents one of the boroughs of London, and on a clear day you can see many of them as the view extends for around 25 miles (40km), to beyond the city limits.

The "Eye" is one of the most popular attractions in the capital

Around 3.5 million visitors a year take this ultimate aerial ride, with up to 800 people on the wheel at any one time. July and August are the busiest months and generally most days are busy between 11am and 3pm, so make a reservation by telephone or in person. Even then, you may wait 30 minutes or so before boarding, unless you buy a Fast Track ticket, which allows you to turn up just 15 minutes before your flight time.

Insider Tip

TAKING A BREAK
Options include cafés and restaurants in and around County Hall. **The Zen Café** is nearest.

✚ 208 B2
✉ County Hall Riverside Buildings , SE1
☎ Ticket hotline: 087 17 81 30 00; www.londoneye.com
🕐 July–Aug daily 10–9:30; Sep–Jun 10–8:30
Ⓜ Westminster, Waterloo
🚌 1, 4, 26, 59, 68, 76, 77, 171, 172, 176, 188, 211, 243, 341, 381, 507, 521, X68, RV1
💷 £19.20

㉖ Tate Britain

In 1897, Henry Tate gave his collection of 65 paintings to the nation – and a building to house them in. That has expanded into 66,000 works of art, and the Millbank gallery is one of the most popular art destinations in London. There is no entrance fee. After extensive renovation, the gallery opened again at the end of 2013.

Gallery Highlights

Tate Britain covers five centuries of British art, from *A Man in a Black Cap* by John Bettes (1545), to works by 20th- and 21st-century artists, such as Francis Bacon and Henry Moore, Gilbert & George, Damian Hirst and Rachel Whiteread. All the paintings at Tate Britain are periodically rehung and sometimes disappear into storage for lack of space – though since the split (the modern works are now housed in the Tate Modern) this is much less of a problem. During any visit, however, you can count on seeing great works by William Hogarth, Sir Joshua Reynolds, Thomas Gainsborough, John Constable and, of course, **J. M. W Turner** (1775–1851). Turner is regarded as the greatest home-grown talent and has his own wing, the **Clore Gallery**. A couple of

Imposing steps up to the gallery

Large, well-lit galleries display Tate Britain's extensive collection

his paintings not to miss are the action-packed *The Battle of Trafalgar, as Seen from the Mizen Starboard Shrouds of the Victory* and *Snow Storm: Hannibal and his Army Crossing the Alps.*

For many visitors the favourites are still the impossibly romantic works of the late 19th-century **Pre-Raphaelites** – principally John Everett Millais, William Holman Hunt and, in particular, Dante Gabriel Rossetti, who founded this avant-garde brotherhood of artists. There are many outstanding paintings on display from this group, but, in particular, look for Millais' powerful *Ophelia* – which depicts the character from *Hamlet* singing as she drowns in a beautiful, flower-lined river – Rossetti's radical *Ecce Ancilla Domini! (The Annunciation)* and *The Haunted Manor* by Holman Hunt.

Equine lovers will want to head for the works of **George Stubbs**, who portrays horses in exquisite and uncannily accurate detail – partly inspired by his scientific research.

TAKING A BREAK

Since the extensive renovation and reorganization, the additional catering services of the museums also serve food to the visitors.

➕ 207 F2 ✉ Millbank, SW1 ☎ 020 78 87 88 88; www.tate.org.uk
🕐 Daily 10–6 (also 1st Fri in month 6–10) 🍴 Café, Rex Whistler restaurant
🚇 Westminster, Pimlico 🚌 2, 36, 87, 88, 185, 436, 507, C10
🎟 Free ⛴ Tate Boat runs every 40 min to Tate Modern (£6.50)

INSIDER INFO

To avoid the crowds, visit on a Monday, when the galleries are at their quietest. Start with the **Turner Galleries** and you could well have rooms full of Turner's finest paintings all to yourself. Consider seeing an exhibition in reverse; **start at the end** and work your way back to the front. Everyone seems to clog up the first room of a show. If there is a special exhibition, the first two weeks are particularly busy.

㉗ Houses of Parliament

Spectacularly located at the edge of the River Thames, beside Westminster Bridge, the Houses of Parliament is the most iconic of all London sights. It is home to the House of Commons and the House of Lords.

Much of the parliament building was rebuilt in the 19th century following a fire in 1834, but Westminster Hall, part of the original palace, dates from 1097. The Victoria Tower (325 feet/98.5m) stands at the southern end and the **Big Ben Clock Tower** (316 feet/96.3m) at the other (Big Ben is actually the name of the bell).

During the elaborate **State Opening of Parliament ceremony**, which usually occurs in November or December, the Queen presides over the non-elected peers of the House of Lords, before the junior members of the process, the elected Members of Parliament (MPs) from the House of Commons, are allowed in. They then slam the door of the Commons chamber in the face of Black Rod, the Queen's representative, to confirm their independence from the Lords.

The Houses of Parliament and Big Ben Tower at night

TAKING A BREAK

Between No 10 and Parliament, the 100-year-old **Red Lion pub** (48 Parliament St, SW1) serves food all day. A bell calls the MPs back to work.

➕ 208 A1 ✉ Parliament Square, SW1
☎ 020 72 19 42 72; www.parliament.uk 🕒 Mon–Fri, months vary; check website for details 🚇 Westminster
🚌 3, 11, 24, 53, 159, 211 🎫 Free

VISITING THE HOUSES OF PARLIAMENT

Debates are open to all. UK citizens can get tickets from their MP; foreign visitors should apply to their Embassy/High Commission. Otherwise, line up outside St Stephen's Entrance, but expect to wait.

㉘ SEA LIFE London Aquarium

Alongside the London Eye, one of the largest aquariums in Europe takes you round the world – underwater. Thanks to expensive improvements in recent years, the tanks range from exotic coral reefs and lagoons to the River Thames and tiny rock pools. As ever, the highlight features close encounters with sharks.

Start your 🔆 tour through **SEA LIFE** at the bottom and work up to the 165,000-gallon (750,000-litre) **Atlantic Tank**, complete with a whale skeleton, where stingrays and blacktip reef sharks play. In nearby touch pools, you can stroke starfish and crabs.

Although the 220,000-gallon (1 million-litre) **Pacific Tank** is impressive, youngsters still tend to prefer the clownfish in **Nemo's Coral Caves**. See piranhas and crocodiles, learn about conservation work and take part in feeding time. Finish with the **Shark Walk** that bridges the Pacific Tank. Although you are on a glass walkway, the sinister giant sandtiger sharks below you feel just too close for comfort!

TAKING A BREAK

At the rear of the building, the nearest restaurant is **Troia** (3F Belvedere Road, SE1), serving healthy Turkish dishes: salads, pasta and vegetarian dishes.

Sharks glide close to visitors in the Pacific Zone shark tank

➕ 208 B2 ✉ County Hall, Westminster Bridge Road, SE1
☎ 0871 6 63 16 78; www.visitsealife.com 🕐 Mon–Sun 10–7
🍴 Options in County Hall 🚇 Westminster, Waterloo 🚌 12, 53, 77, 148, 171, 211, 341 💷 £20.70 (cheaper after 3pm or if you book online tickets)

In the Centre of Power

The House of Commons passes the important legislation while the influence of the House of Lords on policy is fairly limited these days. Parliament's most glamorous annual highlight is the ceremonial State Opening of parliament by the Queen in October or November.

❶ Victoria Tower: When Victoria Tower was built in 1858 (75 feet/ 23m long and 334 feet/102m tall), it was the highest tower in the world.

❷ House of Lords: The Upper House is made up of members of peers appointed by the Queen.

❸ St Stephen's Hall: The House of Commons met here from 1547–1837

❹ Westminster Hall: The only remnant of the old Westminster Palace. It was here that the trials of Richard II and Thomas More took place.

❺ Elizabeth Tower: The inimitable symbol of London: Built in 1858/ 1859, the tower known as Clock Tower until 2012 is 320 feet (97.5 m) high. The clock face is almost 26 feet (8m) in diameter, the hands are almost 13 feet (4m) long and the famous bell **Big Ben** weighs 13 tons. The sound of the bell has become associated around the world with the BBC.

❻ House of Commons: It is here that the elected MPs meet. Tradition dictated that there be "two sword lengths" between the government representatives and the opposition. There is not enough space for all the MPs to sit down.

The State Opening of Parliament is a very dignified and ceremonial occasion, and steeped in tradition

Houses of Parliament

Calm before the storm – a look inside the empty House of Commons

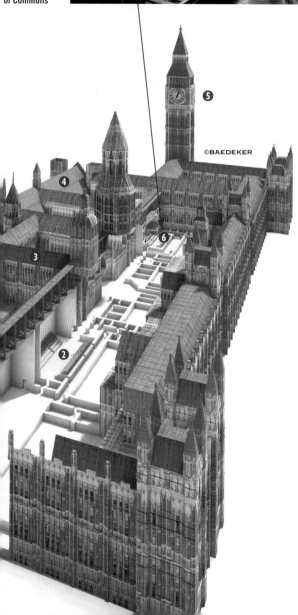

©BAEDEKER

㉙ Tate Modern

Although a relative newcomer as an art museum, Tate Modern is a world-class gallery and one of London's top attractions. The gallery encompasses the spectrum of modern art movements from 19th-century Impressionism to the challenging work of young British artists of the late 20th and early 21st centuries.

Once inside the strikingly converted power station, many visitors find the scale of the Turbine Hall, which occupies the bulk of the building, amazing: it resembles a vast cathedral, measuring 500 feet (152m) in length and 115 feet (35m) in height. A bridge leads from Level 4 to the new extension that offers another 11 exhibitions.

Permanent Collection

The collection is exhibited on Levels 2 to 4. Level 2, "Poetry and Dream", is dedicated to the paintings and sculptures of Surrealism. You can also see works by Pablo Picasso, Giorgio de Chirico and Jannis Kounellis. **Level 3** is devoted to **"Transformed Visions"**, with motifs depicting people, violence and war, e. g. Mark Rothkos' "The Seagram Murals". The west half of level 4 offers "Structure and Clarity", celebrating Cubism and Minimalism, with artists such as Piet Mondrian and Elssworth Kelly. The east half is entitled **"Energy and Process"** and exhibits works by Kazimir Malevich, Richard Serra and Gerhard Richter.

You can take part in one of the free guided tours of the museum, daily 11–3. You are more independent with the Multimedia Guide (£4) and as you walk round can listen to interviews with artists such as Joseph Beuys

Above: The Millennium Bridge links the Tate Modern to St Paul's Cathedral

Left: Sculpture at the gallery includes The Kiss by Rodin (1901–1904)

INSIDER INFO

- To avoid the crush, visit on weekday mornings, or take advantage of the late opening on Fridays and Saturdays – by 8:30pm the crowds thin out.
- **Level 5** houses the Interactive Zone, with hands-on games, multimedia and films on art
- The well-organized **shop** on the entrance level has a good selection of art books.
- The **Millennium Bridge**, which links St Paul's Cathedral to Tate Modern, is the best way to approach the gallery, taking visitors across the Thames and straight into its heart.

and Louise Bourgeois. The Tate Modern also offers WLAN and a museum app.

Breathtaking Views

For many visitors, the views of London from the upper floors of the gallery are as exciting as the art. From the East Room of **Level 7**, there is a superb panorama north, over the Millennium Bridge to St Paul's Cathedral. The view from the east window looks down upon Shakespeare's Globe (➤ 114) and spreads across towards Docklands. From the south window, you can look across to the London Eye (➤ 101).

TAKING A BREAK

Enjoy the view from the restaurant on Level 6, or the espresso bar on Level 3; down at the riverside, **Café 2** with its view of the Thames is more affordable.

Galleries within Tate Modern are open and uncluttered

🚉 209 E3 ✉ Bankside, SE1 ☎ 020 78 87 80 08; www.tate.org.uk 🕐 10–6 (Fri–Sat also 6–10pm), last admission 45 min before closing 🍴 Café, restaurants 🚇 Southwark, Waterloo (East), Blackfriars, London Bridge 🚌 45, 63, 100, 344, 381, RV1 💷 Free; admission charge for special exhibitions on Level 4

At Your Leisure

A cruise boat heads along the Thames near County Hall and the London Eye

30 River Trips

A trip along the Thames is a tremendous way to see the city, away from the Underground and traffic-clogged streets. Piers in central London from where you can take trips are **Embankment, Bankside, Festival, Tower Millennium, London Eye** (Waterloo) and **Westminster Millennium**. Services east to **Greenwich** (with connections to the Thames Barrier) pass through urban and industrial landscape, but offer views of **Greenwich** (➤ 184). Services upstream to Hampton Court via Kew (➤ 170), **Putney, Richmond** and on to **Kingston** are more rural, the river meandering through parks and alongside some of London's more village-like residential enclaves. An evening cruise is also a lovely way to see the city. Note that timetables vary from month to month, so be sure to go to the piers or telephone for latest details.

Insider Tip

From Westminster

Millennium Pier
Upriver to Kew (1½ hours), Richmond (2 hours) and Hampton Court (3 hours)
🚇 200 B2 ☎ 020 79 30 20 62; www.wpsa.co.uk.

Downriver to Tower Millennium Pier (35–45 min) and Greenwich (45 min)
🚇 208 B2 ☎ 020 77 40 04 00; www.citycruises.com.

From Embankment Pier
Downriver to Greenwich (1 hour)
🚇 208 B3
ℹ www.thamesclippers.com

From Tower Millennium Pier
Upriver to Embankment (25 min)
Downriver to Greenwich (30–40 min)
Evening cruises On a dinner and cabaret cruise (3 hours) you can sightsee while wining, dining and dancing aboard the *London Showboat*. The cruise operates Wed–Sun
🚇 208 B3 ☎ 020 78 21 11 86; www.thamesclippers.com

Fun and Thrills
Great fun for kids: The 🔟 **London Duck Tours**, which use yellow amphibious ex-World War II vehicles that start on land near the London Eye, tour London's landmarks, then splash down into the Thames for a 75-minute cruise. For a high-speed ride, **Thames Rib Experience** tours the sights, then opens the throttle.

London Duck Tour
☎ 020 79 28 31 32;
www.londonducktours.co.uk.

Thames Rib Experience
☎ 020 79 30 57 46;
www.thamesribexperience.com.

31 Westminster & Waterloo Bridges

Westminster Bridge (built in 1862) is one of over 30 across the Thames, but in 1750 the original bridge on this site was only the second crossing, built after London Bridge. Near Westminster Bridge stop at Westminster Pier to check on the times, prices and destina-

Westminster Bridge, with the Houses of Parliament

tions of the river trips (opposite) available.

From **Waterloo Bridge** you will have one of the finest views of London. Looking east, the dominant landmarks are **St Paul's Cathedral** (➤ 74), **St Bride's Church** spire, **Tower 42**, **Lloyd's Building** (➤ 181) and – in the far distance – **Canary Wharf**. In the near distance, on the right, stands the **Oxo Tower** (➤ 112) and **The Shard** (➤ 115). As you walk to the north side of the bridge, the grand building to the right is **Somerset House** (➤ 89), the only remaining example of the 18th-century mansions that once lined the **Strand**. It now houses the **Courtauld Institute Gallery's** permanent art collection.

Westminster Bridge
✚ 208 B2

Waterloo Bridge
✚ 208 B3

32 County Hall

The **London Film Museum** is great fun; it offers an entertaining look at British film history, emphasizing how many blockbusters have been – and still are – made in Britain, from *Superman* and *Indiana Jones* to *Sherlock Holmes* and *Harry*

Potter. "Charlie Chaplin: The Great Londoner" traces the life of this local hero from near-poverty to Hollywood legend. Other permanent displays are devoted to *Alien*, *The Borrowers* and *Dr Who*. A small branch of the museum opened in Covent Garden in 2011 (at Russell Street and Wellington Street, WC2. Tube: Covent Garden).

✚ 208 B2
✉ County Hall, Riverside Buildings, SE1
🍴 Café 🚇 Westminster, Waterloo
🚌 12, 24, 26, 76, 77, 148, 176, 243, 341, 381, 507, X68

London Film Museum
☎ 020 72 02 70 40; www.londonfilmmuseum.com
🕐 Mon–Fri 10–5, Sat 10–6, Sun 11–6 💷 £13.50

🔟🍴 London Dungeon
For the ultimate in spooky, adrenaline-filled adventures, the London Dungeon experience takes you deep below the streets of London into the murky and grisly world of torture and pain. It is fun, though, as long as you don't mind a bit of gore and facing some innate fears! The rather startling line-up of attractions include: **Boat Ride to Hell**, which plunges you into a total darkness filled with scary characters; encounters with **Jack the Ripper**, London's notorious 19th-century murderer and **Sweeney Todd**, the city's murderous barber; an all too real look into what it felt like to be running for your life during the **Great Fire of London**. You are also witness to the plot led by **Guy Fawkes** to blow up the Houses of Parliament.

✚ 208 B2 ✉ County Hall, Westminster Bridge Road, London SE1 7PB
☎ 087 14 23 22 40; www.thedungeons.com
🕐 Times vary month to month, but generally open daily 10–5:30 (longer in school holidays)
🚇 Waterloo G12, 24, 26, 76, 77, 148, 176, 243, 341, 381, 507, X68 💷 £16.95

🔢 Southbank Centre
Back in 1951, the Festival of Britain looked forward by celebrating the nation's culture and creativity. That legacy lives on in the buildings that line the curving south bank of the Thames. Open 364 days of the year, Southbank Centre (▶ 118) has something for everyone, from a glass of wine on Festival Terrace to hundreds of free events in the Royal Festival Hall foyers.

You can browse the shops and, of course, attend events in the venues themselves, from concerts at the Royal Festival Hall, Queen Elizabeth Hall and the Purcell Room to major art exhibitions, which are held regularly at the Hayward Gallery.

✚ 208 C3
☎ 084 48 75 00 73; www.southbankcentre.co.uk
🚇 Waterloo 🚌 Waterloo 1, 4, 26, 59, 68, 76, 77, 168, 171, 172, 176, 188, 211, 243, 341, 381, 501, 507, 521, NG8, RV1

🔢 Oxo Tower
This art deco building contains a mixture of private and public housing, bars and restaurants (▶ 117)

The Oxo Tower

Inside the Imperial War Museum

and designer workshops. The tower's windows are cleverly placed to spell out the word "OXO" (a brand of stock cube), a ploy by the architect to evade rules against riverside advertising. The eighth-floor terrace has superb views.

✚ 209 D3
✉ Barge House Street, SE1
☎ 020 70 21 16 86; www.coinstreet.org
🕐 Observation area, Level 8: daily 11–10; studios and shops Tue–Sun 11–6
Ⓤ Blackfriars, Waterloo
🚌 45, 63, 100, 381
✋ Free (all areas)

36 Imperial War Museum

This fascinating but sobering museum is much more than a display of military might or a glorification of war – despite the name, the monstrous guns in the forecourt and the militaristic slant of the vehicles on display in the main hall.

The museum's real emphasis and strengths are the way in which it focuses on the effects of war in the 20th century on the lives of soldiers and civilians alike. This is achieved through a comprehensive collection of artefacts, documents, photographs, works of art, and sound and film archive footage. The most moving testimonies come from oral descriptions recorded by ordinary people whose lives were deeply affected by their wartime experiences. If you have never experienced war, this museum will deepen your understanding.

✚ 209 D1 ✉ Lambeth Road, SE1
☎ 020 74 16 50 00; www.iwm.org.uk
🕐 Daily 10–6 🍴 Café
Ⓤ Lambeth North, Elephant and Castle, Waterloo 🚌 1, 12, 45, 53, 63, 68, 168, 171, 172, 176, 188, 344, C10
✋ Free

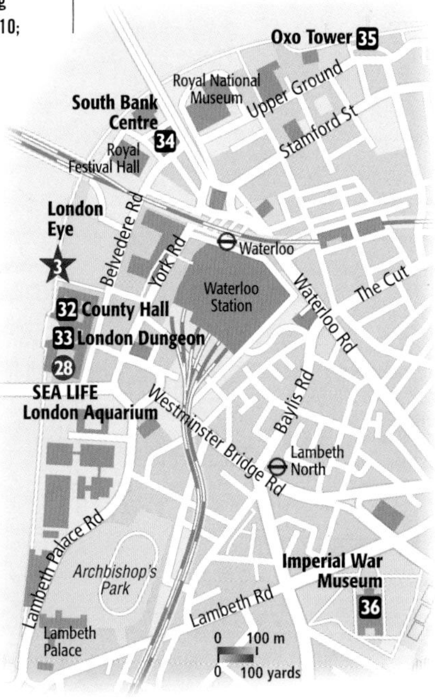

The Globe is a faithful recreation of the original Elizabethan theatre

➕ 209 E3 ✉ 21 New Globe Walk, Bankside, SE1
☎ 020 79 02 14 00; box office 020 74 01 99 19;
www.shakespeares-globe.org
🕐 The Exhibitions: daily 10–5, longer in summer. Tours are regular. During matinees, tours visit the archaeological site of The Rose, Bankside's first playhouse. Check website
🍴 Coffee bar, café and restaurant
Ⓜ Mansion House, London Bridge
🚌 Blackfriars 45, 63, 100; Southwark Street 381, RV1 💷 £13.50, with the Rose £16

37 Shakespeare's Globe

How about visiting Shakespeare's theatre? The Globe Theatre is a very successful reconstruction of the original theatre (whose original site lay some 330 yards/300m away) in which Shakespeare was an actor and shareholder, and in which many of his plays were first performed. The project was the brainchild of Sam Wanamaker, the American film actor and director, who died before its completion. The theatre is built of unseasoned oak held together with 9,500 oak pegs, topped by the first thatched roof completed in the city since the Great Fire of London in 1666. It is also partly open to the elements, as was the original Globe, with standing room in front of the stage where theatregoers can heckle the actors in true Elizabethan fashion. A visit to the exhibition and a tour of the theatre (or nearby site of the contemporary Rose Theatre) is very worthwhile and will certainly make you want to see a play.

38 Borough Market

A must for visitors to London, Borough Market demonstrates Britain's passion for food. Wedged under railway viaducts between Borough High Street and the Thames, it offers an amazing selection. After 800 years, this is now very much a **gourmet food market**, with 70 stalls and stands. British producers bring their best meat and fish, cheeses and breads, cakes and ales. There are also fine European products. Taste jams and honeys, hams and cheeses, watch resident chef Hayley's cooking demonstrations (Thu from 11am), and enjoy a gourmet sandwich and glass of cider.

➕ 210 A3 ✉ Southwark Street, SE1
☎ 020 74 07 10 02; www.boroughmarket.org.uk
🕐 Thu 11–5, Fri 12–6, Sat 8–5
Ⓜ London Bridge
🚌 21, 35, 40, 43, 47, 48, 133, 141, 149, 344
💷 Free

Queen Victoria St · ⊖ Mansion House · Cannon St · Upper Thames St · Cannon Street · Cannon Street Station · ⊖ Monument · Lower Thames St · Millenium Bridge · Shakespeare's Globe 37 · Southwark Bridge · Thames · London Bridge · Tower Millenium Pier · 29 Tate Modern · HMS Belfast 40 · London Bridge · Southwalk St · Borough Market 38 · The Shard 39 · Duke St Hill · 41 Design Museum

0 100 m
0 100 yards

39 The Shard

The London skyscraper finished in 2012 and inaugurated with a laser show is a fascinating sight and the city's new attraction. Star architect Renzo Piano designed the 1,000-foot (310m) high, glass-clad pyramid. Two high-speed lifts take you up to the observation decks on floors 68–72 at a height of 800 feet (244m). Book your tickets (issued with the exact date and time) in advance. Bags should not exceed a standard size, otherwise you will not be allowed inside and there is no cloakroom. The security guards will also scan you and your belongings before you enter.

🚇 210 A2 ⊠ Joiner Street ☎ 084 44 99 71 11; www.theviewfromtheshard.com
🕐 Summer 9am–10pm, from Oct Sun–Wed 10–7, Thu–Sat 10–10 (last admission 1–1½ hr before closing time) 🚇 London Bridge
🚌 17, 43, 47, 48, 141, 149, 343, 381, CV1
💷 £29.95 (on the day itself), £24.95 (booked online at least 24 hr in advance)

40 HMS *Belfast*

This World War II vessel, the biggest cruiser ever built by the Royal Navy, took part in the Normandy landings, and remained in service until 1963. Preserved in the state she enjoyed during active service, the ship is now moored on the Thames in front of London's "Leaning Tower of Pizza", the City Hall. She houses displays connected with recent Royal Navy history, but it is the ship itself that is the true attraction. You can explore from the bridge to the engine and boiler rooms nine decks below, taking in the cramped quarters of the officers and crew, the galleys, punishment cells and sick bays, as well as the gun turrets, magazines and shell rooms. More than just a warship, she was a floating community of up to 950 sailors.

🚇 210 B3 ⊠ Moored off Morgans Lane, Tooley Street, SE1
☎ 020 79 40 63 00; www.iwm.org.uk
🕐 Mar–Oct daily 10–6 (last admission 5); Nov–Feb 10–5 (last admission 4)
🍴 Many near by 🚇 London Bridge, Tower Hill, Monument 🚌 42, 47, 78, 343, 381, RV1
💷 £14.50; children 15 or under free

41 Design Museum

The Design Museum is the world's leading museum devoted to contemporary design, from furniture to graphics, architecture to industrial design. It needs more space, so will be moving to West London in November 2015, where it will house the Design Museum's collection of 2,000 contemporary and 20th-century pieces, covering the history of design in mass production, from lighting and domestic appliances to communications technology. The regular and intriguing exhibitions continue, exploring themes such as fashion, furniture and architecture, but also everyday design used in road signs, kitchenware and computers. Above the current museum is the pricey, designer-orientated Blueprint Café, with its views of Tower Bridge.

🚇 210 C2 ⊠ 28 Shad Thames, SE1
☎ 020 74 03 69 33, www.designmuseum.org
🕐 Daily 10–5:45 (last entry 5:15)
🚇 London Bridge 🚌 42, 47, 78, 188, 381
💷 £10.85

HMS *Belfast* is moored on the Thames near Tower Bridge

Where to...
Eat and Drink

Prices
The quoted prices are per person for a meal and do not include drinks or service.
£ under £ 25   ££ £25–50   £££ over £50

The Archduke £/££
Under the railway arches by Waterloo Station, this is an unusual but atmospheric spot. As well as visitors to the South Bank, it caters for locals, who come for the live jazz six nights a week. It's open all day for light lunches and relaxed dinners, serving omelettes and salads, fish and vegetarian dishes. The speciality is steaks: prime British Isles beef, hung for 28 days, char-grilled and served with a choice of sauces – Béarnaise, peppercorn, herb and garlic butter.

➕ 208 C2 ✉ Concert Hall, South Bank, SE1 ☎ 020 79 28 93 70; www.blackandblue restaurants.com ⏰ Sun–Thu 12–11, Fri–Sat 11am–11:30pm 🚇 Waterloo, Embankment

Butler's Wharf Chop House £/££
Go for views of Tower Bridge and the Modern British food. The well-priced set menu offers everything you can think of, from charcoal-grilled steaks and beer-battered haddock with hand-cut chips to steamed wild Scottish mussels in white wine and a Dickensian steak and kidney pudding – with an oyster. Prices are lower in the Chop House Bar.
➕ 210 C2 ✉ 36e Shad Thames, SE1 ☎ 020 74 03 34 03; www.danddlondon.com ⏰ Mon–Sat 12–3, 6–11, Sun 12–9:45 🚇 London Bridge, Tower Hill

Cantina del Ponte £/££
This lively eatery, decorated in simple Italian style, is located on the wharf by Tower Bridge and has fabulous views back over the City. The mainly Italian-inspired menu offers a large selection of meat and fish dishes. In summer, ask for a table on the terrace.
➕ 210 C2 ✉ Butler's Wharf Bldg, 36c Shad Thames, SE1 ☎ 020 74 03 54 03; www.cantina.co.uk ⏰ Lunch: Mon–Thu 12–3, 6–11, Fri–Sat 12–10:30 🚇 London Bridge, Tower Hill

Cantina Vinopolis £
Vinopolis is dedicated to good wine and food. With its bare brick walls and modern furniture, its Cantina restaurant has a Mediterranean slant: foie gras with apricot chutney, roast lamb, and fresh pappardelle with wild mushrooms. Vinopolis has three other spots for eating and drinking: Brew Wharf (with its own micro-brewery), Wine Wharf (wine bar) and Bar Blue (cocktails).
➕ 209 F3 ✉ 1 Bank End, SE1 ☎ 020 79 40 83 33; www.cantinavinopolis.com ⏰ Thu–Sat 12–3, 6–10:30, Mon–Wed 6–10:30 🚇 London Bridge

Fish! Restaurant ££/£££
Begin the day with kippers for breakfast. At Fish!, freshly caught fish are made into classical dishes: grilled scallops, seafood salad or fish & chips. Come to brunch on Sunday and enjoy smoked shellfish, a swordfish sandwich or a tuna burger as you look out at Southwark Cathedral and the bustling Borough Market.
➕ 210 A3 ✉ Cathedral Street, Borough Market, SE1 ☎ 020 74 07 38 03; www.fish kitchen.com ⏰ Breakfast Fri–Sat 9–11, Sun brunch: 10–2; restaurant: Mon–Thu11.30–11, Fri–Sun 12–11.30 🚇 London Bridge

Oxo Tower ££/£££

Choose from three places on the OXO Tower's eighth floor: the restaurant, hip bar and brasserie. The brasserie menu is modern and very international: Thai crayfish cakes, slow-braised lamb shank, gnocchi, grilled Asian spiced quail, charcuterie. The restaurant is more British: halibut, smoked bacon and mussel chowder, roast pork chop with a mustard and Calvados cream sauce. The bar rocks.

🖰 209 D3 ✉ 8th Floor, OXO Tower Wharf, Barge House Street, SE1 ☎ 020 78 03 38 88; www.harveynichols.com 🕔 Mon–Sat 6pm–11pm, Sun 6:30pm–10pm 🚇 Blackfriars

RSJ ££

The name RSJ refers to the rolled steel joist that crosses the ceiling of this long-established, family-owned, restaurant. Among its numerous charms are a comfortably warm but contemporary interior, good, modern Anglo-French cooking strong on seasonal dishes and a much applauded wine list. The fixed-price lunch is excellent value. Highly recommended.

🖰 209 D3 ✉ 33 Coin Street, SE1 ☎ 020 79 28 45 54; www.rsj.uk.com 🕔 Lunch: Mon–Fri 12–2:30. Dinner: Mon–Sat 5:30–11 🚇 Waterloo

Swan at the Globe £/££

Enjoy stunning river views from the Georgian building that forms part of the Globe Theatre complex on the South Bank (➤ 113). This airy, bright theatre bar serves light lunch and supper dishes such as pasta and salads, as well as cakes and sandwiches. The brasserie on the first floor has the same river views, and offers an à la carte menu, as well as good-value pre- and post-theatre menus.

🖰 209 F3 ✉ 21 New Globe Walk, Bankside, SE1 ☎ 020 79 28 94 44; www.loveswan.co.uk/ shakespearesglobe 🕔 Theatre bar: Mon–Wed 8–11pm, Thu–Fri 8–12, Sat 11–12:30, Sun 11–10; Restaurant: Mon–Sat 12–2:30, 6–10, Sun 11–6 🚇 Cannon Street, London Bridge, Mansion House

The Table Café £/££

The architect who designed and owns this deliberately plain restaurant is passionate about food, sourcing as much produce as possible close to London. Dishes range from roast organic chicken with preserved lemon couscous to wild rabbit and hazelnut sausages, squid and mussel gratin, and properly-aged organic steaks from North Wales. There are also imaginative lunches and brunches.

🖰 209 E3 ✉ 83 Southwark Street, SE1 🕔 020 74 01 27 60; www.thetablecafe.com 🕔 Mon–Fri 7:30–5. Dinner: Tue–Thu 6–10:30, Fri–Sat 6–11. Weekend brunch: 8:30–4 🚇 Southwark, London Bridge

BARS & PUBS

Anchor & Hope £

Probably the best time to go to this popular gastropub is for a late lunch or pre-theatre meal, as they have a no-booking policy and you will need to be patient if you want a table in the evening. The good hearty British cuisine is all very well cooked and includes some imaginative choices such as earthy pigeon and foie gras terrine and rich shin of beef in red wine, infused with rosemary and juniper.

🖰 209 D2 ✉ 36 The Cut, SE1 ☎ 020 79 28 98 98 🕔 Mon 5pm–11, Tue–Sat 11–11, Sun 12:30–5 🚇 Southwark, Waterloo

Gordon's Wine Bar £

Dating from 1890 and claiming to be the oldest established wine bar in town, this dark, cobwebby place is a gem. Rub shoulders with commuters, wine lovers and inquisitive visitors who come not only to drink in the atmosphere but to sample an excellent range of wines, plus traditional ports and madeiras. A healthy buffet salad bar, hot meals and a traditional roast on Sunday are served.

🖰 208 A3 ✉ 47 Villiers Street, WC2 ☎ 020 79 30 14 08; www.gordonswinebar.com 🕔 Mon–Sat 11–11, Sun 12–10 🚇 Embankment, Charing Cross

Where to...
Shop

Oxo Tower Wharf and **Gabriel's Wharf** represent one of the more unusual and fun shopping areas in London (Barge House Street, SE1, www.coinstreet.org). Watch internationally recognized artists and craftspeople working on everything from jewellery and hats to fabrics and fashion.

Explore Oxo Tower Wharf for funky gifts. **Joseph Joseph**, actually twin brothers Antony and Richard Joseph, design cheerful and refined kitchenware, such as their clever space-saving NEST collection that is also distributed through major departments stores (1.20/1.21 first floor courtyard, www.josephjoseph.com). Victoria Whitbread and Jackie Piper of **Whitbread Wilkinson W2 Products** (2.01/2.02 second floor courtyard, www.w2products.com) designed the iconic Pantone mug, as well as a range of design-led contemporary gift and homeware collections.

For cult watches, head for **Mr Jones Design**, developed by Crispin Jones as "jewellery for the mind" (1.11, first floor riverside, www.mrjoneswatches.com). Close by, jeweller **Josef Koppmann** creates one-of-a-kind treasures from 24-carat gold and sterling silver (1.22 first floor courtyard, www. josefkoppmann.com).

Unique is the only description for **j-me's** witty and stylish designs for everyday items from magazine racks to tape dispensers (1.15 first floor courtyard, www.j-me.co.uk). **Suck UK** has equally clever designs for skateboard mirrors, sun jars, drumstick pencils and musical rulers (103 first floor riverside, www.suck.uk.com).

Where to...
Go Out

With a variety of venues, the **Southbank Centre** (▶ 112) is the world's largest arts centre of its kind. For music and dance, check out the **Royal Festival Hall**, and the **Queen Elizabeth Hall**, with its Purcell Room.

Further downstream, with top quality plays, the **Royal National Theatre** (tel: 020 74 52 30 00; www.nationaltheatre.org.uk) comprises three separate spaces: the Lyttelton, Olivier and Cottesloe theatres.

The **BFI South Bank** (tel: 020 79 28 32 32; www.bfi.org.uk) is the British Film Institute's home (cinema archives), and has three screens for mainstream and subtitled foreign films, and has various projects dedicated to helping young filmmakers.

Close by, the BFI runs the **London IMAX Cinema**, a 500-seat, state-of-the-art cinema (tel: 033 03 33 78 78) for 3D films on the UK's largest screen.

The other giant on the South Bank is **Shakespeare's Globe** (▶ 113). Nearby, two venues share a name. At the **Old Vic** (tel: 0844 8 71 76 82; www.old victheatre.com), artistic director Kevin Spacey maintains its star-studded history. By contrast, the **Young Vic** (tel: 020 79 22 29 22; www.youngvic.org) offers edgy productions at affordable prices.

In summer, look out for the **E4 Udderbelly**. This 400-seat, pop-up venue hosts a variety of alternative comedy, circus, music, theatre and unusual performance styles in Jubliee Gardens, near the Royal Festival Hall. In December, the German-style **Christmas Market** is popular.

Knightsbridge, Kensington & Chelsea

Getting Your Bearings	120
The Perfect Day	122
TOP 10	124
Don't Miss	130
At Your Leisure	137
Where to …	140

 **Little Treats**

Back to the Sixties
Soak up the London feeling of this period –
with the bright clothing on show at the fashion
exhibition in the **V&A Museum** (▶ 126)!

Learn to fly
Regardless whether young or old, in the
Red Arrows' 3D flight simulator at the **Science
Museum** (▶ 131) everyone feels like a jet pilot.

Futuristic, modern
Each year, a different artist designs the
pavilion in **Hyde Park** for the Serpentine Gallery
(▶ 138) and writes architectural history.

Perfect Days in...

Getting Your Bearings

Portobello Road Market 48

These premier residential districts were once leafy villages, favoured by the wealthy for their healthy distance from the dirt and pollution of early London. Today they still retain an ambience of exclusivity: their houses are grand, the streets still leafy, and the area has attracted many consulates and embassies to its genteel environs.

Portobello Rd

Kensington Park Rd

Pembridge Rd

Bayswater

Queensway

Notting Hill Gate

Bayswater Rd

Kensington Church St

Kensing Gard

The Broad Walk

Kensington Palace 6

Rc P

Kensington Rd

Palace Gate

High Street Kensington

Cr

Kensington first gained its fashionable reputation in the late 17th century when royalty moved to Kensington Palace. The palace remains a royal home – though parts are open to the public – and the gardens are among London's prettiest. Kensington Gardens occupy the western swathe of Hyde Park, which extends all the way to Marble Arch, affording a magnificent green space at the very heart of the city. In the middle is the Serpentine, an artificial lake.

Much of Kensington is scattered with monuments to Queen Victoria's husband, Prince Albert, who died prematurely in 1861. The Albert Memorial on the edge of Kensington Gardens is the principal example, but more subtle reminders of the royal consort survive elsewhere. It was the Prince's idea that profits from the Great Exhibition (held in Hyde Park in 1851) should be used to establish an education centre in the area. The colleges and institutions of South Kensington were the result, among them three of the capital's foremost museums: the V&A Museum, the Science Museum and the Natural History Museum.

Knightsbridge is Kensington's neighbour to the east and, if anything, is even more exclusive as a residential address. It also has a smart commercial aspect, including the department store Harrods. More affluent residents use the shop as a local store, but most Londoners and tourists are content with a voyeuristic look at the richness and variety of its stock, its lavish interiors and the tempting food halls.

Getting Your Bearings

TOP 10
⭐ 6 Kensington Palace ➤ 124
⭐ 8 V&A Museum ➤ 126

Don't Miss
42 Harrods ➤ 130
43 Science Museum ➤ 131
44 Natural History Museum ➤ 134

At Your Leisure
45 Saatchi Gallery ➤ 137
46 Albert Memorial ➤ 137
47 Hyde Park & Kensington Gardens ➤ 138
48 Portobello Road Market ➤ 139

The Perfect Day

If you're not quite sure where to begin your travels, this itinerary recommends a practical and enjoyable day out exploring Knightsbridge, Kensington and Chelsea, taking in some of the best places to see. For more information see the main entries (► 124–139).

🕙 10:00am

㊷ Harrods (left, ► 130) is essential viewing even if you don't want to spend any money. Don't miss the food halls, the pet department, the exotic Egyptian Hall and the splendid Egyptian escalators. Have a coffee in one of the many in-store cafés.

🕦 11:30am

Wander along Brompton Road, lined with upmarket shops, to the ⑧ **Victoria and Albert Museum** (► 126). Alternatively, if you don't fancy the 800m (half-mile) walk, catch a No 14, 74 or C1 bus, any of which will drop you near the museum. The other museums are across the road. The Victoria and Albert Museum, the national museum of art and design, is filled with all manner of beautiful objects; the ㊹ **Natural History Museum** (► 134) covers the earth's flora, fauna and geology; and the ㊸ **Science Museum** (► 131) investigates every imaginable aspect of science. The best approach is to choose one museum and give it a couple of hours – don't try to tackle too much in one go.

🕐 1:30pm

Have a leisurely lunch in the area at one of the museum cafés or in a patisserie or pub in nearby Brompton Road.

🕝 2:45pm

Walk north up Exhibition Road, turn left into Kensington Gore to the Royal Albert Hall and admire the ㊻ **Albert Memorial** opposite (► 137). If the weather is fine, head into Kensington Gardens and across to the Round Pond and Kensington Palace. Otherwise, buses No 9, 10 or 52 run towards Kensington High Street along Kensington Gore; get off at the Broad Walk (it's just a couple of stops along) and walk straight into the gardens near the palace. (Note that in winter the last admission to Kensington Palace is at 4pm.)

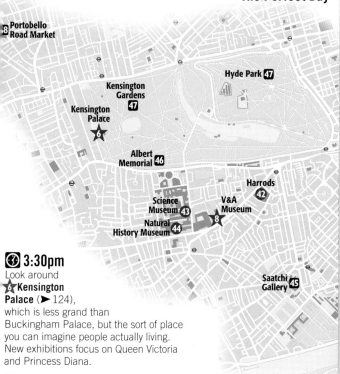

Portobello
Road Market

Hyde Park **47**

Kensington
Gardens
47

Kensington
Palace
★ 6

Albert
Memorial **46**

Harrods
42

Science
Museum **43**

V&A
Museum
8

Natural
History Museum **44**

Saatchi
Gallery **45**

🕒 3:30pm

Look around
★ **Kensington
Palace** (➤ 124),
which is less grand than
Buckingham Palace, but the sort of place
you can imagine people actually living.
New exhibitions focus on Queen Victoria
and Princess Diana.

🕒 5:00pm

Enjoy the walk through **47 Kensington
Gardens** and into **47 Hyde Park** (below,
➤ 138). From spring to autumn, you can take a
rowing boat out on the Serpentine. Have a break, perhaps afternoon tea,
in the Serpentine Bar & Kitchen.

⭐6 Kensington Palace

Since the death of Diana, Princess of Wales in 1997, visitors have flocked to see this elegant mansion overlooking Kensington Gardens. Diana was not the only princess to live here; Kensington Palace also played an important role in the life of Queen Victoria. A major revamp of the public areas includes new exhibitions about its royal residents.

The mansion began life as a country house in 1605, but was converted into a palace by Sir Christopher Wren for King William III and Queen Mary II following their accession to the throne in 1689 and their decision to move from damp, riverside Whitehall. Later resident monarchs included Queen Anne, George I and George II, while Queen Victoria was born, baptized and grew up in the palace. It was also here that she was woken one morning in June 1837 to be told that her uncle (William IV) had died and that she was Queen.

The south front of Kensington Palace was designed in 1695 by Nicholas Hawksmoor

Visiting the Palace

Today, visitors see the opulent state rooms as well as additional apartments not previously open to the public. The "Victoria Revealed" displays explore Queen Victoria's story of love, duty and loss. The route includes the Birth Room, where she was born in 1819 and the Red Saloon, where she held her first Privy Council meeting. The stone stairs, where she first saw Prince Albert in 1836 are also on the tour. As well as her own writings, the Queen's 63-year-reign is recalled by personal objects, from baby shoes to her wedding dress. Interactive displays and Explainers, or

The King's Gallery holds the famous Van Dyck portrait of Charles I

storytellers, provide insights into the life of this woman, who was a wife and mother, as well as the monarch.

The palace has also been home to other members of the royal family. The late Princess Margaret, sister of the present Queen, lived here, as did Princess Diana. Both were very much in the public eye and new exhibitions tell their stories. There are also displays about royal residents from centuries ago: King William III and Queen Mary II, Queen Anne and King George II.

The beautiful gardens still have many original features that date back to their creation in 1728. These include the Round Pond and the Broad Walk, with its marble statue of Queen Victoria. Designed by her daughter, Princess Louise, it shows the queen in her coronation robes, when she was just 18 years of age.

TAKING A BREAK

With its large windows, the **Orangery** is a delightful place to relax over a meal or just a snack (opening hours same as Kensington Palace).

☩ 202 B3 ✉ The Broad Walk, Kensington Gardens, W8
☎ 0844 4 82 77 77 (from the UK); www.hrp.org.uk
🕑 March–Oct daily 10–6 (last entry 5pm); Nov–Feb daily 10–5 (last entry 4pm)
🍴 Café and restaurant in the Orangery
🚇 High Street Kensington, Queensway, Notting Hill 🚌 Bayswater Road 94, 148, 390; Kensington High Street 9, 10, 49, 52, 70, 452 💷 £15

INSIDER INFO

- The visitor entrance is on Broad Walk, on the east side of the palace, so you can enter the palace directly from Kensington Gardens.
- **Book tickets online** to get a discount and to save time when you arrive at the palace.
- An exhibition focuses on Princess Diana's style, with some examples of her dresses.
- Don't miss the lovely Sunken Garden, created a century ago.

⭐8 V&A Museum

The V&A: this is how everyone refers to the Victoria and Albert Museum. It was founded in 1857 to make art accessible, educate working people and inspire designers and manufacturers. Or, if you prefer, think of it as a testament to mankind's creativity and love of beautiful objects. This is one of Europe's greatest museums, with 12 acres (4.8ha) of exquisite exhibits that span some 4,000 years and are drawn from Britain and across the world.

This is the sort of place where you want to take everything home: some Meissen, perhaps, a Persian carpet, or the Heneage Jewel once owned by Queen Elizabeth I. The range of objects is staggering – sculpture, ceramics, glass, furniture, metalwork, textiles, paintings, photography, prints, drawings, jewellery, costume and musical instruments. In addition to the wealth of beautiful works of art, the V&A also has the most peaceful atmosphere and most interesting shop of all the major London museums.

Exploring the Museum
Behind the magnificent facade of the 1899 building are over 140 galleries spread across seven floors.

The ornate exterior of the museum

The plaster cast copy of Trajan's Column displays many details which have, in the meantime, disappeared from the original in Rome

The collection is organized in various themes: by art form, such as sculpture; geographically, such as South Asia; or chronologically, as in the Medieval rooms. Strolling aimlessly is a recipe for visual indigestion, so start your visit at the information desk. Ask about special exhibitions (there may be a fee); pick up a map which lists 20 highlights (donation requested, £1) and mark up your particular areas of interest. The last decade has seen major renovations, with individual galleries closing for a while, such as the Fashion Galleries, which reopened in 2012.

The ground floor is the most crowded; fewer people visit the upper floors. Start at the top and work down. Although the building can be confusing, don't worry if you get lost: every gallery you come across is full of inspirational objects.

Medieval and Renaissance Galleries
Opened in 2009, the 10 galleries span the period from AD300–1600 and occupy three floors right at the front of the building. Highlights include the 12th-century **Becket Casket**, an enamelled box depicting the gruesome "Murder in the Cathedral" of St Thomas Becket; the 17th-century choir screen from the Cathedral of St John at 's-Hertogenbosch in the Netherlands; and sculptures by Donatello.

Raphael Cartoons: Level 1
The V&A's Raphael Cartoons were commissioned by Pope Leo X in 1515. The word cartoon refers to a preparatory drawing for works in other media. Monumental in scale, these were for tapestries depicting scenes from the lives of St Peter and St Paul, designed to hang in the Sistine Chapel in the Vatican.

Knightsbridge, Kensington & Chelsea

South Asia: Level 1

The **Nehru Gallery** covers a wide range, from textiles and paintings, to a white jade wine cup belonging to Shah Jahan (a 17th-century Mogul emperor of India and builder of the Taj Mahal). Don't miss *Tipu's Tiger* (*c.* 1790), a life-size wooden automaton depicting a tiger eating a man. A musical box inside the tiger's body can reproduce the growls of the tiger and screams of the victim.

Casts and copies from the Italian Renaissance in the Dorothy and Michael Hintze Gallery

Islamic Middle East: Level 1

Spanning the period from the 8th to the early 20th century, the focus of the **Jameel Gallery** is the huge Ardabil Carpet. Made in Iran in the 16th century, the deep colours are due to the density of knots. To preserve this wool and silk master-piece, the carpet is lit only on the hour and half-hour.

Cast Courts: Level 1

In the 19th century, art students were less able to travel to see masterpieces at first hand, so they came here – and they still do – to study and sketch these reproductions: Trajan's Column (Rome), the Portico de la Gloria (Santiago de Compostela) and Michelangelo's *David* (Florence). After renovation work, this gallery should now be open again.

Photographic Gallery: Level 1

The museum houses the national collection of photography, from the 1850s to the present day. Some of the 500,000 images are displayed, along with special themed exhibitions.

Levels 2 and 4

Covering British art and design from 1500–1900, the extensive **British Galleries** provide a visual history of the country. The wedding suit of King James II (1673) positively glitters with silver embroidery. The Great Bed of Ware was made in 1690 not for a nobleman, but for the Crown Inn in

Insider Tip

Hertfordshire. It measures 10 feet wide by 11 feet long (3m by 3.3m)!

Level 3

The most popular areas here are Jewellery and Theatre & Performance. The **Jewellery** rooms reflect the human love of ornament. At the entrance is a Bronze Age gold collar that was found in Ireland; further on is the Manchester tiara, made in 1903 for Consuela, Duchess of Manchester. Take time to watch videos on the making of jewellery.

The **Theatre & Performance** rooms also have videos, of performances and directors explaining their work. Costumes on show range from Brian Eno's 1970s black outfit, with pink feathers, to the grey satin Edwardian dress worn by Dame Maggie Smith in *The Importance of Being Earnest*.

Level 6

The revamped **Ceramics** galleries opened in 2009. Functional and ornamental, ornate and simple, the items here show how clay has been used over some 4,500 years for pottery, stoneware and porcelain. The collection is the world's most extensive, with examples of Dutch Delftware, Meissen and Japanese porcelain, plus a Bernard Leach bowl (*c*.1925) and a vase decorated by Picasso (1950s). If you miss one of the demonstrations in the workshop, there are videos of artists at work.

TAKING A BREAK

The **V&A Café** is in the ornate Morris, Gamble and Poynter Rooms (daily 10–5:15, until 9:30 Friday evenings). In summer, sit outside in the **Garden Café**.

➕ 203 E1 ✉ Cromwell Road, SW7
☎ 020 79 42 20 00; information: www.vam.ac.uk
🕓 Daily 10–5:45, Fri until 10 🍴 Cafés
🚇 South Kensington 🚌 C1, 14, 74, 414
💷 Free

INSIDER INFO

- Take a **free introductory tour**. Lasting about an hour, there are six per day. **Late-night viewing** is on Friday. The Theatre & Performance rooms have their own tours, also free, at 2pm Mon–Fri (excluding bank holidays).
- As part of the Create Programme, workshops and courses are organized for young people aged 16–24. Subjects include fashion design, for example, and participants receive valuable tips from experts in the respective areas.
- At the information desk, ask about 👪 **family events**; you can borrow a back-pack full of fun things, including jigsaws, stories, puzzles, construction games and objects to handle. The activities focus on subjects such as "architecture" for example, which encourage the children to explore not only the exhibits but the museum building as a whole. There are hands-on exhibits in the Theatre & Performance area.

42 Harrods

Harrods is a London institution. It began when Charles Henry Harrod, a grocer and tea merchant, opened a small shop in 1849. Today it contains more than 300 departments spread across seven floors, together striving to fulfil the Harrods motto *Omnia Omnibus Ubique* – all things, for all people, everywhere.

Harrods works hard to maintain its reputation as London's premier department store. Liveried commissionaires (known as Green Men) patrol the doors and if you are deemed to be dressed inappropriately you'll be refused entry. Rucksacks, leggings, shorts or revealing clothing are to be avoided.

The store's most popular departments are the cavernous ground-floor **food halls**, resplendent with decorative tiles and vaulted ceilings, where cornucopian displays of fish, fruit and myriad other foodstuffs tempt shoppers. Handsomely packaged teas and coffees, and jars bearing the distinctive Harrods logo are available: good for gifts or souvenirs. In fact, there is an entire section of Harrods souvenirs, from sturdy shopping bags and china mugs in the distinctive green and gold to a Harrods bear. Each year, a new version is introduced, so these are popular with collectors.

Also worth a special look are the **Egyptian Hall**, complete with sphinxes (also on the ground floor) and the **Egyptian Escalator** that carries you to the store's upper floors. One perennial favourite is the 🏠 **pet department** (on the fourth floor), whose most publicized sale was a baby elephant in 1967; the shop keeps smaller livestock these days. After dark, Harrods is impossible to miss, with thousands of lights illuminating the exterior.

Harrods' food halls are the mo
famous of the store's departm

TAKING A BREAK

There is a total of 30 places to eat and drink, covering a wide spectrum of prices. Choices range from a simple coffee, pizza or burger to sushi or steak, or champagne and caviar.

➕ 206 A4
✉ 87–135 Brompton Road, SW1
☎ 020 77 30 12 34; www.harrods.com
🕐 Mon–Sat 10–8, Sun 12–6
🍴 Bars and restaurants, including a deli, pizzeria and rotisserie
🚇 Knightsbridge
🚌 C1, 9, 10, 14, 19, 22, 52, 74, 137, 414, C1

⓼ Science Museum

Science is "knowledge ascertained by observation and experiment". As well as showing the "how" and "why" of science, this museum shows how this knowledge has changed our lives. From the complex to the simple, everything is explained and presented in user-friendly ways. Adults and children, the technically minded and the science phobe: all are catered for. With interactive displays, IMAX films and simulators, the museum is crowded during school holidays.

The museum's popular "Who Am I?" exhibit

You can easily spend the whole day here and still not see everything. Start at the information desk, where you can pick up a map and find out what shows and tours are on.

Ground Floor
Stroll through the **Energy Hall**, which tells the story of steam. The main draws here are examples of the monumental engines that powered the Industrial Revolution. Continue through **Exploring Space**, with its rockets and views of earth from space.. Here is an impressive collection of inventions and "firsts", from Stephenson's *Rocket*, the record-breaking 1829 locomotive, to the scorched and battered Apollo 10 Command Module that orbited the moon in May 1969.

Wellcome Wing
At the far end is the Wellcome Wing, with its deep-blue glass wall. Revamped in 2010 for the centenary celebrations of the museum, this has some of the most high-tech exhibitions, with touch screens galore. On the ground floor,

Knightsbridge, Kensington & Chelsea

the **Antenna** gallery reflects the latest developments and news from the world of science. Here, too, you can buy tickets for the **IMAX** theatre and for *Legend of Apollo*, with its 4-D sensation of being on a space mission. On the floors above, **Who am I?** looks at the body, brain and genes. Why do people smile? Why is somebody clever? See how you will look as you age – or what you would look like as the opposite sex! Go up again for the **Atmosphere** gallery, which is all about climate science. Themes include energy, the history of the earth and future technology.

Splitting the atom

The "Splitting the Atom" exhibition

Third Floor

This area is one of the most popular. The Fly Zone simulators (additional charge) provide thrills for those who love speed; the **Flight** gallery chronicles the history of manned flight from the Montgolfiers' balloons to supersonic engines. **Launchpad** is hands-on science and loads of fun. There are over 50 interactive exhibits for you to experiment with yourself. Cycle to create electricity and learn to work with basic tools, such as a pulley, screw, lever and wheel.

Other Galleries to Explore

There are many more diverse galleries to visit – and many of these are less crowded. **The Secret Life of the Home** (basement) shows how the everyday household items we take for granted have evolved and how they operate. This then-and-now of machines and appliances ranges from radios to fridges, hearth cooking to electric kettles. Compare the 1780 toilet from Hampton Court Palace with Thomas Crapper's Valveless Waster Preventer (1900), flushed with a pull chain. Other galleries include the Science and Art of Medicine, Telecommunications, Science in the 18th century, Agriculture and Measuring Time.

TAKING A BREAK

Bring your own picnic: there are two special picnic zones. Alternatively, try either the

😊 FOR KIDS

The museum is a lot of fun for the whole family, and offers something for every age group. Some galleries have been specially designed with youngsters in mind.

- **The Garden** (basement) is a play area for 3- to 6-year-olds, with a climbing frame and water play.
- **The Fly Zone** (third floor) has simulators that provide excitement for teenagers. Fly 3D provides the sensation of piloting a jet in the Royal Air Force's Red Arrow aerobatics team. In Fly 360°, you are at the controls!
- **Launch Pad** (third floor) is a hands-on environment showing the fun side of science, specially aimed at 8- to 14-year-olds.

The central atrium, seen from the second floor walkway

Deep Blue, with its underlit tables, in the Wellcome Wing or the **Revolution Café** (self-service) in the Energy Hall.

➕ 203 E1 ✉ Exhibition Road, SW7
☎ 020 79 42 40 00; www.sciencemuseum.org.uk 🕐 Daily 10–6
🍴 Restaurant and cafés Ⓢ South Kensington 🚌 C1, 9, 10, 14, 49, 52, 70, 345, 360, 414 💷 Free. IMAX, simulators and some special exhibitions: £6–12

INSIDER INFO

- Pick up a map and look for the symbol of a **black hand with a pointing finger**. This indicates the galleries that have **interactive exhibits**. As well as doing things for yourself, Explainers are on hand to answer questions.

- There are regular **free events**. Throughout the day, **Launchpad** offers science shows, complete with experiments. Most days there are three guided tours: **Flight** at 1pm, **Challenge of Materials** at 2pm, and **Making the Modern World** at 3pm. On weekends, there are special tours, such as **Spaced Out**, an interactive tour of the Exploring Space gallery (check for times).

Insider Tip

- Although **entry to the museum is free**, you have to **pay** for popular activities, such as the **IMAX 3-D cinema** and simulator rides. The **Explorer ticket** includes all these extras (£20, children £17.50).

⓸ Natural History Museum

The Natural History Museum tells the story of life and the earth, from the most distant past to the modern day. Flora and fauna are in the Green Zone and Blue Zone; geological material is in the Red Zone. The Orange Zone, the Darwin Centre, opened in 2009. Here, visitors can see some of the work that goes on behind-the-scenes, learn about the collection and study of the museum's 73 million specimens.

Before you enter, take a look at the museum building. Designed in the late 19th century to look like a cathedral, it was the first in Britain to be entirely faced in terracotta. Inside and out, it is decorated with terracotta animals and plants. A total contrast is the Darwin Centre, to the left, whose glass walls enclose the eight-storey white Cocoon.

The 🚇 **National History Museum** is enormous and it is easy to spend an entire day here. Buy a map (£1), which has a helpful list of 15 "Don't miss" exhibits. Ask about free tours and events. The Visit Planners (wearing purple shirts) can help you make the best use of your time.

The Natural History Museum is home to more than 73 million specimens

Central Hall

In this two-storey-high entrance hall, centre stage is held by the cast of a fossilized skeleton of a Diplodocus dinosaur. Some 85 feet (26m) long, it has stood here for over a century. At the far end, up the stairs, a marble statue of **Charles Darwin** sits in contemplation, while visitors pose for photos with the "Father of Evolution".

Blue Zone

Dinosaurs. These galleries are among the most popular in the museum, with a host of models, fossils and videos that bring these extinct creatures to life. A raised walkway enables visitors to get close to the exhibits, such as a massive Triceratops and a Dromaeosaurus, or running lizard, only 5.9 feet

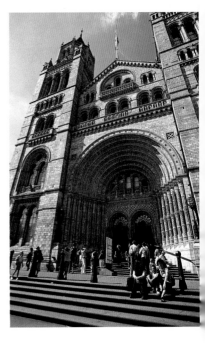

(1.8m) tall. Best of all is the animatronic Tyrannosaurus rex that growls and moves, looking ready to bite nearby prey!

Mammals. Learn about the differences between mammals on land and in the oceans. A rhinoceros and a polar bear, the cat family and little pygmy shrews: all are dwarfed by the life-size model of the blue whale (92 feet/28m long).

An unusual host: in the Central Hall a Diplodocus dinosaur welcomes visitors

Orange Zone Darwin Centre

At the information desk, pick up a NaturePlus card (for calling up information on the touchscreens), then go to the top of the building and enter the **Cocoon**. This high-tech area is a "show and tell" of how scientists do their work. Your virtual guides are curators, who greet you by

video and explain their passion for, say, butterflies or plants. Walk down the ramp and peer into labs; use the 40 touch screens to discover more about nature, perhaps about the mosquito, then store the information on your **NaturePlus** card. There are films and Nature Live talks in the Attenborough Studio.

Green Zone
Ecology. How Life Works is the theme of this visually impressive area, where video displays show, for example, the Water Cycle and a talking leaf explains how vital plants are to the life of the planet.

Creepy Crawlies. In this gallery, devoted to bugs and beasties, you'll learn more than you ever wanted to know about insects, spiders, crustaceans and centipedes. It will leave you wondering just what lurks in your home.

Red Zone
The entrance to the Red Zone is on the ground floor, at the side of the museum. Take the escalator up into the huge hollow earth sculpture; then work your way back down through the galleries.

The Power Within. These rooms are all about volcanoes and earthquakes. Don't miss the memorable mock-up of a supermarket, where you can feel the tremors in a simulation of the 1995 Kobe earthquake in Japan that killed 6,000 people.

Earth's Treasury. Here the focus is on minerals, metals, gems and rocks. After peering at minerals that glow in the dark, priceless diamonds, emeralds and sapphires – and fakes – you will never look at a humble rock in quite the same way again.

TAKING A BREAK
The self-service **Restaurant** is open all day, for breakfast, lunch and afternoon tea. For a snack, try the Central Hall Café, near the main entrance. The quietest spot is the Deli Café, by the side entrance (Exhibition Road).

➕ 203 D1   ✉ Cromwell Road, SW7   ☎ 020 79 42 50 00; www.nhm.ac.uk
🕐 Daily 10–5:50 (last admission 5:30)   🍴 Cafés, restaurant, snack bar
Ⓢ South Kensington   🚌 C1, 14, 49, 70, 74, 345, 360, 414   💷 Free

INSIDER INFO

👫Children keen to learn will love a visit to a museum; the following tips will help heighten the enjoyment:
- Arrive early if you can, in order to avoid all the school classes.
- Read online about the special family events on offer.
- Hire an explorer backpack with binoculars, magnifying glass and activity booklet.
- Children over 8 will enjoy the tour (daily 30 min) through the **Spirit Collection**, where they meet the giant squid Archie.

Insider Tip

At Your Leisure

45 Saatchi Gallery

One of the world's most vibrant art galleries, the Saatchi Gallery has moved around London over the past 25 years. Now its home is just off Sloane Square. The Saatchi Gallery's aim to "bring contemporary art to the widest audience possible" includes free entry to the temporary, curated exhibitions, usually featuring up-and-coming artists from around the world. Inside are 15 stripped-to-the-bone galleries on three levels, with plenty of room for large installations. In the past, the Saatchi has shown artists such as Andy Warhol, Richard Serra and Damien Hirst. The shows are very popular.

🕀 206 A2 ✉ Duke of York's HQ, King's Road, SW3 ☎ 020 78 11 30 85; www.saatchigallery.co.uk 🕐 Daily 10–6; last entry 5:30 🍴 Café 🚇 Sloane Square 🚌 11, 19, 22, 49, 137, 211, 319 💷 Free

46 Albert Memorial

It is worth making a detour to visit this memorial, the most florid and exuberant of all London's monuments. It was inaugurated in 1872 by Sir George Gilbert Scott, winner of a competition to design a national memorial to Prince Albert of Saxe-Coburg-Gotha (1819–1861), Queen Victoria's husband, who died of typhoid aged just 41, a blow from which Victoria never quite recovered. What Albert – who didn't want a memorial – would have made of the neo-Gothic extravaganza is hard to imagine: his spectacularly gilded statue is well over two times life size, and the edifice as a whole rises 165 feet (50m), its apex crowned by the figures of Faith, Hope and Charity. Also portrayed are astronomy, poetry and sculpture, plus more down-to-earth interests of the Prince, including agriculture, manufacturing and commerce. The 169 sculptures around the base are figures from history – there's not one woman among them. Directly opposite is

The Saatchi Gallery on the King's Road

Knightsbridge, Kensington & Chelsea

the Royal Albert Hall, planned by the Prince as a venue for concerts and exhibitions. Today, it is best-known for its summer music festival – The Proms – (➤ 144).

➕ 203 D2 ✉ At Kensington Gore entrance to Kensington Gardens, SW7 ☎ 0300 0 61 20 00; www.royalparks.org 🚇 High Street Kensington, Knightsbridge 🚌 9, 10, 52

47 Hyde Park & Kensington Gardens

Taken together, these open spaces total some 625 acres (253ha) and provide a huge urban playground. Hyde Park, originally a hunting ground for Henry VIII, was opened to the public in the early 17th century. Today, you will see runners,

for boating and bathing. You can still enjoy both: rowing boats and pedaloes are available for a fee on the northern bank; swimming is in a designated area off the south shore.

To the west of the Serpentine in Kensington Gardens is the 👪 **Diana, Princess of Wales Memorial Fountain.** Small children splash around in the water-filled oval ring of Cornish granite. Nearby, the **Serpentine Gallery** shows a changing programme of often controversial modern art.

Among the other art in the park, the most famous is the statue of **Peter Pan** (1912), which was paid for by the story's author, J. M. Barrie, who

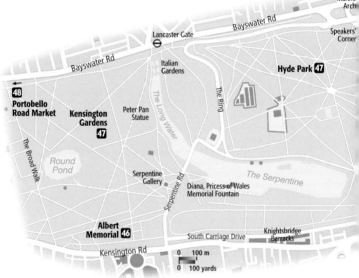

cyclists and riders on horseback, informal games of touch rugby and cricket, and concerts. **Speakers' Corner**, near Marble Arch, is the place to air your views. Anyone is entitled to stand up and (within certain parameters) speak their mind; Sunday afternoons are the busiest time.

Further west is the 👪 **Serpentine**, an artificial lake created in the 1730s by Caroline, wife of George II,

lived close by. It's just off a walkway near the Long Water, the northwest extension of the Serpentine. At the western end of the gardens are Kensington Palace (➤ 124) and a 👪 playground, designed for children up to the age of 12.

Hyde Park

➕ 203 F3 🕐 Daily 5am–midnight 🚇 Hyde Park Corner, Knightsbridge, Lancaster Gate, Marble Arch

The red building "Alice's" on the corner of Portobello Road Market

Kensington Gardens
➕ 203 D3 ⏰ Daily 5am–dusk
🚇 High Street Kensington, Bayswater, Queensway, Lancaster Gate

Serpentine Gallry
➕ 203 D3 ☎ 020 74 02 60 75; www.serpentinegallery.org
⏰ Daily 10–6 during exhibitions
🚇 Lancaster Gate 💷 Free

48 Portobello Road Market

Portobello is London's largest market, the long street and its environs offering a huge variety of food, craft and flea market-style stalls – as well as the specialist antiques shops (and stalls) that first made it famous. For the full experience, go on a Saturday when there are over 1,000 traders. The market generally splits into several sections. At the southern end, near Notting Hill Gate Tube station, are real antiques (from antiquities to Wedgwood) as well as bric-a-brac. After Westbourne Grove, stalls line the street, with everything from china to cigarette cards. Further north, after Elgin Crescent, the focus is food. Fresh fruit and vegetable stalls are interspersed with stands selling freshly made crêpes, paella and other food to eat on-the-go. Further north, towards the "Westway" elevated road and Ladbroke Grove Tube station, the wares are inexpensive: CDs, retro clothes and homewares. The market is often extremely crowded, so you should beware of pickpockets.

➕ 202 A4
⏰ General market: Mon–Wed 9–6, Thu 9–1, Fri–Sat 9–7. Antiques/bric-a-brac market: Fri–Sat. Some antiques shops open Mon–Sat
☎ www.portobelloroad.co.uk/the-market
🚇 Notting Hill Gate, Ladbroke Grove
🚌 7, 23, 27, 28, 31, 52, 70, 328

Citizens' Monument: the Diana Princess of Wales Memorial Fountain in Hyde Park

Where to...
Eat and Drink

Prices

The quoted prices are per person for a meal and do not include drinks or service.

£ under £ 25   ££ £25–50   £££ over £50

Chutney Mary £/££

One of the first restaurants in London to give a modern touch and ambience to Indian cuisine, still going strong after almost 25 years.

✚ 202 south of A1
✉ 535 Kings Road, SW 10
☎ 020 7351 3113; www.chutneymary.com
🕐 Dinner: Mon–Sat - 6:30–11:30 (last orders 11:45); Sun 6:30–10.30 (last orders 10:45); Lunch: Sat, Sun 12:30–2:45 (last orders 3:00)
🚇 Fulham Broadway

Babylon £/££

For that special occasion, **Babylon** has wonderful views and cutting-edge British food, 100 feet (30m) above busy Kensington High Street. As a break from shopping, book for the well-priced Saturday lunch: try the pumpkin risotto or fillet of black bream with North African spices, followed by a chocolate pot with ginger ice cream.

✚ 202 B2
✉ 99 Kensington High Street, W8
☎ 020 73 68 39 93; www.roofgardens.virgin.com
🕐 Mon–Sat 12–2:30, 7–10:30, Sun 12–2:30
🚇 High Street Kensington

Bluebird ££

A flower shop, café, bar and epicerie are all part of the Bluebird experience on the King's Road. There is a great buzz from the smart restaurant. The menu is simply conceived and includes an eclectic range of modern European dishes. There is a strong seafood selection and more rustic choices such as chicken and mushroom pie. They have a special Sunday lunch menu.

✚ off 206 A2
✉ 350 King's Road, SW3 ☎ 020 75 59 10 00; www.bluebird-restaurant.co.uk
🕐 Mon–Fri 12–2:30, 6–10:30, Sat–Sun 12–3:30, 6–10:30 (Sun 9:30)
🚇 Sloane Square

Bumpkin South Kensington £

Chefs in the open-plan kitchen at this popular neighbourhood restaurant focus on fresh seasonal British produce with a modern slant: duck liver parfait with pickled gherkin, braised Barnsley lamb chop with creamy mashed potato, treacle tart with vanilla ice cream. Regular favourites include pies, fish and chips and, on Sunday, roasts.

✚ off 203 D1 ✉ 102 Old Brompton Road, SW7
☎ 020 73 41 08 02; www.bumpkinuk.com
🕐 Daily 11–11 🚇 South Kensington

Cadogan Arms £

With its brick fireplace, leather-covered bench seats and walls covered with hunting trophies, this has an old-fashioned British look. Dishes are also traditional: pint mugs stuffed with prawns, roast partridge with all the trimmings and sticky toffee pudding with rum caramel.

✚ off 206 A2 ✉ 298 King's Road, SW3 ☎ 020 73 52 65 00; www.cadoganarmschelsea.com
🕐 Mon–Sat 11–11, Sun 11–10:30
🚇 Sloane Square, South Kensington

Gallery Mess ££

This was part of the **Duke of York's Barracks**, but is now part of the hip **Saatchi Gallery**. Contemporary artworks dot the interior, with its historic vaulted ceilings, exposed brickwork and designer furniture. Comforting dishes include smoked salmon with bread and butter, salmon and cod fishcake, steak sandwich and the Eaton Mess dessert.

🚇 206 A2 ✉ Saatchi Gallery, King's Road, SW1 ☎ 020 77 30 81 35; www.saatchi-gallery.com/gallerymess 🕐 Mon–Sat 10am–11:30pm, Sun 10–7 🚉 Sloane Square

Hereford Road £/££

The menu is straight from the fashionable nose-to-tail school, with an emphasis on the "best of British": hearty, rarely used cuts and offal, all carefully prepared, such as braised oxtail and devilled kidneys, as well as smoked eel and whole guinea fowl (with a dandelion salad). Wines are mainly French, many by the glass, and the set lunch is value for money.

🚇 202 B5 ✉ 3 Hereford Road, W2 ☎ 020 77 27 11 44; www.herefordroad.org; 🕐 Daily 12–3, 6–10:30 (Sun to 10pm) 🚉 Notting Hill Gate

Le Pain Quotidien £

At the large communal wooden table, even solo guests have company. Fresh organic bread is served with a topping of white bean, lemon hummus, or ricotta with dried figs and roasted pine nuts, Other delights include the mixed berry or chocolate tarts. From 5pm, meat and vegetarian dishes top the menu.

🚇 206 A2 ✉ 201–203 Kings Road (corner Oakley Street), SW3 ☎ 020 36 57 69 41; www.lepainquotidien.co.uk 🕐 Mon–Fri 7am–9pm, Sat 8–9pm, Sun 8am–7pm 🚉 Sloane Square, South Kensington

Racine ££

Only in France does it get any more French than in this popular Knightsbridge **brasserie**, just opposite the South Kensington museums. There's an authentic bustle and a rather masculine decor of dark wood and deep brown leather. Pick the hearty bourgeois fare such as rabbit in mustard sauce, steak and *frites*, or perhaps langoustines.

🚇 203 E1 ✉ 239 Brompton Road, SW3 ☎ 020 75 84 44 77; www.racine-restaurant.com 🕐 Mon–Fri 12–3, 6–10:30, Sat–Sun 12–3:30, 6–10 🚉 South Kensington

Zafferano £££

In an understated room, the plain walls, terracotta floor, comfortable chairs and closely set tables all contribute to an air of classy informality. Star chef **Giorgio Locatelli** established Zafferano as London's leading Italian restaurant and, although he has now gone, the cooking is still excellent. The food here is presented with tremendous understanding and flair. Uncluttered and simply conceived dishes based on the finest ingredients, exact technique and clear flavours are the driving force behind both the lunch and dinner menus. Expect classics with a twist such as veal shin ravioli with saffron. For a romantic setting, book a table in the first room.

🚇 206 B3 ✉ 15 Lowndes Street, SW1 ☎ 020 72 35 58 00; www.zafferanorestaurant.com 🕐 Lunch: Mon–Fri 12–2:30, Sat–Sun 12:30–3. Dinner: Mon–Sun 7–11 🚉 Knightsbridge

BARS & PUBS

Boisdale of Belgravia (15 Eccleston Street, SW1. Tube: Victoria) has an amazing range of 170 single malt whiskies, and there's live jazz nightly. The **Anglesea Arms** (15 Selwood Terrace, SW7. Tube: South Kensington) has outdoor seating, a panelled pubby interior and a wide selection of beers. **The Kensington Wine Rooms** (127–129 Kensington Church Street, W8. Tube: High Street Kensington), a wine shop and wine bar, offers 40 wines by the glass.

The **Attic in Bumpkin**, Notting Hill (209 Westbourne Park Road, W11. Tube: Westbourne Park) is a hideaway for the in-crowd. Open in summer only is the **Gin Bar**, a pop-up bar in a 1950s Citroen van by the Serpentine, serving cocktails (Hyde Park, W2).

Insider Tip

Where to...
Shop

This area has some of London's best and most varied shopping, from department stores and market stalls to designer boutiques and museum shops. Opening hours are generally 10am to 6 or 7pm. On a Sunday this usually becomes noon to 5pm. Many stores have late-night shopping once a week; usually on Wednesday or Thursday, which provides an extra hour for customers.

KNIGHTSBRIDGE

There are two main shopping streets in Knightsbridge: Brompton Road and Sloane Street. Both are accessed from Knightsbridge Tube station. On the corner where these two streets meet is the department store, **Harvey Nichols** (109–125 Knightsbridge, SW1, www.harvey nichols.com). Known as "Harvey Nicks", this has long been a destination for fashionistas, with eight floors of clothes for men and women, accessories, perfumery and cosmetics. At the top, the Fifth Floor has a restaurant, food hall, bar and café with outdoor terrace.

To the south, designer names line both sides of Sloane Street. **Salvatore Ferragamo**, **Missoni**, **Versace**, **Valentino** and **Pucci** are just some of the beautiful and expensive shops along the way.

By contrast, the shops along the Brompton Road are more affordable, though these are still upmarket. Among familiar international names are British stalwarts: **Jigsaw** (at 31, www.jigsaw-online.com) and **LK Bennett** for well-designed style (at 39–41, www.lkbennett.com), **Monsoon** for colourful ethnic-influenced fashion (at 49, www. monsoon.co.uk) and **Mulberry**, best

known for leather goods (at 171, www.mulberry.com). The department store **Harrods** is on the itinerary of most first-time visitors to London (► 130). Past Harrods are more shops. **Emporio Armani** (at 191, www.emporioarmani.com) also has a café; **Reiss** (at 163, www.reissonline.com) started out selling menswear in the City but now caters for women as well. Turn left into Beauchamp Place (pronounced Bee-chum), a short street that is lined with top-of-the-range boutiques that are fun for window-shopping, even if you can't afford the prices.

Further on, Brompton Road veers left. Follow this to the area known as Brompton Cross where you will find a choice of stores that includes the **Conran Chelsea**, in the distinctive 1909 Michelin building. Design guru Sir Terence Conran's flagship store features fun, contemporary home furnishings, as well as design classics.

SLOANE SQUARE & THE KING'S ROAD

In this area, posh Sloane Square rubs shoulders with the King's Road, where independent shops maintain a presence, despite the encroachment of chain stores. Everyone goes to **Peter Jones**, the department store that is on the square, opposite the Sloane Square Tube station.

The most expensive shopping is on the north side of the square, on Sloane Street. Here, British names include **Thomas Pink** (at 162, www. thomaspink.com), shirtmakers for both men and women, **Pringle of Scotland** (at 141, www.pringle scotland.com) for knitwear, especially cashmere, and **Hackett** (at 137–138, www.hackett.com), for classic British menswear. There are also boutiques selling Italian and French designers.

On the east side of Sloane Square is **David Mellor** (at 4, www.david

mellordesign.com).Look through the large windows and you will see beautifully crafted kitchenware and tableware. There is more on the floor below, and many of the lines, particularly cutlery, are David Mellor designs.

To the west, you can't miss **Peter Jones** department store (www.peter jones.co.uk). It is part of the **John Lewis Group** (including John Lewis on Oxford Street), known for its good prices. There are seven floors of fashions for men, women and children, plus homeware, electrical and technology departments. Its Top Floor restaurant (self-service) has great views over London.

The King's Road comes into Sloane Square from the west. Across it, opposite the side of Peter Jones, is the entrance to **Duke of York's Square**. Next to the **Saatchi Gallery** (➤ 137), this relaxed pedestrianized area offers cafés with outdoor seating and shops ranging from edgy **Allsaints** (at 14, www.allsaints.com) to Spanish children's wear **Neck & Neck** (at 34, www.neckandneck. com).

As for the King's Road itself, the choice is wide and eclectic, with something for everyone. French brand **Kooples** (at 36, www.the kooples.co.uk) caters for the young and slim; **Hobbs** (at 84, www.hobbs. co.uk) is a British group offering a more grown-up look. The classic tailoring of Jermyn Street is available at **Hawes & Curtis** (at 39, www. hawesandcurtis.com), makers of shirts and accessories for men and women. Reiss (at 114, www.reiss. com) used to sell only men's clothing; now, it also stocks fashionable lines for women. Another home-grown name is **Jack Wills** (at 72, www.jackwills.com), but the styles here are decidedly more casual.

For a total contrast, pay a visit to **Ad Hoc** (at 153, www.adhoclondon. co.uk), a boutique full of "street fashion" that teenagers love – hats, costume jewellery, wigs, hosiery and all sorts of unsuitable garments.

For women who want to look good while they exercise, **Sweaty Betty** (at 125, www.sweatybetty. com) has the clothes – for cycling, swimming, yoga and running.

The shops continue, way down the King's Road. Keep on going, either by foot or by bus, and when you feel weary, stop for something to eat and drink at **Bluebird** (at 350), a neighbourhood favourite with its café and food market (➤ 140).

KENSINGTON HIGH STREET & KENSINGTON CHURCH STREET

Kensington High Street is a good shopping area with mainly middle-of-the-range stores. To the east of High Street Kensington Tube station are large branches of **Topshop**, **Zara** (the Spanish fashion giant) and **Uniqlo** (the well-priced Japanese brand), plus Whole Foods Market and the discount store **TK Maxx**.

To the west of **Marks & Spencer** and the station are familiar international names, such as **Gap**, but the street is particularly good for shoe stores. Among them you will find **Sole Trader** (at 96a, www.soletrader. co.uk), **Clarks** (at 98, www.clarks. co.uk), **Ecco** (at 102, www.ecco. com) and **Aldo** (at 141, www.aldo shoes.com). Another speciality is stores selling sport and outdoor clothing. Continue west to find several clustered together, including **Columbia Sportswear** (at 170, www. columbia.com), **Snow & Rock** (at 188, www.snowandrock.com) and **Rohan** (at 204–206, www.rohan. co.uk).

On Kensington Church Street, fashion boutiques give way to antiques shops and art galleries as you head up the hill to Notting Hill Gate. On Saturdays, the Tube station here is busy with people making their way to **Portobello Road Market**, one of London's most famous (➤ 139).

Where to...
Go Out

NIGHTLIFE

Archangel and **AAA** are two clubs in one. **AAA** has live music from rock and folk to alternative, while **Archangel**, its upstairs sister bar, is the cooler cocktail bar. Both also serve food (11–13 Kensington High Street, W8, tel: 020 79 38 41 37. Tube: Kensington High Street).

If you like jazz, try the **606 Club** (90 Lots Road, SW10, tel: 020 73 52 59 53; www.606club.co.uk. Tube: Fulham Broadway), where groups such as the bluesy, modern jazz Julian Siegel Quartet play. It's open seven nights a week.

For 20- to 30-year-olds, the eclectic **nottinghillartsclub** is an arts venue, combining leading-edge, pioneering music alongside avant-garde graphic arts-based exhibition programmes and concept visuals. The nightly programme ranges from Latin funk and disco to world music and even circus acts (21 Notting Hill Gate, W11, tel: 020 74 60 44 59; www.notting hillartsclub.com. Tube: Notting Hill Gate). There are also free Saturday afternoon sessions.

MUSIC & THEATRE

Ever since it was built in 1871, the **Royal Albert Hall** (Kensington Gore, SW7, tel: 0845 4 01 50 45; www.royalalberthall.com. Tube: South Kensington) has been one of the world's most versatile spaces, staging everything from concerts (classical to rock), sports events (boxing to tennis), ceremonies and meetings. Legendary names appearing here include **Frank Sinatra, The Beatles** and **Elton John, Nelson Mandela**, the **Dalai Lama** and

President Bill Clinton. There are top-class shows every day, but the annual highlight is **The Proms**, as the Henry Wood Promenade Concerts are known, one of the world's greatest music festivals. Over seven weeks, starting in mid-July, visiting international orchestras, soloists and conductors join the BBC Symphony Orchestra to perform a wide range of music. If you are prepared to wait, you can buy inexpensive standing-only tickets, otherwise you can choose from a range of more expensive seats or even boxes. There are 13 bars and three restaurants that open two hours before performances.

Whether shocking, disturbing or just plain brilliant, the **Royal Court** (Sloane Square, SW1, tel: 020 75 65 50 00. Tube: Sloane Square), home of the English Stage Company, has nurtured some of Britain's best modern playwrights, and is the place for modern theatre at its very best. A multimillion-pound refurbishment has uplifted the experience for theatregoers, replacing cramped conditions in the two theatres with superb facilities and state-of-the-art stage technology.

The **Holland Park Theatre** (Holland Park, W8, tel: 0845 2 30 97 69. Tube: Holland Park) is a popular open-air venue that operates only in the summer months. With the ruins of the 17th-century **Holland House** as a backdrop, and occasional accompaniment from the peacocks wandering freely through the park, the theatre plays host to the Royal Ballet, as well as offering a well-regarded opera season.

Despite a seating capacity of 70, **The Gate Theatre** is an ambitious setting for emerging writers, actors and directors. Stars who appeared here early in their careers include **Jude Law** and **Rachel Weisz**. It's above the Prince Albert pub (11 Pembridge Road, W11, 020 72 29 07 06. Tube: Notting Hill Gate).

Covent Garden, Bloomsbury & Soho

Getting Your Bearings   146
The Perfect Day   148
TOP 10   150
Don't Miss   154
At Your Leisure   160
Where to...   164

 **Little Treats**

In the blossoming garden

A treat for a summer day: reading a good book in **Regent's Park** (➤ 160).

Feast under the starry sky

On Fridays and Saturdays, you can savour French delicacies in the elegant courtyard of the **Wallace Collection** restaurant (➤ 162).

Film location 1972

"Frenzy" was shot at **Covent Garden** (➤ 150) when fruit and vegetable traders, including Hitchcock's father, were still based here.

Getting Your Bearings

Exploration of these districts underlines London's amazing variety: within the space of a few streets an area's character can change from classy to run down, from retail to residential, and from busy and exciting to genteel and refined.

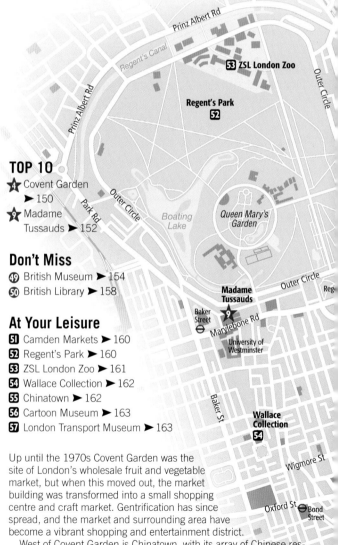

TOP 10

⭐ Covent Garden ► 150

⭐ Madame Tussauds ► 152

Don't Miss

㊾ British Museum ► 154

㊿ British Library ► 158

At Your Leisure

51 Camden Markets ► 160

52 Regent's Park ► 160

53 ZSL London Zoo ► 161

54 Wallace Collection ► 162

55 Chinatown ► 162

56 Cartoon Museum ► 163

57 London Transport Museum ► 163

Up until the 1970s Covent Garden was the site of London's wholesale fruit and vegetable market, but when this moved out, the market building was transformed into a small shopping centre and craft market. Gentrification has since spread, and the market and surrounding area have become a vibrant shopping and entertainment district.

West of Covent Garden is Chinatown, with its array of Chinese restaurants, and Soho, with its history of Bohemian poets and the Swinging

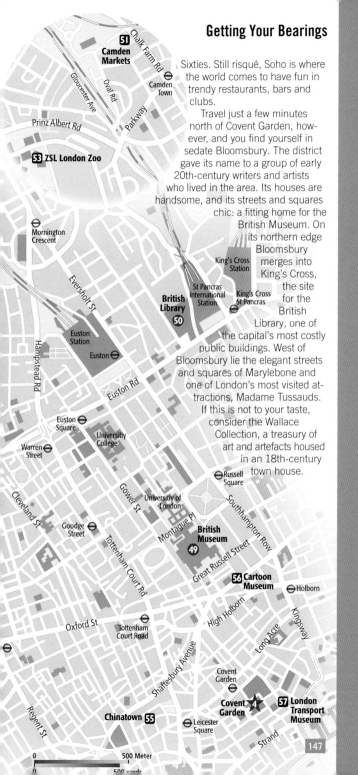

Getting Your Bearings

Sixties. Still risqué, Soho is where the world comes to have fun in trendy restaurants, bars and clubs.

Travel just a few minutes north of Covent Garden, however, and you find yourself in sedate Bloomsbury. The district gave its name to a group of early 20th-century writers and artists who lived in the area. Its houses are handsome, and its streets and squares chic: a fitting home for the British Museum. On its northern edge Bloomsbury merges into King's Cross, the site for the British Library, one of the capital's most costly public buildings. West of Bloomsbury lie the elegant streets and squares of Marylebone and one of London's most visited attractions, Madame Tussauds. If this is not to your taste, consider the Wallace Collection, a treasury of art and artefacts housed in an 18th-century town house.

51 Camden Markets

Chalk Farm Rd
Gloucester Ave
Oval Rd
Prinz Albert Rd
Parkway
Camden Town

53 ZSL London Zoo

Mornington Crescent
Eversholt St
Hampstead Rd
King's Cross Station
St Pancras International Station
King's Cross St Pancras

British Library 50

Euston Station
Euston
Euston Rd
Euston Square
University College
Warren Street
Russell Square
Cleveland St
Gower St
University of London
Southampton Row
Goodge Street
Tottenham Court Rd
Montague Pl
British Museum 49
Great Russell Street
56 Cartoon Museum
Holborn
Oxford St
Tottenham Court Road
High Holborn
Long Acre
Kingsway
Shaftesbury Avenue
Covent Garden
Covent Garden
57 London Transport Museum
Regent St
Chinatown 55
Leicester Square
Strand

0 500 Meter
0 500 yards

Perfect Days in...

The Perfect Day

If you're not quite sure where to begin your travels, this itinerary recommends a practical and enjoyable day out exploring Covent Garden, Bloomsbury and Soho, taking in some of the best places to see. For more information see the main entries (➤ 150–163).

🕘 9:00am

Arrive at the **49 British Museum** (above, ➤ 154) for when the Great Court opens at 9am. Here you can have a cup of coffee, get a map and find out about what talks and tours are on during the day. At 10am you will be able to start exploring the museum itself, full of beautiful pieces from bygone civilizations, including the Parthenon Sculptures (Elgin Marbles).

🕛 12:00 noon

From Russell Square catch a No 91 bus or take a 30-minute walk through Bloomsbury to the **50 British Library** (➤ 158). Look at the outside of the building from the spacious piazza then admire some of the world's loveliest old books and manuscripts. Have a light lunch in one of the cafés here.

🕝 2:30pm

From the British Library, take the No 30 bus along the Euston Road, which becomes the Marylebone Road. Near Baker Street station is **⭐ Madame Tussauds** (opposite top, ➤ 152). The waxworks are popular year-round and you will probably have a wait in the long queue to get in, so try to buy your ticket online in advance.

- **51** Camden Markets
- **53** ZSL London Zoo
- **53** ZSL London Zoo
- **52** Regent's Park
- **50** British Library
- **9** Madame Tussauds
- **49** British Museum
- **54** Wallace Collection
- **56** Cartoon Museum
- **57** London Transport Museum
- **55** Chinatown
- **Covent Garden**

⏰ 4:00pm

Take the No 13 bus from Baker Street to Strand for ⭐**Covent Garden** (Neal's Yard, below, ➤ 151). There is plenty to do in the area, with street entertainers, the market and shops (➤ 167). The **57 London Transport Museum** (➤ 163) is far more than just a collection of historic vehicles; it tells the story of the city's growth and how that changed society. As for eating and drinking, Covent Garden has a great choice of restaurants, pubs and bars. It's a short walk from here to many West End theatres (➤ 168).

⭐4 Covent Garden

Covent Garden is a favourite destination with visitors, as well as Londoners, for its mix of shops, restaurants and entertainment – from street buskers and theatres to the world-renowned Royal Opera House. The bustle dates back to the 1630s, when it was developed to a design by the architect Inigo Jones. In the 1970s, the fruit and vegetable traders moved out of the lovely old market building; the area was redeveloped and is now busy seven days a week.

The district's heart is the Piazza, surrounding the market that houses small shops and the crafts stalls of the Apple Market. Close by are the **Royal Opera House**, home of the Royal Opera and Royal Ballet (➤ 168), the London Transport Museum (➤ 163) and the indoor Jubilee Market (bric-a-brac, clothes, crafts, leather goods). One of the highlights is the variety of 🛇 **street entertainers**, from Chinese orchestras to acrobats, mime artists and didgeridoo players. For a peaceful interlude, head for St Paul's Church with its gardens on the west side of the piazza. Known as the Actors' Church, it has a long association with the theatrical community. Inside are memorials to stars, such as Dame Edith Evans (1888–1976) and Vivian Leigh (1913–1967).

Street performer in Covent Garden

Left: bronze of a ballerina outside the Royal Opera House; right: shoppers in the markets

TAKING A BREAK
You are never far from something to eat in this area. Good choices are **Bill's Produce Store** (➤ 164) and **Café des Amis** (➤ 164).

➕ 208 B4 🚇 Covent Garden 🚌 Along Strand 6, 9, 11, 13, 15, 23, 91, 176

INSIDER INFO

- Most visitors tend to stay in the vicinity of the piazza, but it's great **fun to explore the small streets** – east to Drury Lane, north to Shorts Gardens and the intersection known as Seven Dials, and west to St Martin's Lane/Monmouth Street.
- **Neal's Yard** looks like a throwback to the hippy 1960s, with **Neal's Yard Remedies** (15 Neal's Yard, WC2, www.nealsyardremedies.com) selling herbal remedies, aromatherapy oils and toiletries. For delicious British cheeses, try **Neal's Yard Dairy** (17 Shorts Gardens, WC2, www.nealsyarddairy.co.uk), and lovers of healthy food should visit **Neal's Yard Salad Bar** (2 Neal's Yard) - a veritable mecca for vegetarians).
- **Stanfords** (12–14 Long Acre, WC2, www.stanfords.co.uk) boasts of being the biggest travel bookshop in the world. This 1901 store is particularly known for its maps of cities and countries round the world, plus the detailed Ordnance Survey maps of Britain. On the ground floor, you can literally walk across the world: the flooring is a map!

Insider
Tip

⭐ Madame Tussauds

One of London's most popular tourist attractions, Madame Tussauds offers you the chance to meet James Bond, see how tall actor-turned-politician Arnold Schwarzenegger really is and have your photograph taken with boxing legend Muhammad Ali – or at least waxwork models of these.

A visit to the ⚑ waxworks museum provides fun-packed entertainment for adults and children alike.

The displays proper start with the **A-List Party**, where you are in with the glitzy in-crowd. You can give Brad Pitt a squeeze or make J-Lo blush (you'll have to visit to find out how!), feature as part of an exclusive photo shoot with Kate Moss for a fictional "glossy" and you may even be interviewed on Madame T's TV.

Next comes the glitz of **Premiere Night**, with a lavish production of screen stars past and present, such as Marilyn Monroe and Zac Efron.

First Floor Displays

Upstairs on the **World Stage** there are models of religious leaders, members of the Royal Family, politicians and world leaders, as well as figures from sport and the arts including David Beckham, Picasso and The Beatles.

From here you plunge into the **SCREAM** the most ghoulish section (unsuitable for children under 12). Torture, execution and murder are dealt with, together with lots of gruesome sound effects, the subject matter portrayed in graphic detail with live actors to add to the fear factor. There is an additional charge for this area.

Opposite top:
Hollywood
actor Johnny
Depp

Opposite:
US President
Barack Obama

Below: As if
it were yester-
day – John,
Paul, George
and Ringo, as
they appeared
at the start of
their careers

FACTS AND FIGURES

- Early techniques involved casts being made of the model's head. Napoleon had to have straws stuck up his nostrils so that he could breathe as his cast was made, and was so distressed he held Josephine's hand throughout.
- All the hair used on the models is real and is regularly washed and styled.
- The wax used is very similar to candle wax, and the exhibition purposely has no windows so that models don't melt in the sunlight.

Watch Shakespeare at work; see the Great Plague and the Fire of London in the **Spirit of London** attraction, where you hop into a two-seater black cab for the fascinating 10-minute ride in a "time-travel taxi" through 400 years of London's history. Say hello to your favourite Marvel Super Heroes at the Marvel Super Heroes 4D attraction. After seeing Hulk, Spiderman and Iron Man, finish with a 9-minute Marvel 4D show.

TAKING A BREAK

For salads and sandwiches, the **Natural Kitchen** is close by (77 Marylebone High Street, tel: 020 30 12 21 23).

🚇 204 B4 ✉ Marylebone Road, NW1
☎ 0871 8 94 30 00; www.madametussauds.com
🕐 Daily 9:30–5:30, longer at peak times
🍴 Café Tussauds for snacks
🚇 Baker Street
🚌 13, 18, 27, 30, 74, 82, 113, 139, 274, 205, 453
💷 £30 (online £22.50)

INSIDER INFO

- The exhibition is hugely popular and you may **have to wait up to three hours** to get in during peak season. To avoid the wait, **book tickets online by credit card**, which allows you to enter by the Priority Access entrance. You also save up to 25% per cent compared to buying on arrival. Book a **Combination Ticket** and you can visit further London attractions, such as the London Eye (▶ 101). Or book a Family Ticket – since children under 14 are only allowed in with an adult.
- The exhibition is **quieter later in the afternoon**: if you arrive by 4pm you'll still have time to see everything.
- **Don't be shy**: you are allowed to kiss your favourite star, whisper in Jennifer Lopez' ear, or even squeeze Brad Pitt's bottom!

ⓐBritish Museum

The British Museum houses one of the world's foremost collections, a wealth of antiquities illuminating the history of civilizations and cultures from across the globe. It is also the world's first national public museum, founded in 1753 around the private collection of Sir Hans Sloane. The magnificent building houses more than six million artefacts, from ancient sculpture and coins to armour and silver. Although most of the galleries are organized chronologically and geographically, some have themes, such as Money.

Great Court

Start in this spectacular concourse area, created by glassing over the museum's central courtyard. In the middle is the beautiful 19th-century **Reading Room**; formerly the British Library (► 158), it now holds temporary exhibitions. The Great Court is also the museum's central information area: pick up a free map (donation requested, £1) and ask about free tours and activities.

Ground Floor

Some of the museum's most famous treasures are here. In Egyptian sculpture (Room 4), for example, is the **Rosetta Stone** (196BC). Discovered in 1799, it provided the key to Egyptian hieroglyphs, allowing much of Egyptian civilization to be understood. The same official decree is carved in three languages: Greek at the bottom, Egyptian hieroglyphs at the top and everyday script between the two. More dramatic is the huge **head of Ramesses (sic) II**: it was carved for the ruler's memorial temple in Thebes in the 13th century BC. Nearby are galleries with wonderful antiquities from Assyria, now northern Iraq. In Room 10 are massive carvings of winged bulls with human heads that once guarded the entrance to **Khorsabad, Palace of Sargon** (721–705BC). Along the walls beautiful reliefs

The colonnaded main building of the British Museum was built in 1844 to replace the earlier Montagu House, which had become too small to house the museum's growing collection

The museum's Great Court

depict a lion hunt; they once adorned the palace of King Ashurbanipal, the last great Assyrian king.

Often referred to as the **Elgin Marbles**, the Parthenon sculptures from the Acropolis in Athens have their own gallery (18). Since Lord Elgin had them brought to London, they have been a constant source of controversy. Modern Greece believes the Marbles should be returned, most of which are from a 5th-century BC frieze on the Parthenon in Athens, and probably depict a festival in honour of Athena. As well as the beauty of the human figures, note the liveliness of the horses.

Upper Floors

Two of the most popular themed rooms focus on items that are important across the world: money and clocks. Rooms 38–39, **Clocks and Watches**, tell the story of telling time. The main draw is a 1610 clock, whose simple mechanics still hammer a bell on the hour. Room 68 is all about **Money**. Over 5,000 years, payment has ranged from grains, shells and metal to modern plastic. Kids love to see "pieces of eight", the Spanish coins made from South American silver that were the first global currency.

Britain and Europe from AD300 to the present day are covered in nine galleries. Highlights include the 7th-century Anglo-Saxon **Sutton Hoo Ship Burial exhibits** (Room 41) that provide a valuable insight into a period about which relatively little is known. Excavated from a mound in eastern England in 1939, the most popular item is a **helmet with face mask**. In Roman Britain (Room 49) the **Mildenhall Treasure** is a shining array of 4th-century Roman silverware, including the 18-pound (8kg) Great Dish, decorated with images of Oceanus, the sea god.

Winged, human-headed bull sculptures from Assyria (865–860BC)

The **Ancient Egypt galleries** here are famous for funerary art and artefacts, with highly-decorated coffins, mummies, sarcophagi, jewellery and scrolls. In Rooms 62–63, the three coffins of Henutmehyt (*c*.1290BC) are particularly impressive. Also look for the case containing a "Predynastic Egyptian Man", nicknamed "Ginger" for the few tufts of red hair on the 5,000-year-old preserved body.

North Side

On Level 2, the **Chinese Ceramics** (Room 95) opened in 2009 to house the **Sir Percival David Collection**. Among the most important items are the David Vases, made in 1351.

The Nereid Monument: an Ancient Greek temple tomb

Mummies are among the most popular exhibits in the museum

Use the touch screens to discover more about these and the priceless assembly of some 1,700 objects. Up on Level 5 are the **Japan galleries** (Rooms 92–94). As well as porcelain, sculptures and samurai armour, there is a reconstruction of a tea house; you may be lucky to visit on a day when a demonstration of the tea ceremony is scheduled.

TAKING A BREAK

Choose from three places to eat in the museum: the **Court Restaurant (► 165)**, the casual **Court Café** or the **Gallery Café**, near Room 12 at the front of the building.

✚ 205 F3 ✉ Great Russell Street, WC1
☎ 020 73 23 80 00; www.britishmuseum.org
🕐 Main galleries: Sat–Thu 10–5:30, Fri 10–8:30. Great Court: Sat–Wed 9–6, Thu–Fri 9–8:30 🍴 Cafés and restaurants 🚇 Holborn, Tottenham Court Road, Russell Square 🚌 Tottenham Court Road, north-bound, and Gower Street, southbound 10, 14, 24, 29, 73, 134; Southampton Row 68, 91, 188; New Oxford Street 7, 8, 19, 25, 38, 55, 98 💷 Free

INSIDER INFO

■ There are numerous free walks and talks every day, such as **"eyeOpener" gallery tours** (30–40 min) led by volunteer guides and lunchtime talks by curators (Tue–Fri 1:15–2). Friday evenings offer a shorter overview in the form of Spotlight Tours (20 min) focusing on one highlight. Multimedia guides (£5) allow a more independent tour, and there are special versions for kids (book online, £3.50). Note that ID is required as a deposit (moderate). Video and still photography are generally allowed.

■ From the website, you can download a list of **highlights of the museum**: choose the 1-hour or 3-hour tour – or "12 objects to see with children". For fascinating listening, download a podcast from the series "A History of the World in 100 Objects". Broadcast on BBC radio, each of the 15-minute programmes is on just one object, such as a **Mexican codex map** or a **Sudanese slit drum**. All are presented by Neil MacGregor, the museum's Director. The free museum map shows where the 100 objects are around the museum.

Insider Tip

㊿ British Library

The British Library ranks among the greatest libraries in the world. The facts and figures about the library are exceptional enough, and the modern architecture and spacious facilities underline this first impression, even before you begin to look at the exhibits. They include some of the world's most valuable printed treasures. Exhibits span almost three millennia, from the Buddhist Diamond Sutra of AD868, the world's oldest printed book, a Gutenberg Bible and the Magna Carta.

The contemporary complex faces a large piazza, with its oversize sculpture "Newton after William Blake" by Eduardo Paolozzi. Inside, there are several rooms open to the public. The main attraction is the John Ritblat Gallery, a showcase for some of the most precious treasures. Because of age and fragility, some items are taken off display periodically. If there is something you really want to see, contact the Library before your visit. The PACCAR Gallery and the Folio Society Gallery are used for temporary exhibitions.

John Ritblat Gallery: Treasures of the British Library

This large room contains some of the library's most valuable items, including maps, religious texts and letters, plus literary and musical manuscripts. The light is kept low to protect the material and the atmosphere is almost hallowed – as indeed it should be in the presence of the **Lindisfarne Gospels**, one of the loveliest early English illuminated manuscripts. Also on display are the notebooks of **Leonardo da Vinci**, in his characteristic "mirror writing" (left to right) and original manuscripts by **Jane Austen** and **Charlotte Brontë**. *Birds of America*, with beautiful life-size illustrations, is one of only 120 remaining copies of John James Audubon's mammoth compendium.

In the music section, you can see the hand-written lyrics for *Help* (John Lennon) and *Yesterday* (Paul McCartney). Put on the headphones and you can listen to these – and to other works, such as Handel's *Messiah*, from 1741.

The binding of the Lindisfarne Gospels (*c.* AD698)

INSIDER INFO

- Visit the **café** or **restaurant**, as from here you can enjoy some of the best views of the central glass tower that houses the 65,000 leather-bound volumes of King George III's library.
- Sit at one of the computer terminals; using the **Turning the Pages software**, you can view the museum's treasures, magnify details and listen to explanations by experts.
- The Reading Rooms are for reference and research. A **Reader Pass** is required for admission; apply online before you visit.

Insider Tip

The **National Philatelic Collections** are also here. Pull out sliding panels to see stamps from across the world. The world's first postage stamps were printed in the UK.

You can't miss the dramatic six-storey glass tower soaring up past the café and restaurant. Inside is the King's Library, some 65,000 leather-bound volumes from the George III Collection.

TAKING A BREAK

In fine weather, the outdoor terrace of the restaurant is the perfect spot for lunch or coffee and cake.

➕ 205 F5 ✉ 96 Euston Road, NW1
☎ 019 37 54 60 60; www.bl.uk
🕐 Mon–Thu 9:30–8, Fri and Sat 9:30–5, Sun and public hols 11–5
🍴 Restaurant, cafés and espresso bar
🚇 King's Cross, St Pancras, Euston
🚌 10, 30, 73, 91 🎫 Free

View of the cafeteria in the British Library, located next to the glass tower containing the George III Collection

VITAL STATISTICS

- The library basement is equivalent to more than five storeys and holds 388 miles (625km) of shelving.
- Some 14 million books are stored in the basement, but the library's total collection numbers more than 150 million items.
- The library receives a free copy of every book, comic, map, newspaper and magazine published in the United Kingdom. This means it receives an average of 3 million items annually.
- The stamps displayed in the sliding panels of the **National Philatelic Collections** are just a selection of the more than eight million in the library's collection.

At Your Leisure

51 Camden Markets

Like a mix of eastern bazaar and flea market, the market stalls (1,000 of them) fill old buildings and extend under railway arches, along the canal and in alleyways. They spread northwards from **Regent's Canal** and on either side of Camden High Street. To the east is **Camden Lock Village**, with a United Nations array of street food. The shopping is inexpensive, for example, scarves, jewellery and knick-knacks. On the other side of the High Street is **Camden Lock Markets**, in and around the Market Hall. The quality is generally higher here.

The stalls continue under the railway arches and into the **Stables Market**. Built in 1854, this complex included workshops, warehouses and stables for the horses that pulled the barges on the canal. That history is recalled with life-size statues of horses, carts and even a blacksmith shoeing a horse. The shopping ranges from T-shirts and bric-a-brac to clothing (cheap and vintage), leather, jewellery, art, vinyl records and collectables.

This enormous area is the antithesis of the modern shopping mall. Come to search for something different and to haggle over prices. It is very crowded at weekends. Start at Camden Town Tube station and con-

tinue north; the top of the market is close to Chalk Farm Tube station.

Entertainment at night includes the theatrical restaurant called **Gilgamesh** (tel: 020 74 28 49 22, www.gilgameshbar.com) and **Dingwall's**, a live music venue for well over 40 years (tel: 020 74 28 59 29, www.dingwalls.com).

🚼 205 E5 ✉ Camden High Street, NW1 ☎ 020 74 85 79 63; www.camdenlockmarket. com ⏰ Daily, usually 10–6 (later Jun–Sep) 🚇 Camden Town, Chalk Farm 🚌 24, 27, 29, 31, 88, 168, 214, 253, 274 🎟 Free

52 Regent's Park

Regent's Park ranks alongside St James's Park as one of central London's loveliest green spaces (➤ 20). Fringed by the glorious Regency architecture of John Nash, it is loved by locals and visitors alike for its rose garden, its open-air theatre, boating lake and ZSL London Zoo (➤ 161).

An oft-overlooked park attraction is a trip on the Regent's Canal. Built in 1820, it runs for 13km (8 miles) between chic **Little Venice** in west London to Limehouse in the Docklands, where it eventually joins the Thames. Little Venice is a par-

Decorated shop front, Camden High Street

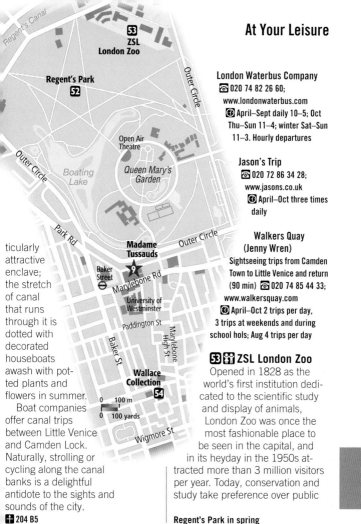

London Waterbus Company
☎ 020 74 82 26 60;
www.londonwaterbus.com
🕐 April–Sept daily 10–5; Oct
Thu–Sun 11–4; winter Sat–Sun
11–3. Hourly departures

Jason's Trip
☎ 020 72 86 34 28;
www.jasons.co.uk
🕐 April–Oct three times
daily

**Walkers Quay
(Jenny Wren)**
Sightseeing trips from Camden
Town to Little Venice and return
(90 min) ☎ 020 74 85 44 33;
www.walkersquay.com
🕐 April–Oct 2 trips per day,
3 trips at weekends and during
school hols; Aug 4 trips per day

53 🏃 ZSL London Zoo
Opened in 1828 as the
world's first institution dedicated to the scientific study
and display of animals,
London Zoo was once the
most fashionable place to
be seen in the capital, and
in its heyday in the 1950s attracted more than 3 million visitors
per year. Today, conservation and
study take preference over public

Regent's Park in spring

ticularly
attractive
enclave;
the stretch
of canal
that runs
through it is
dotted with
decorated
houseboats
awash with pot-
ted plants and
flowers in summer.
　Boat companies
offer canal trips
between Little Venice
and Camden Lock.
Naturally, strolling or
cycling along the canal
banks is a delightful
antidote to the sights and
sounds of the city.
🖶 204 B5

display and changing fashions mean that the zoo is a much quieter place. Nonetheless, it is still a popular and important visitor attraction, offering the chance to see around 16,000 animals from 725 species, many of which are endangered in the wild.

On arrival, check out the daily events, such as feeding times and demonstrations, when you can get close to reptiles, spiders and monkeys. With special VIP tickets (book in advance), you are allowed to get up close to the giraffes and penguins, an experience that is not only fun for children. In the **Children's Zoo**, youngsters can explore the animal world from the tops of the trees down to the roots. Favourites include the big cats, the families in the Gorilla Kingdom, and the dazzling array in the revamped walk-through indoor rainforest.

🚩 204 C5 ✉ Regent's Park, NW1
☎ 020 77 22 33 33; www.zsl.org
🕐 March to mid-July daily 10–5:30; mid-July to Aug 10–6; Sep–Oct daily 10–5:30; Nov–Feb daily 10–4 (last admission 1 hour before closing)
🎟 £23 (online booking less expensive)

54 Wallace Collection

In an elegant mansion on a leafy square, this rich collection could well be one of London's best-kept secrets. Collected by one family in the 18th and 19th centuries, it was bequeathed to the nation. Like the British Museum, the inner courtyard was glassed in with a roof, creating a sculpture garden, with a classy restaurant.

Every room is filled with treasures, though most people's favourite is the **Great Gallery**, where a wonderful collection of works by Titian, Rubens, Murillo, Van Dyck and others is on display. The collection's best-known work, Frans Hals's *The Laughing Cavalier*, is also here. While obviously a figure of substance, the man in question is neither laughing nor a cavalier. Near by is another portrait of an unknown sitter, Velázquez's *Lady With A Fan*.

Known for its variety, the collection also offers high quality: one of the world's finest collections of 18th-century Sèvres porcelain, 18th-century French furniture, and impressive armour, from the 10th-century sword to the impressive suit of 15th-century equestrian armour, for both rider and horse.

🚩 204 B3 ✉ Hertford House, Manchester Square, W1 ☎ 020 75 63 95 00; www. wallacecollection.org 🕐 Daily 10–5
🍴 Wallace restaurant 🚇 Bond Street
🚌 2, 13, 30, 74, 82, 94, 113, 189, 274 🎟 Free

55 Chinatown

In the heart of London, Chinatown's streets are always busy, as diners head for the 80 or so restaurants.

Gerrard Street, at the heart of London's Chinatown, is crammed with good restaurants and shops

Transport Museum exhibits

The cuisine gets ever more authentic and pan-Asian: Malaysian and Mongolian, as well as Szechuan and Cantonese. The Chinese New Year celebrations are among the largest outside Asia (► 14). If your feet are feeling the strain, little shops offer to recharge your batteries with a session of reflexology, massage or alternative medicine.

➕ 205 F2 ✉ Around Gerrard Street, W1
🚇 Leicester Square 🚌 14, 19, 24, 29, 38, 176

🏛 Cartoon Museum

London's first dedicated cartoon museum is over 15 years old. The collection numbers some 1,500 original works from top cartoonists and artists from the 18th century to the present day. Exhibitions change over the year: you could see political cartoons and caricatures, children's comics or newspaper strip cartoons. Every second Saturday during the summer, from noon till 4, there is a **family fun day** with different programmes and workshops, where you can draw your own cartoons and talk to the cartoonist in residence.

➕ 208 A5 ✉ 35 Little Russell Street, WC1
☎ 020 75 80 81 55; www.cartoonmuseum.org
🕐 Tue–Sat 10:30–5:30, Sun 12–5:30
🚇 Holborn 🚌 1, 8, 19, 25, 38, 55, 98
🎫 £5.50

57 🏛 London Transport Museum

Far more than just a collection of transport memorabilia, this museum focuses on the role of transport in the life of London – over the past 200 years, now and in the future. When the world's first underground railway line was opened in 1863, steam engines pulled the carriages.

Metropolitan number 23, the only engine left from that era, is here. Today, the transport system carries over three million passengers every day. Simulators provide the experience of driving a Tube train, while the 3-D display "Connections" shows how the system above ground relates to that underneath. Among the historic taxis, trains and buses is everyone's favourite, the red **Routemaster** bus, with the open platform at the back. See how the design for the Tube map was perfected over the years. If you think you know London, have a go at the "Knowledge", the test cab drivers have to pass to get a licence. Don't miss the gift shop, which is full of quality souvenirs of London.

➕ 208 B4 ✉ Covent Garden, WC2 ☎ 020 75 65 72 99; 020 73 79 63 44; www.ltmuseum.co.uk
🕐 Daily 10–6 (Fri 11–6), last admission 5:15
🍴 Café 🚇 Covent Garden
🚌 Along Strand 9, 11, 13, 15, 23, 139
🎫 £15; under 16s free

Where to...
Eat and Drink

Prices
The quoted prices are per person for a meal and do not include drinks or service.
£ under £ 25   ££ £25–50   £££ over £50

Amphitheatre ££

Inside the Royal Opera House, this is a sumptuous place for lunch, with a fine terrace (May–Aug). The food is British with a modern twist: dinner dishes include royal breasts of pigeon with spinach and mushroom pithivier.

208 B4 ⊠ Bow Street, WC2 ☎ 020 72 12 92 54; www.roh.org.uk Lunch: Mon–Sat 12–3. Dinner: opens 90 min prior to performance (ticket holders only) Covent Garden

Barshu £/££

In Chinatown, Barshu serves authentic Sichuan food. Alongside fiery dishes with chillies and Sichuan pepper are more subtle ones: stir-fried lobster with ginger and spring onion, and fragrant stir-fried beef. Hearty, complex Sichuan soups are traditionally served at the end of the meal. Expect Chinese decor, from the statue of the Buddha in the main dining room to hanging lanterns and traditional opera masks. For less fiery dishes, cross the street to sister restaurant Ba Shan.

205 E2 ⊠ 28 Frith Street, W1 ☎ 020 72 87 88 22; www.bar-shu.co.uk Sun–Thu 12–11, Fri–Sat 12–11:30 Tottenham Court Road, Leicester Square

Bill's Produce Store £

In a fashionable modern shopping development just off Long Acre, Bill's is a branch of a popular Brighton restaurant and deli, with an emphasis on fun. It's a funky mix of town and country, with big wooden tables, displays of fruit and flowers, cheerful staff and well-prepared familiar dishes, from eggs Benedict to fishcakes, lasagne, curry and a good hamburger.

208 A4 ⊠ 28 St Martin's Courtyard, WC2 ☎ 020 72 40 81 83; www.bills-website.co.uk Mon–Fri 8am–11pm, Sat 9am–11:30pm, Sun 9am–10:30pm Covent Garden

Brasserie Max £££

In the fashionable Covent Garden Hotel, this is a special occasion spot serving high-class modern dishes such as pheasant, duck and pistachio terrine with cranberry compote, twice-baked Stilton soufflé, halibut with a pine nut and sage crust, panettone and white chocolate pudding with a warm berry compote. For the same experience at a lower price, try the three-course set menu, the pre-theatre menu, or a complete English afternoon tea (3–5:30pm).

208 A4 ⊠ 10 Monmouth Street, WC2 ☎ 020 78 06 10 07; www.firmdale.com Mon–Sat 7am–midnight, Sun 8am–11pm Covent Garden, Leicester Square

Café des Amis £

This bar and restaurant is a fixture in Covent Garden, hidden in an alleyway next to the Royal Opera House. Regulars return for the straightforward, familiar dishes: French onion soup, moules marinières, roast duck breast with an orange liqueur sauce, crab risotto. The star dessert is a chocolate "soup'" served with black pepper ice cream. Eat outside in summer. Booking essential.

208 A4 ⊠ 11–14 Hanover Place, WC2 ☎ 020 73 79 34 44; www.cafedesamis.co.uk Mon–Sat 12–11:30 Covent Garden

Court Restaurant £/££

Dining under the glass roof of the British Museum over the Great Court is a treat. Dishes are inventive, from smoked chicken, chicory and paw paw with a chilli salsa to pan-fried snapper, with plantain crisps, tomato and peanut sauce. The full afternoon tea is an alternative to a grand hotel, and for exhibition goers, a dinner menu is served on Thursday and Friday (5:30–8pm).

✚ 208 A5 ✉ British Museum, Great Russell Street, WC1 ☎ 020 73 23 89 90; www.britishmuseum.org ⏰ Daily 12–3; afternoon tea 3–5:30 Ⓜ Russell Square

Les Deux Salons £

With its black-and-white chequered floor and booths, this all-day brasserie is handy for the theatre, art galleries and major sights in central London. Order rustic French fare: terrines, duck cassoulet, traditional Mediterranean fish soup, charcoal grilled lamb chops, crème brûlée, bitter chocolate mousse. Alternatively, just relax over a classic and filling English afternoon tea. A well-priced, three-course pre-theatre menu is also served Monday to Saturday (5–6:30pm).

✚ 208 A3 ✉ 40–42 William IV Street, WC2 ☎ 020 74 20 20 50; www.lesdeuxsalons.co.uk ⏰ Mon–Sat 12–11, Sun 11–6 Ⓜ Charing Cross

Great Queen Street £/££

This is a typical example of the trend towards keeping things simple: plain walls, tables with no cloths, paper napkins and chunky tumblers rather than wine glasses. The dishes are similarly unfussy: Jerusalem artichoke soup, braised shoulder of lamb, venison pie, rib of beef for two, bitter chocolate terrine with chestnut cream. The food is carefully prepared, and the atmosphere is buzzing. It's important to make a reservation.

✚ 208 A4 ✉ 32 Great Queen Street, WC2 ☎ 020 72 42 06 22 ⏰ Mon–Sat 12–2:30, 6–10:30, Sun 12–3 Ⓜ Covent Garden

Hawksmoor Seven Dials £/££

If anything shows how British food has changed over the years, it has to be this outstanding steak house, serving steaks dry-aged for 35 days. These are cooked the old-fashioned way on a searingly hot charcoal grill. Tradition is everything, from bone marrow to chips fried in goose fat. Think "old school" with modern twist. The set pre-theatre and lunch menus are good value.

✚ 208 A4 ✉ 11 Langley Street, WC2 ☎ 020 74 20 93 90; www.thehawksmoor.co.uk ⏰ Mon–Thu 12–3, 5–10:30, Fri–Sat 12–3, 5–11, Sun 12–9 Ⓜ Covent Garden

J Sheekey ££

One of the oldest and best-known seafood restaurants in the capital, Sheekey's has been around since 1896. It is run by the team responsible for such gastronomic temples as The Ivy and Le Caprice. This is the place to go for traditional British fish dishes. A selection of modern creations add an extra dimension to the menu.

✚ 205 F1 ✉ 28–34 St Martin's Court, WC2 ☎ 020 72 40 25 65; www.j-sheekey.co.uk ⏰ Mon–Sat 12–3, 5:30–12, Sun 12–3:30, 6–11 Ⓜ Leicester Square

Monmouth Coffee Company £ [Insider Tip]

This is one of Soho's best-kept secrets. From the front it is nothing more than a shop selling bags of coffee beans, but at the back are eight tables. It's the perfect place to stop, relax and sample some great coffees and a delectable selection of pastries. There are also branches in Borough Market and Bermondsey.

✚ 205 F2 ✉ 27 Monmouth Street, WC2 ☎ 020 73 79 35 16; www.monmouthcoffee.co.uk ⏰ Mon–Sat 8–6:30 Ⓜ Covent Garden

Norfolk Arms £

This corner pub, close to the British Museum, has been transformed into a popular spot to eat as well as drink. Snack on the wide range of hearty, pan-European tapas and charcuterie, or settle in for a full meal: fish pie with lots of salmon, haddock, pollock, prawns and scallops, braised short ribs, venison and porcini ragout. It's popular for its imaginative desserts (baked apple crumble cheesecake, chocolate and pear torte), as well as its Sunday roast, with Yorkshire pudding.

✚ 205 F5 ✉ 28 Leigh Street, WC1 ☎ 020 73 88 39 37; www.norfolkarms.co.uk 🕐 Mon–Sat 12–3, 6–10:15, Sun 12–10 🚇 Russell Square, King's Cross, Euston

Quo Vadis £/££

Now owned by Sam and Eddie Hart, after a spell under the control of Marco Pierre White, this contemporary restaurant has moved to a classic British menu with a modern twist. Seafood and roasts are the stalwarts, but there are pasta, salads and egg dishes, too. Elegant yet simple decor, with sumptuous leather sofas, make for a sophisticated and relaxing dining experience. The set lunch and pre-theatre menu offer good choices.

✚ 205 E2 ✉ 26–29 Dean Street, W1 ☎ 020 74 37 95 85; www.quovadissoho.co.uk 🕐 Lunch: Mon–Sat 12–3. Dinner: daily 5:30–11 🚇 Piccadilly Circus, Tottenham Court Road

Rules ££

A wonderfully quintessential British restaurant, Rules has an air of slightly aged grandeur. It is the city's oldest restaurant (1798) and offers up a mouth-watering selection of classic British dishes, with an emphasis on game, oysters and pies. It has been frequented by many famous characters throughout its long life, including Charles Dickens and actor Lord Olivier.

✚ 208 A4 ✉ 35 Maiden Lane, WC2 ☎ 020 78 36 53 14; www.rules.co.uk 🕐 Mon–Sat 12–11:45, Sun 12–10:45 🚇 Covent Garden

Wahaca £

At Wahaca you'll experience an authentic version of Mexican food. Everything is freshly made and many of the dishes are tapas-sized for a light snack or substantial dinner.

Choose from street dishes such as organic chorizo and potato quesadillas with thyme or slow-cooked pork tacos with a spicy Yucatecan marinade. It's canteen-style dining so it is not possible to book ahead.

✚ 208 A3 ✉ 66 Chandos Place, WC2 ☎ 020 72 40 18 83; www.wahaca.co.uk 🕐 Mon–Sat 12–11, Sun 12–10:30 🚇 Charing Cross

Wright Brothers Soho Oyster House £/££

With their own Cornish oyster beds and a wholesale fish business, Wright Brothers know their seafood. In the heart of the West End's Theatreland, their restaurant on a quiet courtyard has an open-plan kitchen and an oyster bar, offering half a dozen varieties of oyster. Dishes let the freshness of the fish do the talking: red mullet with spiced chickpeas, and whole baked sea bass for two or three people. Staples include fish soup, whitebait with tartare sauce, potted shrimps, and fish pie.

✚ 205 D2 ✉ 13 Kingly Street, W1 ☎ 020 74 34 36 11; www.thewrightbrothers.co.uk 🕐 Mon–Sat 12–12, Sun 12–11 🚇 Oxford Circus, Piccadilly Circus

BARS & PUBS

Bars abound and open till late. Go back to the 1950s at **Bourne & Hollingsworth** (28 Rathbone Place, W1), a basement cocktail bar with live bands Thu–Sat. By contrast, also in a basement, **Hakkasan** is cool (8 Hanway Place, W1), with its outstanding cocktail menu. At **Academy** (12 Old Compton Street, W1) some of London's star bartenders prepare choices from the 120-drink menu. **Mark's Bar at Hix** (66–70 Brewer Street, W1) is smooth and plush, like a private club (dress smartly). If the idea of a glass of bubbly in a railway station appeals, head for the glamorous **St Pancras Grand Champagne Bar** (St Pancras Station, NW1), Europe's longest, offering 20 styles of champagne by the glass.

Where to...
Shop

COVENT GARDEN

The shopping in this area (➤ 150) ranges from quirky to designer. Start at either Covent Garden or Leicester Square Tube stations: everything is within an easy walk. In the Piazza itself, the **Market Hall** is good for gifts, from toiletries and jewellery to crafts. **Benjamin Pollock's Toy Shop** (44, The Market, WC2, www.pollocks-coventgarden.co.uk), is an emporium full of handmade puppets and toys.

Floral Street is home to British designer **Paul Smith** (at 40, www.paulsmith.co.uk), as well as **Full Circle** (at 13, www.fullcircleuk.com), with younger and less expensive styles. Long Acre is lined with quality stores: among international names are UK ones, such as **Jigsaw** (at 21, www.jigsaw-online.com), **Ben Sherman** menswear (at 49, http://brand.bensherman.com) and **Whistles** (at 24, www.whistles.co.uk).

Off Long Acre is St Martin's Courtyard. This new enclave of upmarket shops includes **Twenty8Twelve**, the boutique owned by actor Sienna Miller and her sister Savannah.

Neal Street is a mix of international names and home-grown talent, such as **Traffic People** (at 69 Neal Street, www.trafficpeople.co.uk). Confusingly, Neal's Yard (➤ 151) is near, but not off of Neal Street.

To the west is Seven Dials. Shops here are youthful and edgy. Just looking at the colourful shoes in **Poste Mistress** (61 Monmouth Street, WC2, www.office.co.uk/postemistress) will cheer you up.

CHARING CROSS ROAD

Book lovers from around the world come to poke about in the bookshops along this street, to the north and south of Leicester Square Tube station. The most famous is **Foyles** (at 113, www.foyles.co.uk), over a century old and still comprehensive in the choice it offers. **Blackwells** (at 100, http://bookshop.blackwell.co.uk), a branch of the Oxford bookstore, has academic as well as general titles. Some of the second-hand bookshops have closed, but **Any Amount of Books** (at 56, www.anyamountofbooks.com) continues to sell everything from inexpensive copies to rare first editions.

Don't miss Cecil Court, with its old-fashioned atmosphere and shops specializing in art, theatre and music books and prints.

SOHO

Back in the Swinging Sixties, **Carnaby Street** was *the* place for trendy shopping, and after a slump, it is once again a good hunting ground for something that little bit different.

Football (soccer) fans can find shirts, kits, boots, souvenirs and accessories for Arsenal, Barcelona and other top teams in **Soccer Scene** (at 56, www.soccerscene.co.uk). **Gola Classics** (at 40, www.gola.co.uk) made its name with football boots, but now sells both sports and fashion footwear. For sexy and daring gear, check out **Miss Sixty** (31 Great Marlborough Street, W1, www.misssixty.com).

Wander down any of the nearby lanes such as Newburgh Street, Marshall Street, Kingly Court and Marlborough Court for more shops, both established and up-and-coming. Convenient Tube stations include Piccadilly Circus, Oxford Circus and Leicester Square.

Where to...
Go Out

With its theatres, cinemas, clubs and bars, London's West End is one of the world's great entertainment centres. By contrast, Camden attracts a younger crowd, looking for alternative music. Check *Time Out* magazine (published Wednesdays) for listings.

THEATRE, OPERA & DANCE

Some of London's most popular theatres are close to Piccadilly Circus, including the **Criterion Theatre**, right by the Tube station. Along Shaftesbury Avenue are four equally historic theatres side-by-side: the **Lyric** (www.nimax theatres.com), the **Apollo** (www. nimaxtheatres.com), the **Gielgud** (www.delfontmackintosh.co.uk) and **Queen's** (www.delfontmack intosh.co.uk).

Covent Garden and the Strand also have top-class theatres, as well as two major opera houses: the **Royal Opera House** (► 150) and the **English National Opera** (London Coliseum, St Martin's Lane, WC2, www.eno.org. Tube: Leicester Square), where works are sung in English. For the best ways to book tickets, see page 46.

London also offers a wide variety of ballet and other forms of dance. The best-known venue is the Royal Opera House, home of the **Royal Ballet** (► 150), but there is also ballet at the London Coliseum (see above). Sadlers Wells hosts international dance companies, from contemporary to hip hop and tango (www.sadlerswells.com).

The **Roundhouse** (Chalk Farm Road, NW1, tel: 084 44 82 80 08; www.roundhouse.org.uk) hosts everything from live music, dance and theatre to circus and news media.

CINEMA

The latest major films are premiered in the West End: **Odeon Panton Street** (11/18 Panton Street, SW1), The **OTHER Cinema** (11 Rupert Street, W1), **UGC Haymarket** (62–65 Haymarket, SW1), **Cineworld** (in The Trocadero, 13 Coventry Street, W1).

CLUBS

In the West End, **Heaven** (Under The Arches, Villiers Street, WC2, tel: 020 79 30 20 20. Tube: Charing Cross), a huge gay club with a laid-back, friendly atmosphere, is also popular with straight men and women. Other popular club venues worth checking out: **Madame Jojo's** (8–10 Brewer Street, W1; tel: 020 77 34 30 40; www.madamejojos.com. Tube: Leicester Square) has morphed as a Soho icon over 50 years. As well as great music every night, audiences also enjoy the live shows: cabaret, burlesque and variety. **Café de Paris** (3 Coventry Street, W1, tel: 020 77 34 77 00; www.cafedeparis.com. Tube: Piccadilly Circus) is a glam dance hall, overlooked by a galleried restaurant.

In Camden, you can hear new bands at the **Dublin Castle** (94 Parkway, NW1, tel: 020 74 85 17 73; www.thedublincastle.com) and great jazz at the **Jazz Café** (5 Parkway, NW1, tel: 020 76 88 88 99; www.jazzcafelive.com). For clubbing, head for the **Electric Ballroom** (184 Camden High Street, NW1, tel: 020 79 16 60 60; www.thejazzcafe.co.uk) or **The Underworld** (174 Camden High Street, NW1, tel: 020 74 82 19 32; www.theunderworld camden.co.uk). Both have popular nightclubs.

Ins Tip

Excursions

Kew   170
Windsor   172

Kew

Kew Gardens lie 10 miles (15km) west of central London. Officially the Royal Botanic Gardens, they are a major research centre, but for visitors they offer beautiful landscapes for walking, playing and picnics.

The 300 acres (121ha) of the Royal Botanic Gardens contain around 30,000 species of plants, including 13 species extinct in the wild. Keen botanists and gardeners will revel in the floral diversity, but non-experts can also easily savour the gardens' overall beauty. Visits outside the summer months can be especially rewarding – September to November produces wonderful autumn colours, camellias flower in January, and February to May sees the first blooms of spring. You need time to see all the botanical highlights. Book a tour with the **Kew Explorer**; it provides an excellent introduction to the gardens.

The Princess of Wales Conservatory

The conservatory features 10 computer-regulated climate zones. Wander from orchids in the humid tropical zone to cacti in the dry tropical zone to appreciate the huge influence of climate on floral types. The most bizarre plants are the "living stone" lithops of Namibia, indistinguishable from stones until they produce brilliantly coloured flowers.

Palm House, Temperate House and Evolution House

This masterpiece of Victorian engineering was constructed between 1844 and 1848 with some 16,000 sheets of glass. Climb one of the wrought-iron spiral staircases to the raised walkways to view its lush rainforest interior containing tropical species such as coconut, banana and rubber. Don't miss the basement with its marine plants and habitats, in particular the coral reef. Kew is one of the few places in Britain with living coral because it is very difficult to cultivate outsides its normal habitat. The Waterlily House, by the Palm House, is Kew's most hot and humid environment, providing a habitat for tropical aquatic plants. In addition to beautiful waterlilies, you can admire spectacular lotuses, gourds and loofahs.

Temperate House, the largest of the glasshouses is an elegant Victorian structure that took almost 40 years to complete. It is divided into various geographical zones. Its highlights include a Chilean wine palm, planted in the

The famous landmark Kew Pagoda, completed in 1762 for Princess Augusta, mother of George III

The Palm House at Kew incorporates 16,000 panes of glass and took four years to build

mid-19th century and now the world's largest indoor plant, and contains subtropical plants such as citrus trees, tea trees and Himalayan rhododendrons. It was closed in 2013 for extensive renovation work. It will open again in summer 2018, together with the Evolution House, which traces the development of the most ancient plants.

Pagoda and Treetop Walkway

The 250-year-old, 10-storey Pagoda is not open to the public. However, children and adults alike enjoy the 55-foot (18m) high 🚼 **Xstrata Treetop Walkway.** It offers a good view of the giant trees, and you can even see Wembley Stadium in north London. For youngsters, there are plenty of 🚼 **other exciting activities**, e. g. climbers and creepers, an interactive botanic indoor playground, and **Treehouse Towers** with huge swings, slides and climbing nets. In the Palm House and Prince of Wales Conservatory, they can also see piranhas, fresh water rays and enormous catfish.

Insider Tip

Kew Gardens
✉ Victoria Gate, Kew, Richmond, TW9 3AB ☎ 020 83 32 56 55; www.kew.org
🕐 Daily 9:30–dusk (telephone for exact closing times).
The glasshouses and galleries close earlier
🍴 Several cafés and restaurants in the gardens and other options nearby
Ⓠ Kew Gardens 🚃 Kew Green (for Main Gate) 65, 391; Kew Bridge 237, 267, 391
🚤 Riverboat to Kew Pier from Westminster, Richmond and Hampton Court
💷 £14.50; in summer after 3.30 £7 (children free)

INSIDER INFO

- Take part in one of the three daily one-hour tours through Kew Gardens. They begin at 11, 12 and 1.30.
- Load the Kew Garden app onto your Smartphone: interactive card, including all garden attractions and QR code scanner for the plant descriptions.

Windsor

A visit to Windsor Castle is the obvious highlight of a trip to Windsor, but the town is attractive in its own right. There is also the chance to visit historic Eton College, traditionally a school for the sons of the rich and famous, and – a treat for the children – the modern theme park of Legoland.

Windsor Castle

Windsor Castle looks the part of a castle to perfection, with towers, turrets, battlements and even uniformed soldiers on guard. It possesses a grandeur that far outshines that of Buckingham Palace (▶ 52). The world's largest inhabited castle, Windsor was founded by William the Conqueror in about 1080, when it formed part of the defences around London. In time it became a royal residence, partly because of the opportunities for hunting afforded by the surrounding countryside. Henry I had quarters in the castle in 1110, and almost 900 years later the sovereign is still resident. Queen Elizabeth II spends most weekends here, as well as much of April and June.

A fire on the night of 20 November 1992, probably started by the heat of a spotlight too close to a curtain, destroyed much of the castle's interior. Several **State Apartments**, including St George's Hall, the Grand Reception Room, the State Dining Room and the Crimson Drawing Room were damaged. The fire burned for 15 hours and it took 1.3 million gallons (6 million litres) of water to extinguish the flames. Restoration took five years and cost £38 million, most of which was met by the Royal Family with money earned from the annual opening of Buckingham Palace and visitor admissions to the precincts of Windsor Castle.

Areas of the castle open to the public include the State Rooms (open all year; check website for closures), Semi-State Rooms (open late September to March only) and St George's Chapel (open daily, for worshippers only on Sun). Their vast array of treasures includes Gobelin tapestries,

Windsor Castle, seen across the river

ornate antique furniture and paintings by artists such as Van Dyck, Rubens, Gainsborough, Dürer, Rembrandt, Reynolds and Canaletto. The 2- to 3-hour tour follows a set route.

Castle Tour Highlights

Queen Mary's Dolls' House is an entire house built in 1924 on a scale of 1:12. Look especially for the tiny leather-bound books in the library, and the vacuum cleaner, crockery, kitchen equipment, miniature works of art on the walls and a sewing machine that actually works.

A statue of Queen Victoria stands in front of Windsor Castle

The **Grand Staircase** and **Grand Vestibule** provide a magnificent introduction to the State Rooms. Both are lined with statues, firearms, armour and huge cases filled with miscellaneous treasures – among them, in the Grand Vestibule, the musketball that killed Admiral Lord Horatio Nelson at the Battle of Trafalgar in 1805 (the uniform he wore is at the National Maritime Museum in Greenwich ➤ 186).

The opulent **Grand Reception Room** was designed for King George IV, a monarch with a passion for ornate French design, which is why everything from walls and ceilings to furniture and chandeliers is intricately gilded and adorned.

St George's Hall – superbly restored since the 1992 fire – is the grandest of the castle's rooms. More than 180 feet (55m) long, it is impressive for its size alone, but is also remarkable for its decoration – crests, busts and suits of armour – and the wonderful oak hammerbeam roof.

Ten monarchs are buried in **St George's Chapel**, a beautifully decorated space distinguished, among other things, by its choir stalls, altar and gilded vaulting. It also contains Prince Albert's Memorial Chapel, built in memory of Victoria's husband who died at Windsor in 1861. It's a startling work, laden with statues, Venetian mosaics and inlaid marble panels.

Special Areas

Two areas are open to the public, only in August and September. You need a head for heights to climb 200 steps up the massive **Round Tower** for splendid views as far as London itself. Also open, and still in use after 750 years, is the **Great Kitchen**.

INSIDER INFO

- The **Changing of the Guard** ceremony takes place at 11am daily (except Sun) from April to July and on alternate days for the rest of the year.
- Ticket price includes an **audio guide**.

In and Around Windsor

If you've more time to spend, **Eton College** is just a 15-minute walk across the river from Windsor. One of Britain's oldest private schools, Eton was founded in 1440, and

Excursions

pupils still wear formal dress. It remains highly prestigious; most pupils come from rich and influential families. David Cameron was the 19th British prime minister to attend. The school yard, oldest classroom, museum and chapel are open to the public, and afternoon guided tours are available.

If you want to give the younger generation a bit of fun, then visit 🏰 **Legoland Windsor**, a popular theme park just 2 miles (3.2km) from the town centre. Even adults will be surprised at all the things that can be made out of lego. A half-hourly shuttle bus operates to Legoland from stops close to Windsor and Eton Central and Riverside railway stations (combination tickets including admission, shuttle bus and rail travel are available from most major railway stations in Britain).

The Crooked House tea rooms in Windsor

Visitor Information Centre
✉ The Old Booking Hall, Central Station, Windsor, SL4 1PJ
☎ 01753 74 39 00; 01753 83 11 18 (recorded information)
🕐 Mon–Sat 10–5, Sun 11–4; extended hours in summer

Windsor Castle
☎ 01753 83 11 18 (24 hour); 020 77 66 73 04; www.royalcollection.org.uk
🕐 March–Oct daily 9:45–5:15 (last admission 4); Nov–Feb 9:45–4:15 (last admission 3). Closed Good Fri, Easter Sun morning. St George's Chapel closed to visitors Sun (subject to full or partial closure at other times) 💷 £17.75

Eton College
☎ 01753 67 11 77; www.etoncollege.com
🕐 Daily term time, tours end March–Oct, Wed, Fri, Sat, Sun at 2 and 3:15
💷 £7.50; buy tickets at Eton College Gift Shop)

Legoland Windsor
✉ Winkfield Road, SL4 4AY ☎ 0871 2 22 20 01; www.legoland.co.uk
🕐 April–Oct, varies according to season; check website 💷 £45.60
(2-day tickets and family tickets available, online booking is less expensive)

GETTING THERE
Windsor is 25 miles (40km) west of central London.
Train (☎ 0845 7 48 49 50) Direct trains to Windsor and Eton Riverside from Waterloo Station, every 30 min. Journey time approximately 55 min. From Paddington Station to Windsor and Eton Central, changing trains at Slough, every 30 min. Journey time approximately 40 min.
Bus (☎ 0844 8 01 72 61) Greenline service 701 and 702 from Victoria Coach Station. Journey time to Windsor c. 80 min.

Walks and Tours

1 Mayfair Squares 176
2 The City 180
3 Greenwich 184
4 Hampstead 188
5 With Bus nos 6 and 15 192

Walks & Tours

1 MAYFAIR SQUARES
Walk

DISTANCE 3 miles (5km) **TIME** 2 hours. Allow extra time for window-shopping, refreshment stops and visiting churches
START POINT Piccadilly Circus Underground station ✚ 205 E1
END POINT Oxford Circus Underground station ✚ 205 D2

Amid the noise and bustle of the surrounding streets, Mayfair (▶47) is an enclave of luxury and elegance. Originally laid out in the early 18th century by wealthy families such as the Grosvenors and Berkeleys, the area is the most expensive in London and retains evidence of past glories, including fine houses, both grand and humble, leafy squares, elegant shopping arcades and the old-fashioned alleyways and cobbles of Shepherd Market.

Look for commemorative blue plaques (▶24), indicating that a famous person is associated with the building, and for shopfronts carrying royal crests; the companies awarded crests supply a member of the Royal Family – read the small print to find out which one.

①–②
Leave **Piccadilly Circus** Tube station via the Piccadilly (South Side) exit. Walk straight along Piccadilly past **St James's Church**, designed by Wren, Princes Arcade, lined with quality shops, and Hatchards, booksellers since 1797. You'll soon reach **Fortnum & Mason**, best known for upmarket groceries and posh hampers. Founded by a servant of Queen Anne in 1707, it oozes old-fashioned elegance, and many of its staff still wear morning suits.

②–③
Cross Piccadilly to Burlington House, an 18th-century mansion, now home to the **Royal Academy of Arts** (▶60). Just beyond is Burlington Arcade, built in 1819. This is the best

known of the exclusive shopping arcades in the area, and the liveried "beadles" enforce regulations against whistling, singing or running. Walk to the back of Burlington Arcade, turn right into Burlington Gardens and after 90m (100 yards) turn left into Savile Row.

Number 3 is famous as the former office of the Apple record company owned by The Beatles. The band gave their last concert from the roof in 1969. Walk along Savile Row and take the first turning left into Clifford Street. Continue to **New Bond Street** at the far end. Turn left into a pedestrian-only area where *Allies*, a bronze sculpture of Winston Churchill and Franklin D Roosevelt, was erected in 1995 to celebrate 50 years of peace after World War II.

▟–▛

Follow New Bond Street, past designer boutiques and exclusive jewellers. At Burlington Gardens, this becomes Old Bond Street; almost immediately, turn right into the Royal Arcade and right again into Albemarle Street. On the left is **Brown's Hotel**, one of London's oldest (1837); guests have included Rudyard Kipling and Alexander Graham Bell, who made the first telephone call in the UK here in 1876. Continue along to Grafton Street; turn left, then left again into Dover Street; turn right into Hay Hill. Cross the street at the bottom into pedestrianized Lansdowne Row and walk through here to Curzon Street.

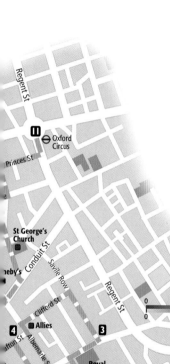

▛–▜

▙–▟
Savile Row is synonymous with made-to-measure tailoring, and Gieves & Hawkes have been in business at No 1 since 1785.

Walk straight along Curzon Street. After 200 yards (183m), No 9 is on the right: this is G. F. Trumper, Court Hairdresser and Perfumer. Established in 1875, it still has the original dark wood and glass – and its "gentlemen's grooming services" still include wet shaving, with a razor and a badger brush. On the

Walks & Tours

Berkeley Square is a green oasis in an exclusive area

left is a covered passageway leading to **Shepherd Market**.

Built in 1735, the buildings look older and smaller in scale than the surrounding area; nowadays, this enclave is busy with small shops and cafés. At Ye Grapes pub, turn immediately right and walk through the pedestrian-only area. Cross cobbled Trebeck Street and turn right up Hertford Street past the **Curzon Mayfair** cinema to Curzon Street. Opposite is **Crewe House** (now the Saudi Arabian Embassy), an example of the fine houses of 18th-century Mayfair.

6–7

Turn left into Curzon Street and then right into elegant Chesterfield Street, left at the top into Charles Street, right at the Red Lion pub on to Waverton Street and right again into Hay's Mews, originally the stables for the coach horses of the wealthy, now converted into highly desirable homes. Take the next right into Chesterfield Hill and at the end turn left, back into Charles Street. Follow this road to its end at Berkeley Square.

7–8

Berkeley Square was made a household name through the song "A Nightingale Sang in Berkeley Square". It was originally laid out in the mid-18th century and retains its attractive, leafy feel, though these days the traffic roaring along the surrounding roads detracts from the prettiness and pollutes the air. Walk up the left (west) side of the square, which has kept the most character. Number 45 was the home of Lord Clive; known as "Clive of India", his military victories were the cornerstone of the British Empire.

At the top left (northwest) corner turn left into Mount Street; after about 200 yards (180m) turn left into peaceful Mount Street Gardens. In the **Church of the Immaculate Conception**, the high altar was designed by Augustus Pugin, who also worked on the Houses of Parliament. Continue straight across the gardens and turn right into South Audley Street. This leads to **Grosvenor Square**, one of London's largest. On the left is the United States Embassy –

Church of the Immaculate Conception

Street. Continue straight ahead past **Claridge's**, one of London's finest hotels, which is often patronized by visiting royalty. Further on, No 25 was home to George Frederick Handel for 36 years; he composed *Messiah* here in 1741. The **Handel House Museum** is on the upper floors. Guitarist Jimi Hendrix lived next door at No 23 from 1968 to 1969.

9–10

At the next junction turn right into New Bond Street. On the left is **Sotheby's**, where anyone can view the often fabulous articles waiting to be sold. At Conduit Street, turn left and immediately left again into St George Street. Continue to **St George's Church**, consecrated in 1725. Handel worshipped regularly here and, since 1978, the annual London Handel Festival has promoted 18th-century music.

it's certainly assertive, although hardly in keeping with the square's period style. There are statues here of US presidents **Roosevelt** and **Eisenhower**.

8–9

Walk diagonally right across the square and leave from the far (northeast) corner along Brook

10–11

At the top of St George Street, the entrance to Hanover Square is marked by the statue of William Pitt "the Younger", who became prime minister in 1783 at the age of only 24. Take Princes Street from the top right (northeast) corner of the square out to Regent Street. Turn left for **Oxford Circus** Tube station.

PLACES TO VISIT

St James's Church
✚ 205 E1
☎ 020 77 34 45 11, www.sjp.org.uk
🕐 Daily 9–6. Free lunchtime concerts (1:10) Mon, Wed, Fri. Also regular programme of evening concerts

Handel House Museum
✚ 204 C2 ✉ Entrance at back, in Lancashire Court
☎ 020 74 95 16 85; www.handelhouse.org
🕐 Tue–Sat 10–6, Sun 12–6 💷 £6

St George's Church
✚ 205 D2 ✉ Hanover Square
☎ 020 76 29 08 74; www. stgeorgeshanoversquare.org
🕐 Mon–Fri 8–4, Sun 8–noon

TAKING A BREAK
Stop at one of the coffee shops or snack bars on Lansdowne Row or try one of the outdoor cafés or pubs in Shepherd Market.

WHEN TO GO
Weekdays are best, as not all of the galleries and shops are open on Saturday and Sunday.

Walks & Tours

2 THE CITY
Walk

DISTANCE 3 miles (5km) **TIME** 2 hours. Allow extra time for
window-shopping, refreshment stops and visiting churches
START POINT Monument Underground station ⊞ 210 A3
END POINT Bank Underground station ⊞ 210 A4

As well as being London's birthplace,
the City of London (▶ 69) is one of
the world's financial powerhouses,
with institutions such as the Bank of
England, the London Stock Exchange
and Lloyd's of London. Only 10,000
people actually live in the City, but
from Monday to Friday, 330,000
work there. Visit on a weekday to get
the buzz; weekends are eerily quiet.
This walk takes in skyscrapers,
churches, galleries and Roman
remains.

❶–❷

Turn left, walk out to the middle of
London Bridge for sweeping river
views: Tower Bridge and HMS
Belfast downstream, and dominating the skyline, the **Shard**, one of
the world's tallest buildings (▶ 19,
115). Although the Romans first
bridged the River Thames almost
2,000 years ago, the current bridge
dates from 1973. The previous
125-year-old bridge was sold to an
American entrepreneur, and re-
assembled as a tourist attraction in
Lake Havasu City, Arizona in 1971.

❷–❸

Walk back towards the
Underground station and take the
first road to the right, Monument
Street, to **The Monument**. It was
designed by Sir Christopher Wren,
architect of St Paul's Cathedral,
in the 1670s as a memorial to the

Great Fire in 1666. It is 203 feet
(62m) tall – the distance on the
ground from its base to the place
where the fire started in Pudding
Lane – and there are 311 steps up
to the viewing platform.

❸–❹

Walk up Fish Street Hill to
Eastcheap at the top and turn
right; the next road on the right
is Pudding Lane, now lined with
modern office buildings. Cross
Eastcheap into Philpot Lane
and look ahead for a view
of the dramatic **Lloyd's Building**.
Designed by Sir Richard (now
Lord) Rogers, it houses the Lloyd's
insurance market, the world's
largest insurance company.
You'll either love or hate the
1984 steel-and-glass giant with

**Views across London from
The Monument**

the entrails of pipes and shafts exposed on the outside – it looks especially dramatic at night.

Towering above the Lloyd's Building, just behind it, is **30 St Mary Axe**, home to the Swiss Re Insurance company, designed by Lord Foster. Nicknamed **The Gherkin,** at 623 feet (190m) it is one of the tallest buildings in the city. At the end of Philpot Lane, cross Fenchurch Street into Lime Street. Take the first street left, Lime Street Passage, to **Leadenhall Market** (➤ 86).

4–5

Leave the market through Whittington Avenue and turn right into Leadenhall Street with its view of the new "Leadenhall Building". At the foot of the **Lloyd's Building**, cross the road

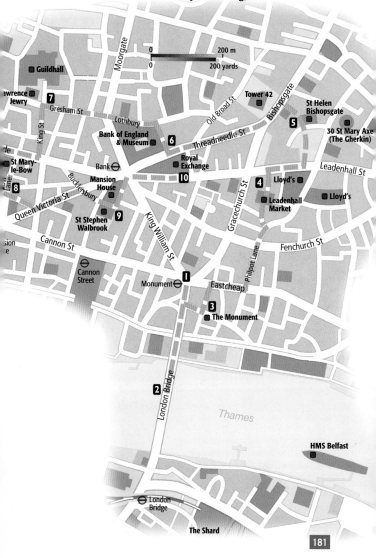

Walks & Tours

The Royal Exchange, founded in 1571

and head north across an open square to **St Helen Bishopsgate**, one of the few churches to survive the Great Fire of London.

5–6

Turn left at the church and along Great St Helen's to Bishopsgate. Look directly ahead to the 601ft (183 m) **Tower 42** and the new **Pinnacle**, which at a height of 945 feet (288m), is one of the City's tallest buildings.

Turn left into Bishopsgate and, at the traffic lights, cross into Threadneedle Street. At Old Broad Street, look left. In a piazza behind the Royal Exchange is the seated statue of George Peabody (1795–1869), a wealthy American philanthropist, who did much for London's poor. Turn right down Bartholomew Lane for the entrance to the **Bank of England Museum** (➤ 86), where you can hold £100,000 of gold in your hands.

6–7

Carry on to the end of Bartholomew Lane, then turn left along Lothbury and into Gresham Street. To your right, behind **St Lawrence Jewry** church, is the **Guildhall**, the symbolic heart of the City. The original 15th-century building has undergone many reconstruc-

tions, but the main hall remains the highlight, decked with shields and banners and displaying figures of the legendary giants Gog and Magog.

Within the Guildhall complex is a curious **Clock Museum**, which includes a skull-shaped pocket watch that belonged to Mary, Queen of Scots; the Guildhall Art Gallery, where important paintings from the Corporation of London's 300-year-old collection are on display; and below ground, London's only Roman amphitheatre, discovered in 1988 and opened to the public in 2003.

7–8

With your back to Guildhall, cross Gresham Street into King Street and continue down to Cheapside where you turn right towards the huge steeple of **St Mary-le-Bow**. The church's original Norman crypt still exists, while the spacious elegance of Wren's work is obvious both in the fine lines of the spire and in the elegant arches and vaulted roof of the interior. Traditionally, only those born within the sound of Bow Bells can call themselves true Cockneys (native Londoners).

In Bow Churchyard, past the church on the left, is a statue of former parishioner Sir John Smith (1580–1631), who married Native American princess Pocahontas. Circle round the back of the church; turn right into Bow

Guildhall is the symbolic heart of the City

TAKING A BREAK

Chamberlain's, 23–25 Leadenhall Market (£/££, tel: 020 76 48 86 90). Seafood Mon–Fri 12–9:30.

WHEN TO GO

Year-round

PLACES TO VISIT

The Monument

🚇 210 A3 ✉ Monument Street, EC3
☎ 020 76 26 27 17 🕐 Daily 9:30–5 💷 £3

St Helen Bishopsgate

🚇 210 B4 ✉ Great St Helen's, EC3
☎ 020 72 83 22 31 www.st-helens.org.uk
🕐 Mon–Fri 9:30–12:30 (entrance via the church office) 💷 Free

Bank of England Museum

🚇 210 A4 ✉ Bartholomew Lane, EC2
☎ 020 76 01 55 45;

www.bankofengland.co.uk/museum
🕐 Mon–Fri 10–5 (last entry 4:45) 💷 Free

Guildhall

🚇 209 F5 ✉ Gresham Street, EC2
☎ 020 76 06 30 30; www.cityoflondon.gov.uk
🕐 guildhall & amphitheatre: Mon–Sat 10–5.
Clock Museum: Mon–Sat 9:30–4:45.
Gallery: Mon–Sat 10–5, Sun 12–4
💷 Guildhall/Clock Museum free:
Gallery/amphitheatre free, Fri tours

St Mary-le-Bow

🚇 209 F4 ✉ Cheapside, EC2
☎ 020 72 48 51 39 🕐 Mon–Wed 7:30–6,
Thu 7–6:30, Fri 7:30–4. Free lunchtime concert Thu 1:05 💷 Free

St Stephen Walbrook

🚇 210 A4 ✉ 39 Walbrook, EC4
☎ 020 76 26 90 00,
http://ststephenwalbrook.net
🕐 Mon–Fri 10–4 💷 Free

Lane. On the right, half-hidden up an alley, is Williamson's Tavern, once the Lord Mayor of London's residence. Further on, another pub, Ye Olde Watling, was used by Sir Christopher Wren's workers on St Paul's Cathedral 300 years ago. Turn left onto Watling Street.

8–9

Walk along Watling Street to Queen Victoria Street. Cross and turn left. On your right are the foundations of the 2nd-century Roman Temple of Mithras (relics are in the Guildhall Museum). Turn right into Bucklersbury to **St Stephen Walbrook** church, built by Wren (1672–1679). Inside is an altar by Henry Moore, as well as telephones commemorating the start in 1953 of a helpline "for the suicidal", which became the Samaritans organization.

9–10

From St Stephen Walbrook church turn along Walbrook and then

right at the end. Cross the street to the traffic island and the huge, temple-like building. Out front with some flowers and benches is an equestrian statue of the Duke of Wellington staring resolutely ahead past two of the City's most important buildings. The **Mansion House**, the official residence of the Lord Mayor of London, is to his left. On the weekly tour (Tue, 2pm), you can see Queen Elizabeth I's Pearl Sword and 84 fine 17th-century Flemish and Dutch paintings. To the Duke's right is the solid bulk of the **Bank of England** surrounded by its windowless walls. Behind him is the grand entrance to the **Royal Exchange**, first granted a charter to trade in all kinds of commerce by Elizabeth I in the 16th century. Dating from 1844, the current building is now a stylish complex of 30 luxury shops, and half a dozen restaurants and cafés. The walk ends here – Bank Underground station is nearby.

3 GREENWICH
Walk

DISTANCE 2 miles (3.2km) **TIME** 2 hours. Allow additional time for visits – you could easily spend a day here
START POINT Greenwich Pier. Allow an hour from Westminster Pier to Greenwich by boat **END POINT** Greenwich Pier

---

Greenwich, a UNESCO World Heritage Site, is 8 miles (13km) east of central London. Go by boat from Westminster, as monarchs did in the past, to the home of the Greenwich Meridian. In 2012, the name of the area was changed to Royal Borough of Greenwich to mark the Queen's Diamond Jubilee. With its royal, maritime and astronomical history, Greenwich is well worth a full day.

❶–❷

From Greenwich Pier, start at the Discover Greenwich Visitor Centre, with its wealth of background history, artefacts and even helmets and sailor's hats to try on. Next door is the *Cutty Sark*, built in Scotland in 1869. The world's sole surviving tea clipper was also the world's fastest in its heyday, bringing Britain tea from China and wool from Australia. With a fair wind, she could cover 360 miles (580km) in a day. After a devastating fire in 2007, restoration was completed in 2012, and it is now open to the public again. Walk back past Greenwich Pier and east along the riverside footpath. On the right, the **Old Royal Naval College** was once the site of Greenwich Palace, where Henry VIII and Queen Elizabeth I were born. Built in the early 1700s, the designers included three of Britain's most famous architects: Sir Christopher Wren, Nicholas Hawksmoor and Sir John Vanbrugh. Generations of officers studied here until the Royal Navy left in 1998; the building now

Aware of its refined aura: Greenwich Park and The Royal Observatory

Greenwich

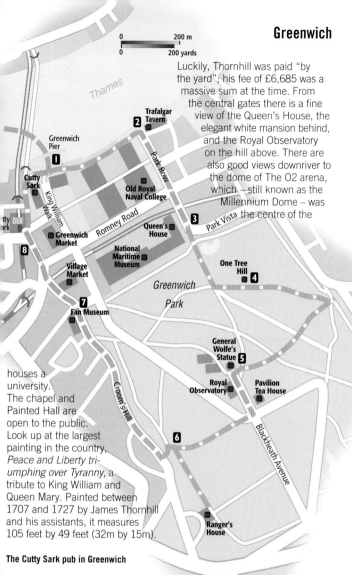

Luckily, Thornhill was paid "by the yard"; his fee of £6,685 was a massive sum at the time. From the central gates there is a fine view of the Queen's House, the elegant white mansion behind, and the Royal Observatory on the hill above. There are also good views downriver to the dome of The O2 arena, which – still known as the Millennium Dome – was the centre of the

Thames

2 Trafalgar Tavern

Greenwich Pier

1

Cutty Sark

Park Row

Old Royal Naval College

King William Walk

tty rk **DLR**

3

Park Vista

Romney Road

Greenwich Market

Queen's House

8

National Maritime Museum

Village Market

Greenwich Park

One Tree Hill 4

7 Fan Museum

General Wolfe's Statue 5

Royal Observatory

Pavilion Tea House

Croom's Hill

6

Blackheath Avenue

houses a university. The chapel and Painted Hall are open to the public. Look up at the largest painting in the country, *Peace and Liberty triumphing over Tyranny*, a tribute to King William and Queen Mary. Painted between 1707 and 1727 by James Thornhill and his assistants, it measures 105 feet by 49 feet (32m by 15m).

Ranger's House

The Cutty Sark pub in Greenwich

festivities when the year 2000 was welcomed in. What is more, you can see the Emirates Air Line (the cable car over the Thames), built in 2012, and across to the towering Canary Wharf tower. One Canada Square, a colossus of stainless steel and glass, has 50 storeys, stands at a height of 771 feet (235m) and is London's third tallest skyscraper. Continue along the river path to Park Row and the **Trafalgar Tavern**.

Walks & Tours

2–3

Turn right; walk up Park Row and cross the main road (Romney Road). On the right are two major attractions. The **Queen's House** was designed by Inigo Jones (1573–1652) for Queen Anne, wife of James I (reigned 1603–25). Influenced by a visit to Italy, Jones created the first Classical-style mansion in England. The highlight is the stunning spiral staircase.

The lively **National Maritime Museum** is a treasure trove of things naval, from Captain Cook's Pacific voyages to the bullet-pierced coat that Nelson wore when he died at the Battle of Trafalgar in 1805. There's even a royal barge. Children love the hands-on opportunities to steer a ship, load cargo or send messages. Exit back into Park Row and enter **Greenwich Park**.

3–4

Walk straight ahead. At the first main junction of the paths, turn left to walk up to the top of the grassy mound called One Tree Hill. Queen Elizabeth I often came here to enjoy the fine view, a custom commemorated in verse carved into the wooden benches.

4–5

From **One Tree Hill** follow the paths, towards the Royal Observatory, the regal brick building with its green dome. You arrive at the **statue of General James Wolfe**, the local hero, killed during his victory at the battle for Quebec City in 1759. He stares out at grand views of London, though St Paul's Cathedral is now dwarfed by skyscrapers.

In 1675, King Charles II founded the **Royal Observatory** to solve the Royal Navy's problem of finding longitude at sea. With one foot in the western hemisphere, the other in the east, visitors line up for photos straddling the Prime Meridian, the line at 0° longitude. Check your watch against chronometers,

The dome of the Old Royal Naval College features a compass

or when the time ball drops at 1pm precisely, as it has daily since 1833. In the Time Galleries, John Harrison's sea clocks include "H4" that solved the longitude problem in 1765. In the neighbouring **Astronomy Centre**, which includes London's only planetarium, you can touch a 4.5 billion-year-old meteorite and learn about the stars.

5–6

With your back to General Wolfe, walk along Blackheath Avenue, past the **Pavilion Tea House**. At the small traffic roundabout (circle), turn right and follow the avenue to the park wall; exit through the small gate. Continue along the gravel drive to Croom's Hill. When open, the 17th-century **Ranger's House** (➤ 187), 200 yards (180m) away to the left, is worth visiting for its medieval and Renaissance works of art.

6–7

Otherwise, turn right and walk downhill, past the 17th- and 18th-century houses. On the left, near the foot of Croom's Hill, is the **Fan Museum**. Set in two 18th-century houses, it is

Greenwich

TAKING A BREAK

The Old Brewery (beside Discover Greenwich), the Pavilion Tea House (Greenwich Park), Observatory Café (Royal Observatory), cafés in Greenwich Market.

WHEN TO GO

Any day; weekends can be very crowded.

GETTING THERE

Options for getting to Greenwich from central London by public transport include the scenic boat trip from the Tower of London, Charing Cross or Westminster to Greenwich Pier; the elevated Docklands Light Railway (DLR; ► 36), part of the London Underground system, with panoramic views of the Docklands (to Cutty Sark station); and rail from Waterloo (to Greenwich station).

PLACES TO VISIT

Cutty Sark

✉ King William Walk, SE10
☎ 020 88 58 44 22; www.1.rmg.co.uk
🕓 Daily 10–5 (last admission 4)
💷 £12

Old Royal Naval College

✉ Entrance from King William Walk, SE10
☎ 020 82 69 47 47; www.ornc.org
🕓 Daily 10–5 💷 Free

Queen's House, National Maritime Museum, Royal Observatory/Planetarium/Astronomy Centre

✉ Greenwich Park, SE10 ☎ 020 88 58 44 22; information line: 020 83 12 65 65; www.1.rmg.co.uk 🕓 Daily 10–5 (last admission 4:30) 💷 £6.35 (moderate charge to have photo taken on the Meridian Line)

Ranger's House

✉ Chesterfield Walk, Greenwich Park, SE10
☎ 0208 2 94 25 48 or 0870 3 33 11 81; www.english-heritage.org.uk
🕓 Apr–Oct Sun–Wed (by guided tour only, at 11 and 2) 💷 £6.70

Fan Museum

✉ 12 Croom's Hill, SE10 ☎ 020 83 05 14 41; www.thefanmuseum.org.uk
🕓 Tue–Sat 11–5, Sun 12–5 💷 £4

Greenwich Market

✉ Greenwich Town Centre, SE10
☎ 020 82 69 50 96; www.greenwichmarket.co.uk/greenwich-market
🕓 Daily 10–5:30

the only museum of its kind in the world. The basis of the exhibition is Helen Alexander's personal collection of 3,500 fans from a wide range of cultures, dating from the 11th century to the present day.

7–**8**

From the Fan Museum, continue straight to the bottom of Croom's Hill, then walk ahead into Stockwell Street with the **Village Market** on your right. Turn right into Greenwich Church Street and continue along it, crossing Nelson Road. Through an alleyway on the right is the lively **Greenwich Market**, whose array of boutiques and cafés surround the 19th-century covered market with its busy art, craft and bric-a-brac stalls. Return to Greenwich Church Street, turn right, cross College Approach, and the *Cutty Sark* is right in front of you.

Detail of the gate at the Old Royal Naval College

4 HAMPSTEAD
Walk

DISTANCE 2.5 miles (4km) **TIME** 2 hours.
Allow more for refreshment stops and visiting the houses
START/END POINT Hampstead Underground station

London is often described as a collection of villages, each with its own character and sense of community. On a hill, north of central London, Hampstead is a fine example: grand old houses and gardens, charming lanes and churches, fashionable boutique shopping, stylish cafés and some of London's favourite historic pubs. All these and more are on this circular walk from Hampstead Tube station.

When the weather is fine, the nearby views from high on Hampstead Heath and the collection of paintings in Kenwood House are a bonus. The village has always attracted artists and writers, such as painter John Constable, poet John Keats and novelist Robert Louis Stevenson. Like many, they were drawn by the healing properties attributed to the local spring.

❶–❷

Exit London's deepest Tube station (192 feet/58.5m) and go straight across Hampstead High Street at the traffic lights. Turn left and walk down the hill. Turn right into Perrin's Court, a tiny, cobble-stoned, traffic-free lane with restaurants, galleries and shops. Halfway along on the right is the narrow entrance to the eclectic Hampstead Antique & Craft Emporium. Here you will find some 30 shops offering silver, jewellery, vintage collectables and antique quilts.

❷–❸

At the end of Perrin's Court, turn right and immediately cross over to Church Row. This is one of London's prettiest streets, with its delightful 18th-century homes and intricate wrought-iron work. At the end is the 250-year-old **St John's Church**. Turn left inside the gate and walk down to the far wall; behind iron railings is the tomb of the painter John Constable (1776–1837), who lived in the village for many years. Walk back up to the church; inside, a bust of poet John Keats is by the lectern on the right.

❸–❹

Exit the church, turn left and cross into Holly Walk. Continue uphill past the graveyard, 200-year-old cottages and **St Mary's**, a Catholic church built by refugees from the French Revolution. General de Gaulle worshipped here during World War II. At the end, turn right at Abernethy House where author Robert Louis Stevenson stayed. Continue uphill, then take the second turning to the left (a sharp one, just down the hill), along the footpath. Ahead is a large sign for **The Holly Bush**; across the street is the 200-year-old pub, on Holly Mount, a classic British "local" with its etched glass windows, open fires and cosy nooks.

❹–❺

Carry on up Holly Bush Hill. The gilded iron gates are the old

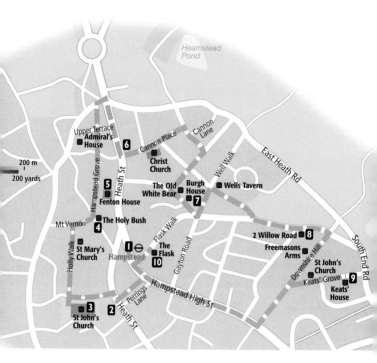

entrance to **Fenton House**; follow its garden wall to today's entrance, on Hampstead Grove. Hampstead's oldest mansion, a 17th-century merchant's house, is known for early musical instruments, but also displays porcelain, Georgian furniture and 17th-century needlework. The garden has changed little in 250 years.

5–6
Continue on Hampstead Grove. At the intersection, look left at the **Admiral's House**, with a roof like a ship's quarterdeck. Two hundred years ago, the owner, a retired officer, fired a cannon to celebrate naval victories. He inspired the character Admiral Boom in *Mary Poppins*. Continue to the end of Hampstead Grove; here Whitestone Pond was a welcome sight for horses hauling wagons up the hill.

Turn sharp right and cross Heath Street at the traffic lights. Turn right again and stroll downhill on the broad gravelled walkway.

6–7
Just before the Friends Meeting House, turn left into Hampstead Square, past Christ Church Hampstead, with its elegant spire. Go straight ahead into Cannon Place; continue on, keeping left and at the far end, turn right and keep right down the steep hill. In the wall on your right is the 1730 Parish Lock-Up. Above was the magistrate's house; here prisoners were kept in solitary confinement to await their fate. Turn right onto Well Road. Cross Christchurch Hill and walk up to New End Square. Turn left at **The Old White Bear**, yet another good pub, and go down the hill. On the left is

Walks & Tours

Burgh House contains a small museum dedicated to John Constable

300-year-old **Burgh House**, with a small café and local history museum, with information on painter John Constable and former resident Dr William Gibbons, an early-18th century physician, who promoted the benefits of the waters from Hampstead's iron-rich mineral springs.

7–8

Just past Burgh House, turn left onto Well Walk. At the end is **The Wells Tavern**, a highly-rated gastro-pub. Turn right along Christchurch Hill; bear right where it joins Willow Road. Today, **No 2 Willow Road** is unremarkable, but this Modernist home was futuristic in 1939, when architect Ernö Goldfinger (1902–1987) built it for his family. Inside are many of his possessions, from modern art to furniture.

8–9

Turn right onto Downshire Hill, passing the **Freemasons Arms**

and elegant Regency homes, then left at **St John's Church** (1820) into Keats Grove. On the right, set back behind lawns is **Keats House** (No 10). The house you visit today was once two homes. Poet John Keats (1795–1821) lived on one side and Fanny Brawne, his fiancée, lived on the other. Outside, a new plum tree was planted in 2009 to commemorate his poem "Ode to a Nightingale", written beneath a plum tree in 1819.

9–10

Go back up to St John's Church, bear left up the hill and turn right onto Rosslyn Hill, the main road, with fashion boutiques and cafés. At the corner of Gayton Road is a six-sided red post box dating from 1870; it is no longer in use, but the post office is across the street. Just before the Tube station, turn right onto Flask Walk, with more small shops, galleries and **The Flask** pub, which inherited its

Insider Tip

name from the flasks of mineral water sold here in Hampstead's heyday as a spa. The fifth typically British pub on this walk, it is a good place to stop for refreshment before returning to Hampstead Tube station.

Fine Weather

On a good day, if you have time, take the 15-minute walk up to the top of **Parliament Hill** (322 feet/98m) for its splendid views across London. Follow the signposted path from East Heath Road, a few steps from No 2 Willow Road.

If you have more time, visit **Kenwood House**, 2 miles (3km) north of Hampstead Village. Designed by Robert Adam, this 18th-century mansion's collection of great paintings includes a self portrait by Rembrandt, Vermeer's *The Guitar Player* and Thomas Gainsborough's portrait of Countess Howe.

In summer, in the grounds by the lake, outdoor concerts, both pop and classical, are a highlight. To get there, take the

No 268 bus from Stop B (close to Hampstead Tube station) towards Golders Green. Get off at Inverforth House and catch the No 210 from Stop L towards Finsbury Park. Get off at Kenwood House. Allow 40 minutes by bus; 30 minutes on foot.

Hampstead Heath offers a peaceful escape from the hustle and bustle of central London

---

TAKING A BREAK
Try the Buttery Café at Burgh House, or the Wells Tavern (30 Well Walk, tel: 020 77 94 37 85).

WHEN TO GO
Hampstead Village is always lively; all the shops are open at weekends.

PLACES TO VISIT

Fenton House
✉ 20 Hampstead Grove, Windmill Hill, NW3
☎ 020 74 35 34 71; www.nationaltrust.org.uk
⊙ March–Oct Wed–Sun 11–5 💷 £6.50

Burgh House
✉ New End Square, NW3 ☎ 020 74 31 01 44;
www.burghhouse.org.uk ⊙ Wed–Sun 12–5
(Sat art gallery only) 💷 Free

No 2 Willow Road
✉ 2 Willow Road, NW3 ☎ 020 74 35 61 66;
www.nationaltrust.org.uk ⊙ March–Oct
Wed–Sun 11–5. Entry by guided tour only at
11, 12, 1 and 2. Places are limited on a first-come, first-served basis. Non-guided viewing
3–5 💷 £6

Keats House
✉ Keats Grove, NW3 ☎ 020 73 32 38 68;
www.cityoflondon.co.uk/keatshousehampstead
⊙ April–Oct Tue–Sun 1–5; Nov–Easter
Fri–Sun 1–5 💷 £5; 16 and under free

Kenwood House
✉ Hampstead Lane, NW3 ☎ 020 83 48 12 86;
www.english-heritage.org.uk
⊙ Daily, 10 – 5; recently reopened
after major renovation work
💷 House and grounds: free

5 THE NO 6 & NO 15 BUS TRIP

Tour

TIME 1 hour, one change at Aldwych
START POINT Marble Arch Underground station ✚ 202 A2
END POINT Tower Hill Underground station ✚ 210 C3

This bus trip from Marble Arch to the Tower of London takes in many of the major London sights including Marble Arch, Piccadilly Circus, Trafalgar Square and St Paul's Cathedral, plus well-known thoroughfares – Oxford Street, Regent Street, Haymarket and the Strand. One easy change is needed. Sit upstairs on the bus and as close to the front as possible for the best views.

❶–❷

Leave **Marble Arch** Underground station by the Subway 1 underpass, Marble Arch and Oxford Street North. Look across to the right to the huge marble edifice on the vast traffic island in the middle of the one-way system – this is the Marble Arch that gives the area its name. Built for the forecourt of Buckingham Palace, it was moved to its current incongruous site in 1851 when the front of the palace was remodelled.

Turn left out of the underpass and catch the No 6 bus at the second stop you come to, stop L. This bus terminates at Aldwych.

The bus goes along Oxford Street, one of London's busiest shopping streets, lined with department stores and wide, pedestrian-friendly pavements. On the left is the facade of **Selfridges**, with its grand pillars. Although this vast store was opened by American millionaire Gordon Selfridge in 1909, it is right up to date and was named as "world's best department store" in 2010.

❷–❸

At Oxford Circus, the bus turns right into Regent Street. Designed by John Nash in 1811, this architecturally homogenous curve is part of a grand urban plan, running from Carlton House, through Trafalgar Square to Regent's Park. Look left along Great Marlborough Street; just off Regent Street, the distinctive black-and-white mock Tudor building is **Liberty** (➤ 67), one of London's finest department stores, open since 1875. After passing 👫 **Hamleys**, Britain's favourite toy shop (➤ 67), neon advertisements announce **Piccadilly Circus**; *Eros* and the fountain are on the right (➤ 61).

❸–❹

The bus turns right down **Haymarket**, named for the market which sold hay for the royal horses stabled in the area

Hop on the bus at Marble Arch

until 1830, and then left and around the south side of Trafalgar Square. The **National Gallery** (▶ 54) is on the left, as is **Nelson** on his **column** and the fine spire of **St Martin-in-the-Fields** rises ahead (P59).

4–5

As the bus turns into the **Strand**, look right. In the **Charing Cross** station forecourt is an ornate Victorian reproduction of an Eleanor Cross. In 1290, King Edward I built 12 crosses on the funeral route of his wife, Eleanor of Castile. Between Lincoln and Westminster Abbey, each marked where her body rested overnight on the journey.

Continuing along the Strand, with its popular theatres, the No 6 bus stops at Aldwych. Alight, walk back 20 yards (18m) to stop D; catch the No 15 bus for Blackwall. Carry on along the Strand, between **St Clement Danes** church (right) and the **Royal Courts of Justice** (left). In the centre of the road, the griffin statue on the **Temple Bar** Memorial marks the City of London boundary. The sovereign stops here on ceremonial occasions to ask the permission of the Lord Mayor of London to enter the City.

5–6

The road now becomes **Fleet Street**, once the publishing

Marble Arch — Marble Arch

Oxford St

Selfridges

⊖ Bond Street

Oxford Circus ⊖
Liberty

Regent St

Eros
Piccadilly Circus ⊖

Haymarket

National Gallery
Trafalgar Square
Nelson's Column
⊖ Leicester Square
St Martin-in-the-Fields
Charing Cross
Charing Cross Station

Strand

Aldwych
Strand

St Clement Danes
Royal Courts of Justice

Temple Bar

Thames

Fleet St

St Bride's Church

0   200 m
0   200 yards

Walks & Tours

centre for the British national press – the newspapers have now moved to modern premises in Docklands. On the left is Ye Olde Cheshire Cheese pub, dating from the mid-17th century. Dr Samuel Johnson, compiler of the first English dictionary, was a customer here, and it became popular with later authors, including Dickens, Thackeray and Mark Twain. Look on the right for the white spire of **St Bride's Church**, one of Sir Christopher Wren's most distinctive creations – it is said that soon after it was built a baker copied the design for a tiered wedding cake and an enduring tradition was born.

6–**7**

After crossing Ludgate Circus, the bus goes up Ludgate Hill, heading straight for the dramatic West Front of **St Paul's Cathedral**, then passes to the right of the cathedral, into Cannon Street. Look to the left for two distinctive office blocks, Tower 42 and 30 St Mary Axe as well as at the new sky-scrapers, The Pinnacle and Leadenhall Building. A few moments later, just after Monument Underground station, look right down Fish Street Hill to see **The Monument** (➤ 180).

The bus then heads along Eastcheap, along Great Tower Street, and into Byward Street. On the right is the church of **All Hallows-by-the-Tower** with its distinctive green roof and farther up **Tower Hill** to the **Tower of London** (➤ 82). From its tower, Pepys watched the Great Fire in 1666; in 1797, John Quincy Adams (later US president) married Louisa Catherine Johnson, still the only foreign-born First Lady. The bus stops across from the Tower of London. Get off, explore or travel from Tower Hill Tube station. Outside is a statue, thought to be of the Roman emperor Trajan (AD98–117), standing before a piece of Roman wall.

WHEN TO GO

Any time, but avoid rush hours (8–9:30am, 4:30–6pm weekdays).

TAKING A BREAK

From Tower Underground station, the Hung Drawn & Quartered pub is a few steps back along the route, at 26–27 Great Tower Street (➤ 91).

Practicalities

Before You Go 196

When You are There 198

Practicalities

WHAT YOU NEED

	USA	Canada	Australia	Ireland	Germany	Ireland	Netherlands	Spain
● Required ○ Suggested ▲ Not required								
Passport/National Identity Card	●	●	●	●	▲	●	●	●
Visa (regulations can change – check before you travel)	▲	▲	▲	▲	▲	▲	▲	▲
Onward or Return Ticket	○	○	○	○	○	○	○	○
Health Inoculations	▲	▲	▲	▲	▲	▲	▲	▲
Health Documentation (➤ 192, Health)	●	●	●	●	●	●	●	●
Travel Insurance	○	○	○	○	○	○	○	○
Driving Licence (national)	●	●	●	●	●	●	●	●
Car Insurance Certificate	n/a	n/a	n/a	●	●	●	●	●
Car Registration Document	n/a	n/a	n/a	●	●	●	●	●

WHEN TO GO

High season   Low season

	JAN	FEB	MAR	APR	MAY	JUN	JUL	AUG	SEPT	OCT	NOV	DEC
	6°C	6°C	8°C	10°C	13°C	16°C	19°C	19°C	16°C	13°C	9°C	7°C
	43°F	43°F	46°F	50°F	55°F	61°F	66°F	66°F	61°F	55°F	48°F	45°F

Sun   Cloudy   Sunshine & showers   Wet

The chart above shows **average daily** temperatures for each month.
London experiences defined seasons. **Spring** (March to May) has a mixture of sunshine and showers, although winter often encroaches on it. **Summer** (June to August) can be unpredictable; clear skies and searing heat one day followed by sultry greyness and thunderstorms the next. **Autumn** begins in September, but clear skies can give a summery feel. Real autumn starts in October and the colder weather sets in during November. **Winter** (December to February) is generally mild and snow is rare, but expect the occasional "cold snap".
Be prepared for the **unpredictability** of the British climate – dress in layers and carry rainwear or an umbrella.

GETTING ADVANCE INFORMATION

Websites
■ British Tourist Authority
www.visitbritain.com
■ London Tourist Board
www.visitlondon.com

■ Accessible London
www.visitlondon.com/
maps/accessibility;
www.disabledgo.com

In the UK
Tourist Information
St Paul's Churchyard
London EC4M 8BX
☎ 020 73 32 14 56
www.visitlondon.com

GETTING THERE

By Air London now has **five airports**, offering a combination of convenience and affordable flights. London Heathrow (LHR) and London Gatwick (LGW) are the principal airports; London Stansted (STN), London Luton (LTN) and London City Airport (LCY) are equally busy and provide easy access. From Europe, Southampton (SOU) provides another option.

There are **direct flights** to London from most European, US and Canadian cities. Flights from Australia and New Zealand stop en route in either Asia or the US. Approximate **flying times** to London: Dublin (1.25 hours), New York (7.5 hours), Los Angeles (11 hours), Vancouver (10 hours), Montréal (7 hours), Toronto (7 hours), east coast of Australia (22 hours), New Zealand (24 hours).

Ticket prices are lower from November to April, excluding Easter and Christmas. Check with the airlines, travel agents, flight brokers, travel sections in newspapers and the internet for current special offers.

By Train An alternative option for travellers from Europe is the train. The Channel Tunnel offers a direct link between London and Paris or Brussels for foot passengers aboard "Eurostar" trains (www.eurostar.com), while the car-carrying train, "Eurotunnel" (www.eurotunnel.com), operates between Calais (France) and Folkestone (England). Rail Europe (www.raileurope.com) is a useful resource for European rail travellers.

By Ferry Passenger and car ferries operate from Ireland, France, Belgium, Netherlands, Germany, Scandinavia and Spain.

TIME

London is on **Greenwich Mean Time** (GMT) in winter, but from late March until late October British Summer Time (BST, i.e. GMT+1) operates.

CURRENCY & FOREIGN EXCHANGE

Currency Britain's currency is the pound (£) sterling. There are 100 pennies or pence (p) to each pound. **Notes (bills)** are issued in denominations of £5, £10, £20 and £50. **Coins** come in denominations of 1p, 2p, 5p, 10p, 20p, 50p, £1 and £2. Sterling **travellers' cheques** are a safe way to carry money. They may be accepted as payment by some hotels, restaurants and large department stores, but it is easier to pay by credit/debit card.

Credit cards (MasterCard, VISA and American Express) are widely accepted, though some small independent shops may not take card payments. Check first.

Exchange You can exchange foreign currency and travellers' cheques at banks and bureaux de change. There are exchange facilities at larger travel agents, in large department stores and hotels, at most main post offices or at dedicated bureaux de change. Be sure to check the rate of exchange and the commission charged before any transaction as they do vary.

Cash Machines (ATMs) These are the easiest way to obtain cash. Before you leave home check with your bank that your card will be accepted in the UK.

In the USA
VisitBritain
☎ 1 800 4 62 27 48
www.visitbritain.us

In Australia
VisitBritain
www.visitbritain.com

In France
VisitBritain
www.visitbritain.com

Practicalities

NATIONAL HOLIDAYS

1 Jan New Year's Day; **Mar/Apr** Good Friday; **Mar/Apr** Easter Monday; **First Mon May** May Day Holiday; **Last Mon May** Spring Bank Holiday; **Last Mon Aug** Late Summer Bank Holiday; **25 Dec** Christmas Day; **26 Dec** Boxing Day

Almost all attractions close on Christmas Day. On other holidays some attractions open, although often with reduced hours. Bear in mind that public transport services are likely to be less frequent on national holidays.

ELECTRICITY

 The power supply is 230/240 volts. Sockets accept only three-(square)-pin plugs, so an adaptor is needed. A transformer is also needed for appliances operating on 110–120 volts.

OPENING HOURS

- ○ Shops
- ● Offices
- ● Banks
- ● Post Offices
- ○ Museums/Monuments
- ○ Pharmacies

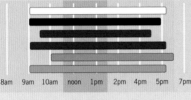

8am 9am 10am noon 1pm 2pm 4pm 5pm 7pm

☐ Day   ☐ Midday   ☐ Evening

Shops Many shops open for longer hours and on Sunday.
Banks High-street banks are also open Saturday morning and bureaux de change are open daily until late.
Museums Smaller museums may close one day a week.
Pharmacies When pharmacies are closed a window sign gives details of the nearest one that operates extended hours or is on 24-hour duty.

TIPS/GRATUITIES

Yes ✓   No ✗

Restaurants (if service not included)	✓	10%
Bar service	✗	
Tour guides	✓	£1– £2
Hairdressers	✓	10%
Taxis	✓	10%
Chambermaids	✓	50p– £1 per day
Porters	✓	50p– £1, depending on number of bags

GENERAL INFORMATION

- There is a **smoking ban** in all public buildings, including pubs, restaurants and Underground stations. It is strictly adhered to.

- **Photography** in public places is legal in the UK, but the police do challenge photographers, especially around sensitive sights.

TIME DIFFERENCES

London (GMT)
12 noon

Berlin (CMT)
1pm

←
New York (EST)
7am

←
Los Angeles (PST)
4am

→
Sydney (AEST)
10pm

STAYING IN TOUCH

Post Post offices are open Mon–Fri 9–5:30, Sat 9–noon. The only exception is Trafalgar Square Post Office, 24–28 William IV Street, open Mon–Fri 8:30–6, Sat 9–5:30. Poste restante mail may also be collected here.

Public telephones Phone booths come in a variety of designs and colours. Coin-operated phones take 10p, 20p, 50p and £1 coins (20p is the minimum charge), but phones taking British Telecom (BT) phonecards or credit cards are often more convenient. Phonecards are available from post offices and many shops.

International Dialling Codes
Dial 00 followed by

Ireland	353
USA / Canada	1
Australia	61
New Zealand	64
Germany	49
Netherlands	31
Spain	34

Mobile providers and services The major mobile phone providers are Vodafone, O2, Orange, T-Mobile and 3. Check before leaving home that the "roaming" function on your phone is activated. The cheapest way to make calls is to buy or rent a local "Pay as you go" SIM card from a company like 0044 (www.0044.co.uk), or get advice at one of the major specialist stores such as Carphone Warehouse (www.carphonewarehouse.com).

For free **WiFi** check McDonalds restaurants, Pret A Manger sandwich shops and JD Wetherspoons pubs. Or use JiWire (www.jiwire.com), which lists more than 4,000 free WiFi hotspots. Refer to www.allinlondon. co.uk to find the nearest Internet café in your area. In the meantime, WLAN is also available in 120 Tube stations (http://my.virginmedia.com/wifi /index.html).

PERSONAL SAFETY

London is generally a safe city and police officers are often seen on the beat in the central areas. They are usually friendly and approachable. To help prevent crime:

- Bag snatchers operate on the Underground. Be careful when stopped at stations.
- Be wary of people approaching you or looking over your shoulder while using ATM machines. Check ATMs for any signs of tampering, as card skimming is a problem.
- Do not carry more cash than you need.
- Do not leave a bag unattended in public places.
- Beware of pickpockets in markets, on the Underground, in tourist sights or crowded places.
- Avoid walking alone in parks or alleys at night

Police assistance:
☎ 999 from any phone

EMERGENCY TELEPHONE NUMBERS
POLICE, FIRE AND AMBULANCE 999
CALLS TO 112, THE EUROPEAN UNION EMERGENCY
NUMBER, ARE AUTOMATICALLY ROUTED TO 999

Practicalities

HEALTH

 Insurance As well as EU nationals, citizens of some 20 countries can get free or reduced-cost medical treatment in Britain with a passport or European Health Insurance Card (EHIC). See www.nhs.uk. Medical insurance is still advised, and is essential for all other visitors.

 Dental Services Visitors qualifying for free or reduced-cost medical treatment (see Insurance above) are entitled to concessionary dental treatment, providing the treatment is by a National Health dentist. Private medical insurance is still recommended, and is essential for all other visitors.

 Weather The sun does shine in London! So don't forget to cover up and apply sunscreen when visiting outdoor sights.

 Prescription and non-prescription **drugs** are available from pharmacies. Pharmacists can advise on medication for common ailments. Pharmacies operate a rota so there will always be one open 24 hours (notices in all pharmacy windows).

 Tap water is **safe to drink**. Mineral water is widely available but it is often expensive.

CONCESSIONS

Students Holders of an International Student Identity Card may obtain concessions on travel, entrance fees and some goods and services. Information can be found at the ISIC site (www.isic.org).
Senior Citizens Senior citizens (usually those aged over 60) will find discounts on travel, entrance fees and some events and shows. You may be asked for proof of age.
Visitor Attractions Pass The London Pass (www.londonpass.com) covers around 55 attractions, restaurants and shops.

TRAVELLING WITH A DISABILITY

Many of the capital's sights have access for wheelchair users but transport can be a problem; not all Underground stations have lifts (elevators) and ramps. Most public houses are not adapted for wheelchairs. Go to www.visitlondon.com/maps/accessibility

CHILDREN

Always ask for reduced admission prices and family tickets. Reductions include free Tube/bus travel for children under 10 years old travelling with an adult. Details from Transport for London, www.tfl.gov.uk. Also check out what's on at www.timeout.com/london/kids.

TOILETS

You can find the cleanest toilets in department stores, hotels and restaurants,

IN TRAFFIC

The British drive on the left, so overseas visitors should always exercise caution. Even at pedestrian crossings, look right, then left, then right again!

EMBASSIES & HIGH COMMISSIONS

USA	Ireland	Australia	Canada	New Zealand
☎ 020 74 99 90 00	☎ 020 72 35 21 71	☎ 020 73 79 43 34	☎ 020 72 58 66 00	☎ 087 00 05 69 62

Street Atlas

For chapters: see inside front cover

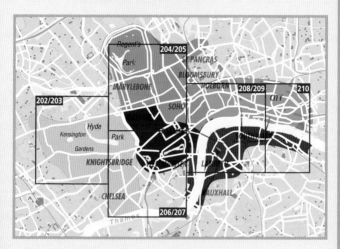

Key to Street Atlas

ℹ	Information	🚌	Bus station
M̂	Museum	✵	Police station
🎭	Theatre / Opera house	⊕	Hospital
♟	Monument	✉	Post office
✝	Church / Chappel	⊖	Underground
✡	Synagogue	🚆	Railway station
☾	Mosque		
P P	Indoor car park / Car park	★	TOP 10
⚠	Youth hostel	26	Don't Miss
☗	Radio or TV tower	22	At Your Leisure

1 : 13 000

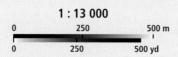

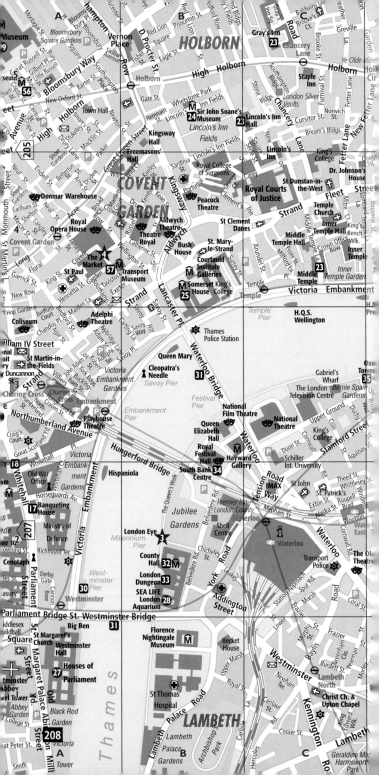

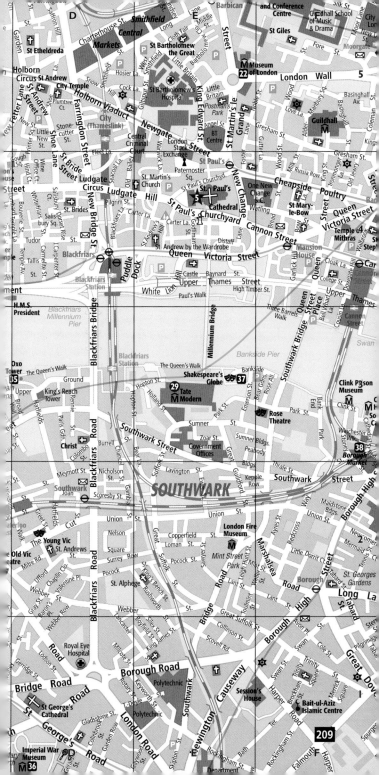

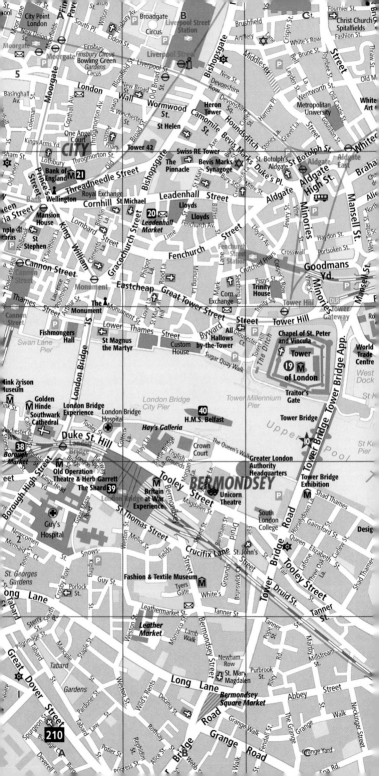

Av	Avenue
Cres	Crescent
Ct	Court
Dr	Drive
Gdns	Gardens
Pl	Place
Rd	Road
Sq	Square
St	Street
Ter	Terrace

Selected street names are not shown on the map due to scale restrictions.

A

Street	Ref
Abbey Orchard St	207 F4
Abbey St	210 C1
Abbots La	210 B2
Abingdon Rd	202 A1
Abingdon St	208 A1
Abingdon Vs	202 A1
Adam & Eve Mews	202 B2
Adam St	208 A3
Adam's Row	204 B1
Addington St	208 B2
Adeline Pl	205 F3
Adelphi Ter	208 A3
Agar St	208 A3
Air St	205 E1
Alaska St	208 C2
Albany St	204 C5
Albemarle St	205 D1
Albert Pl	202 C2
Albion Close	203 F5
Albion St	203 F5
Alder-Manbury Sq	209 F5
Alderney St	206 C2
Aldford St	204 B1
Aldgate High St	210 C4
Aldwych	208 B4
Alexander Pl	203 E1
Alexander Sq	203 E1
Alexander St	202 B5
Alfred Ms	205 E3
Alfred Pl	205 E3
Alice St	210 B1
Alie St	210 C4
Allen St	202 A2
Allington St	207 D3
Allsop Pl	204 A4
Ambrosden Av	207 D3
Angel St	209 E5
Ansdell Ter	202 B2
Aquinas St	208 C3
Archery Clo	203 F5
Argyll Rd	202 A2
Argyll St	205 D2
Arlington St	207 D5
Arne St	208 A4
Arteslan Rd	202 A5
Artillery Lane	210 C5
Artillery Row	207 E3
Arundel St	208 C4
Ashburn Gdns	202 C1
Ashley Pl	207 D3
Atherstone M	203 D1
Atterbury St	207 F2
Augustus St	205 D5
Austin Friars	210 A5
Avery Row	204 C2
Avon Pl	209 F1
Aybrook St	204 B3
Aylesford St	207 E1
Ayres St	209 F2
Ayrton Rd	203 D2

B

Street	Ref
Bainbridge St	205 F3
Baker St	204 A4
Balcombe St	204 A4
Balderton St	204 B2
Baldwins Gdns	208 C5
Balfour Pl	204 B1
Bank End	209 F3
Bankside	209 E3
Bark Pl	202 B4
Barnham St	210 B2
Baron's Pl	209 D2
Barrett St	204 B2
Barter St	208 A5
Bartholomew Clo	209 E5
Basil St	206 A4
Basinghall Av	209 F5
Basinghall St	209 F5
Bateman St	205 E2
Bath Ter	209 E1
Bathurst Ms	203 E5
Bathurst St	203 E5
Battle Bridge La	210 B3
Bayley St	205 E3
Baylis Rd	208 C1
Bayswater Rd	202 B4
Bear Gdns	209 F3
Bear St	205 F1
Beauchamp Pl	203 F1
Beaufort Gdns	203 F1
Beaumont St	204 B3
Bedford Av	205 F3
Bedford Court	208 A3
Bedford Gdns	202 A3
Bedford Row	208 B5
Bedford Sq	205 F3
Bedford St	208 A3
Bedford Way	205 F4
Beeston Pl	206 C3
Belgrave Ms N	206 B4
Belgrave Ms S	206 B3
Belgrave Ms W	206 B3
Belgrave Pl	206 B3
Belgrave Rd	206 D2
Belgrave Sq	206 B4
Bell La	210 C5
Bell Wharf La	209 F4
Belvedere Rd	208 B2
Bentinck St	204 C3
Berkeley Sq	204 C1
Bermondsey St	210 B1
Berners Ms	205 E3
Berners St	205 E3
Berwick St	205 E2
Bessborough Gdns	207 F2
Bessborough Pl	207 F1
Bessborough St	207 E2
Betterton St	208 A4
Bevis Marks	210 B5
Bickenhall St	204 A3
Bidborough St	205 F5
Billiter St	210 B4
Binney St	204 C2
Birchin La	210 A4
Birdcage Wlk	207 D4
Bishop's Bridge	202 C5
Bishopsgate	210 B4
Blackburn Mews	204 B1
Blackfriars Bridge	209 D3
Blackfriars La	209 D4
Blackfriars Rd	209 D2
Blacklands Ter	206 A2
Blandford Ms	204 B3
Blandford St	204 B3
Blenheim St	204 C2
Blomfield St	210 A5
Bloomfield Ter	206 B2
Bloomsbury Pl	208 A5
Bloomsbury Sq	208 A5
Bloomsbury St	205 F3
Bloomsbury Way	208 A5
Bolsover St	205 D4
Bolton St	207 D5
Borough High St	210 A2
Borough Rd	209 E1
Bourdon St	204 C1
Bourne St	206 B2
Bouverie St	209 D4
Bow La	209 F4
Bow St	208 A4
Boyfield St	209 E1
Boyle St	205 D1
Brad St	208 C2
Braham St	210 C4
Bray Pl	206 A2
Brd Ct	208 A4
Bread St	209 F4
Bream's Bldgs	208 C5
Bremner Rd	203 D2
Bressenden Pl	207 D3
Brewer St	205 E1
Brick St	206 C5
Bridge Pl	207 D3
Bridge Rd	209 D1
Bridge St	208 A2
Bridle La	205 E2
Bridstow Pl	202 A5
Broad Sanctuary	207 F4
Broad Wlk	204 C4
Broadbent St	204 C1
Broadway	207 E4
Broadwick St	205 E1
Brockham St	209 F1
Brompton Pl	203 F2
Brompton Rd	203 E1
Brompton Sq	203 F1
Brook Ms North	203 D4
Brook St	203 E4
Brooke St	208 C5
Brooke's Ct	208 C5
Brook's Ms	204 C2
Brown Hart Gdns	204 B2
Brown St	203 F5
Brune St	210 C5
Brunswick Ct	210 B2
Brunswick Gdns	202 B3
Brushfield St	210 C5
Bruton Lane	205 D1
Bruton Pl	204 C1
Bruton St	204 C1
Bryanston Ms E	204 A3
Bryanston Ms W	204 A3
Bryanston Sq	204 A3
Bryanston St	204 A2
Buck Hill Wlk	203 E4
Buck Pl	207 D4
Buckingham Gate	207 D4
Buckingham Palace Rd	206 C2
Buckingham St	208 A3
Bucknall St	205 F2
Budge's Wlk	203 D4
Bulmer Pl	202 A4
Bulstrode Pl	204 B3
Bulstrode St	204 B3
Burbage Clo	210 A1
Burdett St	208 C1
Burlington Arc	205 D1
Burlington Gdns	205 D1
Burrell St	209 D3
Bury Pl	208 A5
Bury St	210 B4
Byward St	210 B3
Bywater St	206 A2

C

Street	Ref
Cadogan Gate	206 A3
Cadogan Gdns	206 A2

Street Index

Cadogan Lane	206 B3	Chandos St	204 C3	Cleveland Ter	202 C5	Crutched Friars	210 C4
Cadogan Pl	206 A3	Chapel Pl	204 C2	Clifford St	205 D1	Ct Pl	202 C2
Cadogan Sq	206 A3	Chapel St	206 B4	Clink St	209 F3	Culford Gdns	206 A2
Cambridge Circus	205 F2	Chaplin Clo	209 D2	Clipstone Ms	205 D4	Culross St	204 B1
Cambridge Pl	202 C2	Chapter St	207 E2	Clipstone St	205 D3	Cumberland Gate	204 A2
Cambridge Sq	203 E5	Charing Cross Rd	205 F2	Cliveden Pl	206 B2	Cumberland	
Cambridge St	206 C2	Charles II St	205 E1	Cloak La	209 F4	Market	205 D5
Camomile St	210 B5	Charles St	204 C1	Cloth Fair	209 E5	Cumberland St	206 C2
Campden Gro	202 A3	Charlotte St	205 E3	Cock La	209 D5	Cundy St	206 C2
Campden Hill		Charlwood Pl	207 E2	Cockspur St	205 F1	Curlew St	210 C2
Gdns	202 A3	Charlwood St	207 D1	Coin St	208 C3	Cursitor St	208 C5
Campden Hill Rd	202 A2	Charterhouse St	209 D5	Cole St	209 F1	Curzon St	206 C5
Campden Hill	202 A3	Cheapside Poultry	209 F4	Coleman St	209 F5	Cutler St	210 C5
Campden Ho Clo	202 A3	Chelsea		Colinbrook St	209 D1		
Campden St	202 A3	Bridge Rd	206 B1	College St	209 F4	D	
Canning Pl	202 C2	Chelsea		Collinson St	209 E1	D Procter St	208 B5
Cannon Row	208 A2	Embankment	206 A1	Colombo St	209 D3	D'Arblay St	205 E2
Cannon St	209 F4	Cheltenham Ter	206 A2	Conduit Ms	203 D5	Dartmouth Clo	202 A5
Capper St	205 E4	Chenies Ms	205 E4	Conduit Pl	203 D5	Dartmouth St	207 E4
Caradoc Clo	202 A5	Chenies St	205 E3	Conduit St	205 D1	David Kenrick Pl	204 B3
Carburton St	205 D4	Chepstow Cr	202 A4	Connaught Pl	204 A2	Davies Mews	204 C2
Cardington St	205 E5	Chepstow Pl	202 A5	Connaught Sq	203 F5	Davies St	204 C2
Carey St	208 C4	Chesham Pl	206 B3	Connaught St	203 F5	Dawson Pl	202 A4
Carlisle La	208 B1	Chesham St	206 B3	Constitution Hill	206 C4	De Vere Gdns	202 C2
Carlisle Pl	207 D3	Chester Ms	206 C4	Conway St	205 D4	Dean Bradley St	207 F3
Carlisle St	205 E2	Chester Rd	204 C5	Cooper's Row	210 C4	Dean St	205 E2
Carlos Pl	204 C1	Chester Row	206 B2	Cope Pl	202 A1	Deanery St	206 B5
Carlton Gdns	207 E5	Chester Sq	206 C3	Copperfield St	209 E2	Dean's Yard	207 F4
Carlton House Ter	207 E5	Chester St	206 C4	Copthall Av	210 A5	Decima St	210 B1
Carmelite St	209 D4	Chester Ter	204 C5	Coptic St	205 F3	Denbigh Pl	207 D2
Carnaby St	205 D2	Chesterfield Gdns	206 C5	Coral St	208 C2	Denbigh St	207 D2
Caroline Pl	202 B4	Chesterfield Hill	204 C1	Cork St	205 D1	Denman St	205 E1
Caroline Ter	206 B2	Chesterfield St	206 C5	Cornhill	210 A4	Denmark St	205 F2
Carter La	209 E4	Cheval Pl	203 F2	Cornwall Gdns	202 C1	Denyer St	203 F1
Carteret St	207 E4	Chicheley St	208 B2	Cornwall Rd	208 C2	Derby Gate	208 A2
Carting La	208 B3	Chichester St	207 E1	Corum St	205 F4	Dering St	204 C2
Cartwright Gdns	205 F5	Chiltern St	204 B3	Cosser St	208 C1	Derra St	202 B2
Cartwright St	210 D3	Chilworth Ms	203 D5	Cottage Pl	203 E1	Devonshire Clo	204 C3
Castle Baynard St	209 E4	Chilworth St	203 D5	Cottesmore Gdns	202 C1	Devonshire Ms S	204 C3
Cathedral St		Chitty St	205 E3	Cottons La	210 B3	Devonshire Ms W	204 C4
Bedale St	210 A3	Christchurch St	206 A1	Coulson St	206 A2	Devonshire Pl Ms	204 B4
Catherine Pl	207 D4	Church Pl	205 D1	Courtnell St	202 A5	Devonshire Pl	204 B4
Catherine St	208 B4	Churchill Gdns Rd	207 D1	Covent Gdn	208 A4	Devonshire Row	210 B5
Causton St	207 F2	Churchway	205 F5	Coventry St	205 E1	Devonshire Sq	210 B5
Cavendish Pl	205 D3	Clabon Ms	206 A3	Cramer St	204 B3	Devonshire St	204 C3
Cavendish Sq	204 C2	Clanricarde Gdns	202 B4	Craven Hill Gdns	202 C4	Devonshire Ter	203 D5
Cavendish St	205 D3	Clarence Gdns	205 D5	Craven Hill Ms	203 D5	Dilke St	206 A1
Caversham St	206 A1	Clarendon Pl	203 E5	Craven Hill	203 D4	Distaff Lane	209 E4
Caxton St	207 E4	Clarendon St	207 D2	Craven Rd	203 D5	Dolphin Sq	207 E1
Cecil Court	205 F1	Clarges Ms	204 C1	Craven St	208 A3	Donne Pl	203 F1
Centaur St	208 C1	Clarges St	206 C5	Crawford St	204 A3	Doon St	208 C3
Central St	208 A5	Claverton St	207 E1	Creechurch La	210 B4	Doric Way	205 E5
Chadwick St	207 E3	Clay St	204 A3	Crispin St	210 C5	Dorset Clo	204 A4
Chagford St	204 A4	Clement's Inn	208 B4	Cromwell Rd	202 B1	Dorset Sq	204 A4
Chalton St	205 F5	Clements La	210 A4	Crosby Row	210 A2	Dorset St	204 A3
Champerdown St	210 C4	Cleveland Gdns	202 C5	Crosswall	210 C4	Douglas St	207 E2
Chancel	209 D3	Cleveland Row	207 D5	Crown Ct	208 A4	Douro Pl	202 C2
Chancery Lane	208 C5	Cleveland Sq	202 C5	Crown Office Row	208 C4	Dover St	205 D1
Chandos Pl	208 A3	Cleveland St	205 D4	Crucifix Lane	210 B2	Dowgate Hill	209 F4

Down St Mews	206 C5	Eccleston Bridge	206 C3	Fisher St	208 B5
Down St	206 C5	Eccleston Ms	206 B3	Fitzhardinge St	204 B2
D'Oyley St	206 B3	Eccleston Pl	206 C3	Fitzroy Mews	205 D4
Draycott Av	206 A2	Eccleston Sq	207 D2	Fitzroy Sq	205 D4
Draycott Pl	206 A2	Eccleston St	206 C3	Fitzroy St	205 D4
Draycott Ter	206 A2	Edgware Rd	203 F5	Flaxman Ter	205 F5
Drayson Ms	202 B2	Edwards Ms	204 B2	Fleet St	208 C4
Druid St	210 C2	Egerton Cres	203 F1	Floral St	208 A4
Drummond Cres	205 E5	Egerton Gdns	203 E1	Foley St	205 D3
Drummond Gate	207 F2	Egerton Ter	203 F1	Fore St	209 F5
Drummond St	205 D4	Eldon Rd	202 C1	Forset St	203 F5
Drury Lane	208 A5	Eldon St	210 A5	Foster Lane	209 E4
Dryden St	208 A4	Elizabeth Bridge	206 C2	Foubert's Pl	205 D2
Duchess of		Elizabeth St	206 B3	Fournier St	210 C5
Bedford's Wlk	202 A2	Ellis St	206 B3	Francis St	207 D3
Duchess St	204 C3	Elvaston M	203 D1	Frankland Rd	203 D1
Duck Ln	205 E2	Elvaston Pl	202 C1	Franklin's Row	206 A2
Dufours Pl	205 E2	Elverton St	207 E3	Frazier St	208 C1
Duke of		Emerson St	209 E3	Frith St	205 E2
Wellington Pl	206 C4	Emery Hill St	207 E3	Furnival St	208 C5
Duke of York St	205 E1	Emperor's Ga	202 C1		
Duke St Hill	210 A3	Endell St	208 A4	**G**	
Duke St	204 B2	Endsleigh Gdns	205 E4	Gainsford St	210 C2
Duke St	207 E5	Endsleigh St	205 F4	Gambia St	209 D2
Duke's La	202 B3	Enford St	204 A3	Ganton St	205 D2
Duke's Pl	210 C4	English Grounds	210 B3	Garden Row	209 D1
Duke's Rd	205 F5	Ennismore		Garlick Hill	209 F4
Duke's Yard	204 C2	Gdns Ms	203 E2	Garrick St	205 F1
Duncannon St	205 F1	Ennismore Gdns	203 E2	Garway Rd	202 B5
Durham Ter	202 B5	Ennismore Gdns	203 E2	Gate St	208 B5
Durweston St	204 A3	Ennismore Ms	203 E2	Gatliff Rd	206 C1
Dyott St	205 F2	Erasmus St	207 F2	Gaywood St	209 E1
		Essex St	208 C4	Gdns Cadogan	206 A3
E		Essex Villas	202 A2	Gdns Pembroke	202 A4
Eagle St	208 B5	Esterbr St	207 E2	Gdns Sq	202 B5
Earlham St	205 F2	Euston Rd	205 F5	Gdns Ter	202 B3
Earls Court Rd	202 A1	Euston St	205 E5	Gdns Victoria St	207 D3
Earl's Wlk	202 A1	Euston Station		George St	203 F5
Earnshaw St	205 F2	Colonnade	205 E5	George St	204 A2
Easley's Ms	204 C2	Euston Underpass	205 D4	George Yard	204 B2
East Stanhope St	205 D5	Evelyn Yard	205 E3	Geraldine St	209 D1
East Tenter St	210 D4	Eversholt St	205 E5	Gerrard St	205 E1
Eastbourne Ms	203 D5	Ewer St	209 E2	Gerridge St	209 D1
Eastbourne Ter	203 D5	Exeter St	208 A4	Gilbert Pl	205 A5
Eastcastle St	205 D2	Exhibition Rd	203 E1	Gilbert St	204 C2
Eastcheap	210 B4	Exton St	208 C2	Gillingham St	207 D2
Eaton Gate	206 B3			Giltspur St	209 E5
Eaton Ms North	206 B3	**F**		Gladstone St	209 D1
Eaton Ms South	206 C3	Fair St	210 C2	Glasgow Ter	207 D1
Eaton Ms West	206 B3	Farm St	204 C1	Glasshouse St	205 E1
Eaton Pl	206 B2	Farmer St	202 A3	Glentworth St	204 A4
Eaton Sq S	206 B3	Farringdon St	209 D5	Gloucaster	
Eaton Sq	206 B3	Fashion St	210 C5	Ms West	202 C5
Eaton Ter	206 B2	Fenchurch Av	210 B4	Gloucester Ct	210 B3
Ebury Bridge Rd	206 C1	Fenchurch St	210 B4	Gloucester Ms	203 D5
Ebury Bridge	206 C2	Fetter Lane	208 C4	Gloucester Pl M	204 A3
Ebury Ms	206 C3	Finsbury Av	210 A5	Gloucester Pl	204 A3
Ebury Sq	206 C2	Finsbury Circus	210 A5	Gloucester Rd	202 C1
Ebury St	206 B2	First St	203 F1	Gloucester Sq	203 E5

Gloucester St	207 D1
Gloucester Ter	202 B5
Gloucester Wlk	202 A3
Godliman St	209 E4
Golden Sq	205 E1
Goodge St	205 E3
Goodmans Yd	210 C4
Gordon Pl	202 A3
Gordon Sq	205 F4
Gordon St	205 E4
Gore St	203 D1
Gosfield St	205 D3
Gough Sq	208 C5
Goulston St	210 C5
Gower Mews	205 F3
Gower Pl	205 E4
Gower St	205 E4
Gr Windmill St	205 E1
Gracechurch St	210 A4
Grafton M	205 D4
Grafton St	205 D1
Grafton Way	205 D4
Graham Ter	206 B2
Grange Ct	208 B4
Grange Rd	210 B1
Grange Wlk	210 B1
Grange Yard	210 C1
Grape St	208 A5
Gravel La	210 C5
Gray St	209 D2
Gray's Inn Sq	208 C5
Great Castle St	205 D2
Great Central St	204 A4
Great Chapel St	205 E2
Great College St	207 F3
Great Cumberland	
Pl	204 A2
Great Dover St	210 A1
Great George St	207 F4
Great Guildford St	209 E3
Great Marlborough	
St	205 D2
Great Maze Pond	210 A2
Great Peter St	207 E3
Great Portland St	205 D3
Great Pulteney St	205 E2
Great Queen St	208 A4
Great Russell St	205 F3
Great	
Scotland Yd	208 A3
Great Smith St	207 F4
Great Suffolk St	209 E2
Great	
Titchfield St	205 D3
Great Tower St	210 B4
Great	
Winchester St	210 A5
Greek St	205 F2
Green St	204 B2

Street Index

Greencoat Pl	207 E3	
Greenham Clo	208 C1	
Greenwell St	205 D4	
Greet St	209 D2	
Grenville Pl	202 C1	
Gresham St	209 F4	
Gresse St	205 E3	
Greville St	208 C5	
Greycoat Pl	207 E3	
Greycoat St	207 E3	
Groom Pl	206 C4	
Grosvenor Cr Ms	206 B4	
Grosvenor Cres	206 B4	
Grosvenor Gdns	206 C3	
Grosvenor Hill	204 C1	
Grosvenor Pl	206 C4	
Grosvenor Rd	207 D1	
Grosvenor Sq	204 B1	
Grosvenor St	204 C1	
Guildhouse St	207 D2	
Gutter La	209 F5	
Guy St	210 A2	

H

Half Moon St	206 C5	
Halkin St	206 B4	
Hallam St	205 D3	
Hallfield Estate	202 C5	
Halsey St	203 F1	
Hamilton Pl	206 C5	
Hampstead Rd	205 D5	
Hanover Sq	205 D2	
Hanover St	205 D2	
Hans Cres	206 A4	
Hans Pl	206 A3	
Hans St	206 A3	
Hanson St	205 D3	
Hanway St	205 E3	
Harewood Pl	205 D2	
Harley Pl	204 C3	
Harley St	204 C3	
Harper Rd	209 F1	
Harriet Wlk	206 A4	
Harrington Rd	203 D1	
Harrington St	205 D5	
Harrow Pl	210 C5	
Harrowby St	203 F5	
Hasker St	203 F1	
Hatfields	209 D3	
Hatherley Gro	202 B5	
Hatton Garden	209 D5	
Hay Hill	205 D1	
Haydon St	210 C4	
Haymarket	205 E1	
Hays La	210 B3	
Hay's Ms	204 C1	
Headfort Pl	206 B4	
Heddon St	205 D1	
Heneage St	210 D5	

Henrietta Pl	204 C2	
Henrietta St	208 A4	
Herbrand St	205 F4	
Hercules Rd	208 C1	
Hereford Rd	202 A5	
Herrick St	207 F2	
Hertford St	206 C5	
Hide Pl	207 E2	
High Holborn	208 A5	
High St	209 F2	
High Timber St	209 E4	
Hill Notting Gate	202 A4	
Hill St	204 C1	
Hillgate Pl	202 A3	
Hillgate St	202 A3	
Hind Ct	209 D4	
Hinde St	204 B2	
Hobart Pl	206 C3	
Holbein Ms	206 B2	
Holbein Pl	206 B2	
Holborn Circus	209 D5	
Holborn Viaduct	209 D5	
Holland St	202 A2	
Holland St	209 E3	
Holland Wlk	202 A2	
Holles St	204 C2	
Hop Gdns	205 F1	
Hopkins St	205 E2	
Hopton St	209 E3	
Horbura Cr	202 A4	
Hornton Pl	202 B2	
Horriton St	202 A3	
Horriton St	202 B2	
Horse Guards	207 F5	
Horse Ride	207 E5	
Horseferry Rd	207 E3	
Horseguards Av	208 A2	
Horselydown La	210 C2	
Hosier La	209 D5	
Houndsditch	210 B5	
Howick Pl	207 E3	
Howland St	205 D3	
Hungerford Bridge	208 B3	
Hungerford La	208 A3	
Huntley St	205 E3	
Huntsworth M	204 A4	
Hyde Park Corner	206 B4	
Hyde Park Cr	203 E5	
Hyde Park Gate	202 C2	
Hyde Park		
Gdns Ms	203 E5	
Hyde Park Gdns	203 E4	
Hyde Park Sq	203 E5	
Hyde Park St	203 E5	

I

Ilchester Gdns	202 B4	
Imperial		
College Rd	203 D1	

Ingestre Pl	205 E2	
Inner Circle	204 B4	
Inver Pl	202 C4	
Inverness Ter	202 C5	
Ironmonger La	209 F4	
Irving St	205 F1	
Iverna Ct	202 B2	
Iverna Gdns	202 B2	
Ivybridge Lane	208 A3	

J

J Prince's St	205 D2	
JCarpenter St	209 D4	
James St	204 B2	
Jameson St	202 A3	
Jay Ms	203 D2	
Jermyn St	205 D1	
Jewry St	210 C4	
Joan St	209 D2	
Jockey's Fields	208 B5	
John Adam St	208 A3	
John Islip St	207 F2	
Johnson's Pl	207 D1	

K

Kean St	208 B4	
Keeley St	208 B4	
Kelso Pl	202 B1	
Kemble St	208 B4	
Kendal St	203 F5	
Kennington Rd	208 C1	
Kens Ch Wlk	202 B2	
Kensington		
Church St	202 A3	
Kensington Court	202 C2	
Kensington Ct	202 B2	
Kensington Gate	202 C2	
Kensington		
Gdns Sq	202 B5	
Kensington Gore	203 D2	
Kensington		
High St	202 A2	
Kensington		
Palace Gdns	202 B3	
Kensington Pl	202 A3	
Kensington Rd	202 C2	
Kepple Row	209 E2	
Keyworth St	209 E1	
Kildare Gdns	202 B5	
Kildare Ter	202 B5	
King Charles St	207 F4	
King Edward St	209 E5	
King Edward Wlk	208 C1	
King James St	209 E1	
King St	207 E5	
King William St	210 A4	
King's Bench St	209 E2	
Kingly St	205 D2	
Kings Arms Yd	210 A5	

King's Bench Wlk	208 C4	
Kings Head	210 A2	
King's Rd	206 A2	
King's Scholar's		
Pass	207 D3	
Kinnerton St	206 B4	
Kipling St	210 A2	
Knightsbridge	206 A4	
Knox St	204 A3	
Kynance Ms	202 C1	

L

Lafone St	210 C2	
Lamb Wlk	210 B1	
Lambeth		
Palace Rd	208 B1	
Lancaster Gate	203 D4	
Lancaster Ms	203 D4	
Lancaster Pl	208 B4	
Lancaster St	209 D1	
Lancaster Ter	203 D4	
Lancaster Wlk	203 D3	
Lancelot Pl		
Langham Pl	205 D3	
Langham St	205 D3	
Langley St	205 F2	
Lansdowne Row	204 C1	
Lant St	209 E2	
Launceston Pl	202 C1	
Laurence		
Pountney La	210 A4	
Lavington St	209 E2	
Law St	210 A1	
Leadenhall St	210 B4	
Leake St	208 B2	
Leathermarket St	210 B2	
Ledbury Rd	202 A5	
Lees Pl	204 B2	
Leicester Court	205 F1	
Leicester Pl	205 F1	
Leicester Sq	205 F1	
Leicester St	205 F1	
Leigh Hunt St	209 E2	
Leinster Gdns	202 C5	
Leinster Ms	202 C4	
Leinster Pl	202 C5	
Leinster Sq	202 B5	
Leinster Ter	202 C4	
Lennox Gdns	203 F1	
Lewisham St	207 F4	
Lexham Gdns	202 B1	
Lexham M	202 B1	
Lexington St	205 E2	
Leyden St	210 C5	
Lime St	210 B4	
Lincoln's Inn		
Fields	208 B5	
Linden Gdns	202 A4	
Linden Palace	202 A4	

Lindsey St 209 E5
Lion Hill 209 E4
Lisle St 205 F1
Little Britain 209 E5
Little Chester St 206 C4
Little Dorrit Ct 209 F2
Little George St 207 F4
Little New St 209 D5
Little Russell St 208 A5
Little Sanctuary 207 F4
Little Portland St 205 D3
Liverpool St 210 B5
Livonia St 205 E2
Lloyd's Av 210 C4
Lodson St 209 D1
Logan Pl 202 A1
Loman St 209 E2
Lombard St 210 A4
London Bridge St 210 A3
London Bridge 210 A3
London Gate 206 B1
London Ms 203 E5
London Rd 209 E1
London St 203 D5
London Wall 209 F5
Long Acre 208 A4
Long Lane 209 E5
Longford St 205 D4
Longmoore St 207 D2
Lothbury 210 A4
Lovat La 210 B3
Love La 209 F5
Lovers' Wlk 204 C1
Lower Belgrave St 206 C3
Lower Grosvenor
  Pl 206 C3
Lower Marsh 208 C1
Lower Sloane St 206 B2
Lower Thames St 210 A3
Lowndes Pl 206 B3
Lowndes Sq 206 A4
Lowndes St 206 B3
Ludgate Circus 209 D4
Ludgate Hill 209 D4
Lupus St 206 C1
Lupus St 207 D1
Luxborough St 204 B4
Lyall St 206 B3

M

Macklin St 208 A5
Maddox St 205 D2
Magdalen St 210 B2
Maiden La 208 A3
Maidstone Bdgs 209 F2
Malet St 205 E4
Maltby St 210 C1
Manchester Sq 204 B2
Manchester St 204 B3

Manciple St 210 A1
Mande-Ville Pl 204 B2
Mansell St 210 C4
Mansfield St 204 C3
Maple St 205 D4
Marble Arch 204 A2
Margaret St 205 D2
Margaret St 207 F4
Mark Lane 210 B4
Market Ms 206 C5
Market Pl 205 D2
Marlborough Rd 207 E5
Marloes Rd 202 B1
Marshall St 205 D2
Marshalsea Rd 209 F2
Marsham St 207 F3
Martlett Court 208 A4
Marylebone
  High St 204 B3
Marylebone Lane 204 B2
Marylebone Rd 204 A3
Marylebone St 204 B3
Mason's Yard 207 E5
Mat Parker St 207 F4
Maunsel St 207 E3
Mayfair Pl 205 D1
McLeod's Ms 202 C1
Medway St 207 E3
Melbury Ct 202 A2
Melcombe St 204 A4
Melior St 210 B2
Melton St 205 E5
Mepham St 208 C2
Mercer St 208 A4
Mermaid Ct 209 F2
Merrick Sq 209 F1
Meymott St 209 D2
Middle St 209 E5
Middle Temple La 208 C4
Middlesex St 210 C5
Midland Rd 205 F5
Milcote St 209 D1
Milford La 208 C4
Milk St 209 F4
Millbank 207 F2
Millstream St 210 C1
Milner St 203 F1
Mincing La 210 B4
Minories 210 C4
Mint St 209 E2
Mitre Ct 208 C4
Mitre Rd 209 D2
Mitre St 210 C4
Monck St 207 F3
Monmouth Rd 202 B5
Monmouth St 205 F2
Montagu Ms N 204 A3
Montagu Ms W 204 A3
Montagu Ms 204 A3

Montagu Pl 204 A3
Montagu Row 204 A3
Montagu Sq 204 A3
Montagu St 204 A2
Montague Pl 205 F3
Montague St 205 F3
Montpelier Pl 203 F2
Montpelier Sq 203 F2
Montpelier St 203 F2
Montpelier Wlk 203 F2
Montrose Pl 206 B4
Monument St 210 A3
Moor Lane 209 F5
Moore St 206 A3
Moorfields 210 A5
Moorgate 210 A5
Moorhouse Rd 202 A5
Moreton Pl 207 E2
Moreton St 207 E2
Moreton Ter 207 E2
Morgan's La 210 B2
Morley St 208 C1
Morpeth Ter 207 D3
Morrocco St 210 B1
Mortimer St 205 D3
Morwell St 205 F3
Moscow Rd 202 B4
Mossop St 203 F1
Motcomb St 206 B4
Mount Row 204 C1
Mount St 204 B1
Moxon St 204 B3
Munster Sq 205 D4
Murphy St 208 C1
Museum St 208 A5

N

Nassau St 205 D3
Neal St 205 F2
Neathouse Pl 207 D3
Needham Rd 202 A5
Nelson Sq 209 D2
New Bond St 204 C2
New Brd St 210 B5
New Bridge St 209 D4
New Burlington Pl 205 D2
New Burlington St 205 D1
New Cavendish St 204 B3
New Change 209 E4
New Compton St 205 F2
New Fetter Lane 208 C5
New Oxford St 208 A5
New Ride 203 F2
New Row 208 A4
New Sq 208 C5
New St 209 D5
New St 210 B5
New Union St 210 A5
Newcombe St 202 A4

Newcomen St 210 A2
Newgate St 209 E5
Newham Row 210 B1
Newham Ter 208 C1
Newington
  Causeway 209 E1
Newman St 205 E3
Newport Court 205 F2
Newton Rd 202 B5
Newton St 208 A5
Nicholson St 209 D2
Noble St 209 E5
Noel St 205 E2
Norfolk Crescent 203 F5
Norfolk Pl 203 E5
Norfolk Sq 203 E5
North Audley St 204 B2
North Crescent 205 E3
North Gower St 205 D5
North Ride 203 E4
North Row 204 B2
North Tenter St 210 C4
North Wlk 203 D4
Northumberland
  Avenue 208 A3
Northumberland
  Pl 202 A5
Northumberland
  St 208 A3
Norwich St 208 C5
Notting Hill 202 A4
Nottingham Pl 204 B4
Nottingham St 204 B3
Nutford Pl 203 F5

O

Observ Gdns 202 A3
Old Bailey 209 D4
Old Bond St 205 D1
Old BRd St 210 A4
Old Burlington St 205 D1
Old Castle St 210 C5
Old Cavendish St 204 C2
Old Compton St 205 E2
Old Jewry 209 F4
Old Palace Yd 208 A1
Old Park La 206 C5
Old Quebec St 204 A2
Oldbury Pl 204 B4
Orange St 205 F1
Orchard St 204 B2
Orme Ct 202 B4
Orme La 202 B4
Ormonde Gate 206 A1
Orsett Ms 202 C5
Orsett Ter 202 C5
Ossington St 202 B4
Ossulston St 205 F5
Osten Ms 202 C1

Street Index

Outer Circle 204 B4
Ovington Gdns 203 F1
Ovington Sq 203 F1
Ovington St 203 F1
Oxendon St 205 E1
Oxford Circus 205 D2
Oxford Sq 203 F5
Oxford St 204 B2

P

Paddington St 204 B3
Page St 207 F3
Palace Avenue 202 B3
Palace Court 202 B4
Palace Gate 202 C2
Palace Gdns Ms 202 B4
Palace Green 202 B3
Palace St 207 D3
Palace 207 D4
Pall Mall East 205 F1
Pall Mall 207 E5
Palmer St 207 E4
Pan-Ton St 205 E1
Paradise Wlk 206 A1
Pardoner St 210 A1
Paris Gdn 209 D3
Park Cr Ms East 204 C4
Park Crescent 204 C4
Park Lane 204 A1
Park Lane 206 B5
Park Rd 202 B5
Park Rd 204 A4
Park Sq E 204 C4
Park Sq W 204 C4
Park St 204 B1
Park St 209 E3
Park St 209 F3
Park West Pl 203 F5
Parker St 208 A5
Parliament Sq 207 F4
Parliament St 207 F4
Passmore St 206 B2
Pater St 202 A1
Paternoster Sq 209 E4
Paul's Wlk 209 E4
Pavilion Rd 206 A3
Peabody Av 206 C1
Peabody Bldgs 209 E3
Peak Pl 207 D5
Pearman St 208 C1
Peel St 202 A3
Pelham St 203 E1
Pembridge Cr 202 A4
Pembridge Ms 202 A4
Pembridge Pl 202 A4
Pembridge Rd 202 A4
Pembridge Sq 202 A4
Pembridge Villas 202 A5
Pembroke Close 206 B4

Pembroke
  Gdns Clo 202 A1
Pembroke Gdns 202 A1
Pembroke Rd 202 A1
Pembroke Sq 202 A1
Pembroke Wlk 202 A1
Pepys St 210 C4
Percy St 205 E3
Peter St 205 E2
Petersburgh Ms 202 B4
Petersham La 202 C1
Petersham M 202 C1
Petersham Pl 202 C1
Peto Pl 204 C4
Petty France
  Broadw 207 E4
Phil-Gdns Clo 202 A2
Phillimore Gdns 202 A2
Phillimore Pl 202 A2
Phillimore Wlk 202 A2
Philpot La 210 B4
Phoenix Rd 205 E5
Piccadilly Circus 205 E1
Piccadilly 205 D1
Picton Pl 204 B2
Pilgrim St 209 D4
Pilgrimage St 210 A1
Pimlico Rd 206 B2
Pitt St 202 A2
Pitt's Head Ms 206 C5
Plumtree Ct 209 D5
Pocock St 209 D2
Poland St 205 E2
Policeman's Wlk 203 F4
Pollen St 205 D2
Ponsonby Pl 207 F2
Ponsonby Ter 207 F2
Pont St 206 A3
Pope St 210 C1
Poplar Pl 202 B4
Porchester Gdns 202 B5
Porchester Pl 203 F5
Porchester Rd 202 B5
Porchester Sq 202 C5
Porchester St 203 E5
Porchester Ter N 202 C5
Porchester Ter 202 C4
Porlock St 210 A2
Porter St 204 A3
Portland Pl 204 C3
Portman Clo 204 B2
Portman Ms 204 B2
Portman Sq 204 B2
Portman St 204 B2
Portsea Pl 203 F5
Portsoken St 210 C4
Portugal St 208 B4
Potier St 210 A1
Praed St 203 E5

Prescot St 210 C4
Prince Consort Rd 203 D2
Prince of Wales
  Ter 202 C2
Prince's Gdns 203 E2
Prince's Ms 202 B4
Princes St 205 D2
Prince's St 210 A4
Prince's Ter Pl 202 B4
Princeton St 208 B5
Printer Sq 209 D5
Providence Court 204 B2
Puddle Dock 209 D4
Purbrook St 210 C1

Q

Queen Anne St 204 C3
Queen Anne's
  Gate 207 E4
Queen Elizabeth
  St 210 C2
Queen St Pl 209 F4
Queen St 206 C5
Queen St 209 F4
Queen Victoria St 209 E4
Queen's Garden 202 C5
Queen's Gate
  Gdns 202 C1
Queen's Gate Gds 203 D1
Queen's Gate Ms 202 C2
Queen's Gate Ms 203 D2
Queen's Gate
  Pl M 203 D1
Queen's Gate Pl 203 D1
Queen's Gate Ter 203 D2
Queen's Gate 203 D2
Queen's Mews 202 B4
Queen's Wlk 207 D5
Queensborough
  Ter 202 C4
Queensway 202 B4

R

R Adam St 204 B3
Radnor Pl 203 E5
Railway App 210 A3
Ralston St 206 A1
Ramillies St 205 D2
Rampayne St 207 E2
Ranelagh Gro 206 B2
Raphael St 203 F2
Rathbone Pl 205 E3
Rathbone St 205 E3
Rawlings St 203 F1
Rd Chepstow 202 A5
Red Lion Sq 208 B5
Red Lion St 208 B5
Red Pl 204 B2
Redan Pl 202 B5

Redcross Way 209 F2
Rede Pl 202 A5
Redfield La 202 B1
Redhill St 205 D5
Reeves Ms 204 B1
Regency St 207 F2
Regent St 205 D2
Remnant St 208 B5
Rennie St 209 D3
Rephidim St 210 B1
Rex Pl 204 B1
Richmond Mews 205 E2
Richmond Ter 208 A2
Ridgmount Gdns 205 E4
Ridgmount St 205 E3
Riding House St 205 D3
Riley Rd 210 C1
Robert St 205 D5
Robert St 208 A3
Rochester Row 207 E3
Rockingham St 209 E1
Rodmarton St 204 A3
Romilly St 205 F2
Romney St 207 F3
Rood La 210 B4
Ropemaker St 210 A5
Rose All 209 F3
Rotary St 209 D1
Rothsay St 210 B1
Rotten Row 203 F3
Rotten Row 206 A5
Roupell St 208 C2
Row Kingsway 208 B5
Royal Avenue 206 A2
Royal Hospital Rd 206 A1
Royal St 208 B1
Rupert St 205 E2
Rushworth St 209 E2
Russel St 208 B4
Russell Sq 205 F4
Russia Row 209 F4
Rutherford St 207 E3
Rutland Gate 203 F2
Ryder St 207 D5

S

S Edwardes Sq 202 A1
Sackville St 205 D1
Saffron Hill 209 D5
Salisbury Dorset
  Rise Ct 209 D4
Salisbury Sq 209 D4
Sandwich St 205 F5
Sardinia St 208 B4
Savile Row 205 D1
Savoy Hill 208 B3
Savoy Pl 208 B3
Savoy St 208 B3
Savoy Way 208 B3

Sawyer St	209 E2	South Ter	203 E1	St Swithins La	210 A4	T
Scala St	205 E3	South Wharf Rd	203 E5	St Thomas St	210 B2	T-Doyle St	209 E1
Scarborough St	210 C4	SouthampSt	208 A4	St Vincent St	204 B3	Tabard St	209 F2
Scarsdale Pl	202 B2	Southampton		St Martins Court	205 F1	Tachbrook St	207 E2
Scarsdale Vs	202 A1	Bldgs	208 C5	Stable Yd	207 D5	Talbot Rd	202 A5
Scoresby St	209 D2	Southampton Pl	208 A5	Stafford Pl	207 D4	Tallis St	209 D4
Scovell Rd	209 E1	Southwark		Stafford St	205 D1	Tanner St	210 B2
Seacoal La	209 D4	Bridge Rd	209 E1	Stafford Ter	202 A2	Tavistock Pl	205 F4
Sedley Pl	204 C2	Southwark		Stag Pl	207 D3	Tavistock St	208 A4
Seething La	210 B4	Bridge	209 F3	Stamford St	208 C3	Taviton St	205 E4
Semley Pl	206 C2	Southwell Gdns	202 C1	Stanford Rd	202 C1	Tedworth Sq	206 A1
Serle St	208 C5	Southwick St	203 E5	Stanhope Gate	206 B5	Temple Av	209 D4
Serpentine Rd	203 E3	Spa Rd	210 C1	Stanhope Gdns	203 D1	Temple La	209 D4
Serpentine Rd	206 B5	Spenser St	207 D3	Stanhope Hyde		Temple Pl	208 C4
Seymour Ms	204 B2	Spring Gdns	207 F5	Pk Gdns	203 E4	Tennis St	210 A2
Seymour Pl	204 A3	Spring St	203 D5	Stanhope M E	203 D1	Tension Way	208 C2
Seymour St	203 F5	Spur Rd	208 C2	Stanhope M W	203 D1	Ter Craven	203 D4
Seymour St	204 A2	Spur Rd	207 D4	Stanhope Pl	203 F5	Terminus Pl	207 D3
Shad Thames	210 C2	Spurgeon St	210 A1	Stanhope Ter	203 E4	Thackeray St	202 B2
Shaftesbury		Sq Kensington	202 B2	Staple St	210 A1	Thanet St	205 F5
Avenue	205 E1	Sq Prince's	202 B4	Starcross St	205 E5	Thayer St	204 B3
Shand St	210 B2	St Alban's Gro	202 C2	Station Approach	208 C2	The Brd Wlk	202 C3
Sheffield Ter	202 A3	St Alban's St	205 E1	Stephen Mews	205 E5	The Cut	209 D2
Sheldrake Pl	202 A2	St Andrew St	209 D5	Stephen St	205 E3	The Dial Wlk	202 C3
Shelton St	208 A4	St Andrew's Hill	209 E4	Sterry St	210 A1	The Flower Wlk	203 D2
Shepherd St	206 C5	St Annes Ct	205 E2	Stillington St	207 E3	The Grange	210 C1
Sherwood St	205 E1	St Ann's St	207 F3	Stone Bldgs	208 C5	The Mall	207 F5
Shoe La	209 D5	St Anselm's Pl	204 C2	Stonecutter St	209 D5	The Queen's Wlk	209 D3
Short Gdns	205 F2	St Barnabas St	206 B2	Stoney La	210 C5	The Ring (West
Short Gdns	208 A4	St Botolph St	210 C4	Stoney St	209 F3	Carriage Dr)	203 E4
Shrewsbury Rd	202 A5	St Bride St	209 D4	Store St	205 E3	Theed St	208 C2
Sicilian Avenue	208 A5	St Cadogan	206 A2	Storey's Gate	207 F4	Thirleby Rd	207 E3
Silex St	209 E1	St George St	205 D2	Strand	208 A3	Thornton Pl	204 A3
Skipton St	209 E1	St George's Dr	207 D2	Stratford Pl	204 C2	Thrale St	209 F2
Sloane Ct East	206 B2	St George's Fields	203 F5	Stratford Rd	202 A1	Thraw St	210 C5
Sloane Ct West	206 B2	St George's Rd	209 D1	Stratton St	205 D1	Threadneedle St	210 A4
Sloane Gdns	206 B2	St George's		Stratton St	207 D4	Three Barrels Wlk	209 F3
Sloane Sq	206 B2	Sq Ms	207 E1	Streatham St	205 F3	Three King's Yd	204 C1
Sloane St	206 A3	St George's Sq	207 E1	Strutton Grnd	207 E3	Three Oak La	210 C2
Smart's St	208 A5	St Giles High St	205 F2	Stukeley St	208 A5	Throgmorton Av	210 A5
Smith Sq	207 F3	St James St	208 A4	Suffolk St	205 F1	Throgmorton St	210 A4
Smith St	206 A2	St James's Pl	207 D5	Suffolk St	207 D1	Thurloe Pl	203 E1
Smith Ter	206 A1	St James's Sq	207 E5	Sugar Quay Wlk	210 B3	Tilney St	206 B5
Smithfield St	209 D5	St James's St	207 D5	Sumner Bldgs	209 E3	Tite St	206 A1
Snow Hill	209 D5	St Katherine's		Sumner St	209 E3	Tooley St	210 A3
Snowsfields	210 A2	Way	210 D3	Sunderland Ter	202 B5	Tor Gdns	202 A3
Soho Sq	205 E2	St Leonhard's		Surrey Row	209 D2	Toria Gro	202 C2
Somers Ms	203 E5	Ter	206 A1	Surrey St	208 B4	Torrington Pl	205 E4
South Audley St	204 B1	St Margaret's La	202 B1	Sussex Gdns	203 E5	Torrington Sq	205 F4
South Carriage Dr	203 E2	St Martin's		Sussex Pl	203 E5	Tothill St	207 F4
South Carriage Dr	206 B4	le Grand	209 E5	Sussex Pl	204 A4	Tottenham
South Crescent	205 E3	St Martin's L	205 F2	Sussex Sq	203 E5	Court Rd	205 E4
South End Row	202 B2	St Martin's St	205 F1	Sussex St	207 D1	Tottenham St	205 E3
South End St	202 B2	St Mary at Hill	210 B3	Sutherland Pl	202 A5	Toulmint St	209 E2
South Molton La	204 C2	St Mary Axe	210 B4	Sutherland St	206 C2	Tower Bridge App	210 C3
South Molton St	204 C2	St Mary's Pl	202 B1	Sutton Row	205 F2	Tower Bridge Rd	210 C2
South Pl	210 A5	St Paul's		Swallow St	205 E1	Tower Bridge	210 C3
South St	204 B1	Churchyd	209 E4	Swan St	209 F1	Tower Hill	210 C3
South Tenter St	210 C4	St Petersburgh	202 B4	Symons St	206 A2	Toynbee St	210 C5

Street Index

Trafalgar Sq	205 F1	Vere St	204 C2	West Eaton Pl	206 B3
Travistock Sq	205 F4	Vernon Pl	208 A5	West Halkin St	206 B4
Trebeck St	206 C5	Vicarage Gate	202 B3	West Ms	204 C4
Trevor Pl	203 F2	Vicarage Gdns	202 B3	West Rd	206 A1
Trevor Sq	203 F2	Victoria		West Smithfield	209 E5
Trinity Sq	209 F1	Embankment	208 A2	West St	205 F2
Trinity St	209 F1	Victoria Gdns	202 A4	West Tenter St	210 C4
Tudor St	209 D4	Victoria Gro	202 C2	Westbourne Cres	203 D5
Tufton St	207 F3	Victoria Rd	202 C2	Westbourne Gdns	202 B5
Turks Row	206 A2	Villiers St	208 A3	Westbourne Grove	202 B5
Turpentine La	206 C1	Vincent Sq	207 E2	Westbourne St	203 D4
Tyers Gate	210 B2	Vincent St	207 F2	Westbourne Ter	203 D5
		Vine St	210 C4	Westminster	
U				Bridge	208 A2
Ufford St	209 D2	**W**		Westmoreland Pl	207 D1
Underpass		Walpole St	206 A2	Westmoreland St	204 C3
Piccadilly	206 C5	Walton St	203 F1	Westmoreland Ter	206 C1
Union St	209 D2	Wardour Ms	205 E2	Weston St	210 A1
University St	205 E4	Wardour St	205 E2	Weymouth Mews	204 C3
Up Belgrave St	206 B4	Warren Mews	205 D4	Weymouth St	204 C3
Up Berkeley St	204 A2	Warren St	205 D4	Whetstone Park	208 B5
Up Brook St	204 B1	Warwick House St	207 F5	Whitcomb St	205 F1
Up Grosvenor St	204 B1	Warwick La	209 E5	White Horse St	206 C5
Up Ground	208 C3	Warwick Row	207 D4	White Lion Hill	209 E4
Up Ground	209 D3	Warwick Sq	207 D2	Whitechapel	
Up Harley St	204 C4	Warwick St	205 D1	High St	210 C5
Up Marsh	208 B1	Warwick Way	206 C2	Whitefriars St	209 D4
Up Montagu St	204 A3	Waterloo Bridge	208 B3	Whitehall Ct	208 A2
Up Thames St	209 E4	Waterloo Pl	207 E5	Whitehall Pl	208 A2
Up Wimpole St	204 C3	Waterloo Rd	208 C2	Whitehall	207 F5
Upbrook Ms	203 D5	Watling St	209 F4	White's Grounds	210 B2
Upper Woburn Pl	205 F4	Waverton St	204 C1	White's Row	210 C5
Upr Phillimore		Webber Row	209 D1	Whitfield St	205 E3
Gdns	202 A2	Webber St	209 D2	Whittlesey St	208 C2
Uxbridge St	202 A3	Weighhouse St	204 C2	Wigmore Pl	204 C3
		Welbeck St	204 C2	Wigmore St	204 B2
V		Welbeck Way	204 C3	Wild Ct	208 B4
Valentine Pl	209 D2	Weller St	209 E2	Wild St	208 A4
Varndell St	205 D5	Wellington St	208 B4	Wild's Rents	210 B1
Vauxhall Bridge		Wells St	205 D3	Wilfred St	207 D4
Rd	207 D3	Well's Way	203 D2	William IV St	208 A3
Vauxhall Bridge	207 F1	Wentworth St	210 C5	William Ms	206 A4
William Rd	205 D5				
Wilton Cres	206 B4				
Wilton Ms	206 C4				
Wilton Pl	206 B4				
Wilton Rd	207 D3				
Wilton Row	206 B4				
Wilton St	206 C4				
Wilton Ter	206 B4				
Wimpole Ms	204 C3				
Wimpole St	204 C3				
Winchester St	207 D2				
Winchester Wlk	209 F3				
Windmill St	205 E3				
Windmill Wlk	208 C2				
Wine Office Ct	209 D4				
Winsland Ms	203 D5				
Winsland St	203 D5				
Winsley St	205 D2				
Woburn Pl	205 F4				
Woburn Sq	205 F4				
Wood St	209 F4				
Woodfall St	206 A1				
Woods Ms	204 B1				
Woodstock St	204 C2				
Wootton St	208 C2				
Wormwood St	210 B5				
Wright's Lane	202 B2				
Wyndham St	204 A3				
Wythburn Pl	204 A2				
Y					
Yeoman's Row	203 F1				
York Bdgs	208 A3				
York Gate	204 B4				
York Rd	208 B2				
York St	204 A3				
York Ter E	204 B4				
York Ter W	204 B4				
Young St	202 B2				
Z					
Zoar St	209 E3				

218

Index

A

accommodation 37–40
Admiral's House 189
Admiralty Arch 58
afternoon tea 42
airport
    city transfers 34–35
airports 34–35, 197
Albert Memorial 137
All Hallows-by-the-Tower 194
antiques 44
art galleries, commercial
    44–45
ATMs (automated cash
    machines) 197
auction houses 44

B

Bank of England 183
Bank of England Museum
    31, 86, 182
banks 197, 198
Bankside Power Station
    95, 97
Banqueting House 62
Barbican Centre 92
bars, pubs 12–13, 42, 66,
    91, 117, 141, 166
The Beatles 26, 31, 144, 152
bed & breakfast 37
Beefeaters 85
HMS *Belfast* 115
Before You Go 196
Berkeley Square 178
Bermondsey Market 31
bicycles 36
Big Ben 11, 104, 106
Blitz 16
Bloomsbury 147
Bloomsbury Group 27
blue plaque scheme 24–27
Bond Street & New Bond Street
    68, 177
Borough Market 31, 45, 114
British Film Institute London
    IMAX Cinema 118
British Library 31, 158–159
British Museum 31, 154–157
Buckingham Palace 21,
    52–53
Burgh House 190, 191
Burlington Arcade 61, 176
Burlington House 60, 176
buses 36
bus trip (Marble Arch to Tower
    of London) 192–194

C

Camden Lock Village 160
Camden Markets 31, 45, 160
Camden Town 24
canal trips 161

Canary Wharf tower 185
car hire 36
Carnaby Street 67, 167
Carnaval del Pueblo 14
Cartoon Museum 163
Cenotaph 63
Changing of the Guard
    (London) 50, 59
Changing of the Guard
    (Windsor) 173
Charing Cross Road 167
Charing Cross station 193
Chelsea 25–26
Cheyne Walk 8
children's activities
    Art Detectives tour
        (National Gallery) 57
    British Museum 155
    Cartoon Museum 163
    Changing of the Guard 59
    Diana, Princess of Wales
        Memorial Fountain 138
    General Information 200
    Harrods (pet department)
        130
    HMS *Belfast* 115
    Knights and Princesses Trail
        (Tower of London) 85
    Legoland Windsor 174
    London Duck Tour (river
        trips) 110
    London Dungeon 112
    London Eye 101
    London Transport Museum
        163
    London Zoo 161
    Madame Tussauds 152
    National History Museum
        134, 136
    Science Museum 132
    SEA LIFE London Aquarium
        105
    Serpentine lake 138
    street entertainers 150
    Tower Bridge lifting 79
    toy shops 61, 63, 192
    V&A Museum 129
    Whispering Gallery (St
        Paul's Cathedral) 75
    Xstrata Treetop Walkway
        171
Chinatown 42, 162–163
Chinese New Year 14
Chiswick House 21
church concerts 30, 87
Churchill War Rooms 60
Churchill, Winston 25
cinema 46, 68, 118, 168
The City
    walk 180–183
Clarence House 58
classical music 46

climate and seasons 196,
    200
Clock Museum 182
clubs 45, 68, 144, 168
Cockneys 182
Columbia Road Flower Market
    92
Comedy Store 68
concessions 200
congestion charging 37
Constable, John 56, 102,
    188–191
Coronation Chair 100
County Hall 111–112
Courtauld Gallery 89
Covent Garden 145,
    150–151, 167
credit/debit cards 197
crime 199
currency 197
Cutty Sark 184, 187

D

dance 168
da Vinci, Leonardo 55
dental services 200
department stores 44
Design Museum 115
Diana, Princess of Wales 74,
    124–125, 138
Diana, Princess of Wales
    Memorial Fountain 21,
    138, 139
Dickens, Charles 25, 88, 98,
    99, 194
disabilities, travellers with
    200
Docklands 187
Docklands Light Railway (DLR)
    36, 187
Downing Street 63
drinking water 200
driving 36–37, 196
drugs & medicines 200
Duck Tours 110

E

eating out 41, 64–66,
    90–91, 116–117,
    140–141, 164–166
Eid in the Square 15
Eleanor Cross 193
electricity 198
Elgin Marbles 155
Elizabeth II, Queen 172
Elizabeth, the Queen Mother
    58, 82
embassies & high
    commissions 200
emergency telephone numbers
    199
Engels, Friedrich 27

Index

entertainment 45–46, 68, 92, 118, 144, 168
Eros 192
Eton College 174
excursions
    Kew 170–171
    Windsor 172–174

F
famous Londoners 24
Fan Museum 186
fashion 44
Fenton House 21, 189, 191
ferries 197
festivals 14–15
financial institutions 180
fish & chips 43
Fleet Street 193
football 28–29
foreign exchange 197
Forster, E. M. 27
Fortnum & Mason 64, 67, 176
free attractions 30
Freemasons Arms 190
Fry, Roger 27

G
Gabriel's Wharf 118
Gatwick Airport 34
Gaulle, Charles de 27
The Gherkin (30 St Mary Axe) 19, 181
Globe Theatre 114, 118
Gog and Magog 182
grand hotels 37
Gray's Inn 88
Great Fire of London 16–17, 70, 74, 76, 112, 180
Green Park 22, 58
Greenwich 31, 184–187
Greenwich Observatory 31, 186–187, 187
Greenwich Park 186 23
Grosvenor Square 178
Guildhall 182–183

H
Ham House 21
Hamleys toy shop 61, 67, 192
Hampstead 24, 188–191
Hampstead Heath 22, 190
Handel House Museum 179
Harrods 44, 122, 130, 142
Harvey Nichols 44, 142
Haymarket 192
Hayward Gallery 112
health 196, 200
Heathrow Airport 34
Hendrix, Jimi 179

Henry VII Chapel, Westminster Abbey 98
Highgate Cemetery 27
Holland Park 22
Holland Park Theatre 144
Horse Guards Parade 48, 58
hotels 37–40
Houses of Parliament 11, 104, 106–107
Hyde Park 21, 138

I
Imperial War Museum 113
Inner Temple 87
Inns of Court 87–88
    Gray's Inn 88
    Inner Temple 87
    Lincoln's Inn 87
    Middle Temple 87
insurance 200
internet access 199
Islington 24–25

J
jazz venues 30, 32
Jermyn Street 61, 67

K
Keats House 190, 191
Keats, John 25, 190–191
Kensington Church Street 143
Kensington Gardens 138
Kensington High Street 143
Kensington Palace 124–125
Kenwood House 22, 191
Kew 170–171
Keynes, John Maynard 27
The King's Road 142
Knightsbridge 142
Kyoto Japanese Garden 23

L
Lawrence, D. H. 25
Leadenhall Market 86, 181
Legoland Windsor 174
Lenin, Vladimir Ilyich 27
Lennon, John 26
Liberty 44, 61, 67, 192
Lincoln's Inn 87
Little Venice 160
Lloyd's Building 18, 180
London Bridge 180
London City Airport 35
London Dungeon 112
London Eye 101
London Film Museum 111
London IMAX Cinema 118
London Pass 37, 200
London Silver Vaults 31
London Transport Museum 163
London Zoo
    (ZSL London Zoo) 161

M
Madame Tussauds 152–153
The Mall 58–59
Mansion House 183
Marble Arch 192
markets 31, 45, 86, 92, 114, 139, 143, 160, 167
Marx, Karl 27
Mayfair 176–179
Middle Temple 87
Millennium Bridge 108
mobile phones 199
The Monument 180, 183, 194
Museum of London 86–87
music venues 30, 32, 45, 68, 92, 118, 144

N
Napoleon III 26
Nash, John 17, 59, 61, 160
National Gallery 31, 54–56, 59, 193
National Gardens Scheme 22
national holidays 198
National Maritime Museum 23, 186, 187
National Portrait Gallery 62
Natural History Museum 18, 134–136
Neal's Yard 151
New Year's Day Parade 14
Nightingale, Florence 25
Notting Hill Carnival 15

O
The O2 arena 45, 185
Old Royal Naval College 184, 187
Old Vic 118
Ono, Yoko 26
open-air theatre 23, 45, 144, 160
opening hours 198
Opera 46, 168
Orwell, George 24
Oxford Street 67
Oxo Tower 112
Oxo Tower Wharf 118

P
Pall Mall 58
parks and gardens 20
Parliament Hill 22, 191
passports and visas 196
Pepys, Samuel 87, 88
personal safety 199
Peter Pan statue 138
Petticoat Lane 92
pharmacies 198, 200
photography 198
Piccadilly 30, 60, 67
Piccadilly Circus 61, 192

Plath, Sylvia 24
Poets' Corner 98–99
police 199
Portobello Road 31, 45, 139
post offices 199
Prime Meridian 184
Princess of Wales 74
The Proms (Henry Wood
  Promenade Concerts)
  46, 144
public transport 35–36
pubs, bars 12–13, 42, 66,
  91, 117, 141, 166

Q
Queen Mary's Dolls' House
  173
Queen's Gallery 53
Queen's House 186–187
Queen Victoria Memorial 52

R
rail services 35, 36, 197
Ranger's House 186, 187
Regent's Canal 160
Regent's Park 23, 160
Regent Street 44, 60, 67,
  192–194
RHS Chelsea Flower Show
  22
river trips 110
road safety 200
Roman amphitheatre 182
Ronnie Scott's Jazz Club
  32, 45
Rosetta Stone 154
Roundhouse 32, 45, 168
Royal Academy of Arts 60
Royal Albert Hall 45, 144
Royal Court 144
Royal Courts of Justice 193
Royal Exchange 182
Royal Festival Hall 45, 112,
  118
Royal Mews 53
Royal National Theatre 46,
  118
Royal Observatory 23,
  185–187
Royal Opera House 150

S
Saatchi Gallery 137
Savile Row 61, 67, 177
Science Museum 131–133
SEA LIFE London Aquarium
  105
Selfridges 44, 67–68, 192
senior citizens 200
Serpentine Gallery 138
Shakespeare 114
  Globe Theatre 114, 118

The Shard (30 Tower Bridge)
  11, 115
Shepherd Market 178
shopping 44–45, 67–68, 92,
  118, 142, 167
sightseeing buses 36
Sir John Soane's Museum 88
Sloane Square 142–143
Sloane Street 142
smoking 198
Soho 145, 167
Somerset House 89
Sotheby's 44, 179
South Bank 96
Southbank Centre 30, 112
Speakers' Corner 21, 138
Spitalfields Market 31, 92
Stables Market 160
Stansted Airport 34
State Apartments, Windsor
  Castle 172
State Opening of Parliament
  104
State Rooms, Buckingham
  Palace 52–53
St Bartholomew the
  Great 17
St Botolph-without-
  Bishopsgate 17
St Bride's Church 111
St Ethelburga 17
St George's Chapel,
  Windsor 173
St George's Church 179
St Helen Bishopsgate 17,
  182, 183
St James's Palace 58
St James's Park 21, 58–59
St James's, Piccadilly 30, 47,
  176–179
St John's Church 188
St Martin-in-the-Fields 41,
  59, 193
St Mary-le-Bow 182–183
St Olave's 87
St Patrick's Day 15
St Paul's Cathedral 74–75,
  194
Strand 111, 193
students 200

T
Tate Britain 31, 102–103
Tate Modern 31, 108–109
taxis 36
telephones 199
Temple Church 87
Thames Barrier 11
Thames, River 10–11
theatre 46, 68, 92, 118,
  144, 168
ticket outlets 46

time 197, 198
tipping 198
toilets 200
tourist information 37, 196
Tower 42 111
Tower Bridge 78–81
Tower Bridge Exhibition 79
Tower Green 83
Tower of London 82–85, 194
Trafalgar Square 30, 58–59
Traitors' Gate 84–85
Travelcards and bus passes
  35–36
travellers' cheques 197
Turner, J. M. W 56, 102

U
Underground (The Tube) 35

V
V&A (Victoria and Albert)
  Museum 31, 126–129
visitor passes 37, 200

W
walks
  The City 180–183
  Greenwich 184
  Hampstead 188
  Mayfair squares 176–179
Wallace Collection 162
Waterloo Bridge 111
websites 196
Wells, H. G. 25
Wembley Stadium 28
Westminster 96
Westminster Abbey 98–100
Westminster Bridge 111
Whispering Gallery 75
Whitehal 63
WiFi 199
Wilde, Oscar 25–26
Windsor 172–174
Windsor Castle 172–174
Woolfe, Leonard 27
Woolf, Virginia 27
Wren, Sir Christopher
  17, 23, 74, 75, 76, 124,
  176, 180, 183

X
Xstrata Treetop Walkway 171

Y
Yeats, W. B. 24
Ye Olde Cheshire Cheese 91
Young Vic 118
youth hostel 37–38

Z
ZSL London Zoo 161

Picture Credits

Credits

1st Edition 2015

Worldwide Distribution: Marco Polo Travel Publishing Ltd
Pinewood, Chineham Business Park
Crockford Lane, Chineham
Basingstoke, Hampshire RG24 8AL, United Kingdom.
© MAIRDUMONT GmbH & Co. KG, Ostfildern

Authors: Lesley Reader, Fiona Dunlop, Elizabeth Carter,
Birgit Weber
Editor: Frank Müller, Anja Schlatterer, Anette Vogt
(red.sign, Stuttgart)
Revised editing and translation: Sarah Trenker
Program supervisor: Birgit Borowski
Chief editor: Rainer Eisenschmid

Cartography: © MAIRDUMONT GmbH & Co. KG, Ostfildern
3D-illustrations: jangled nerves, Stuttgart

Printed in China

Despite all of our authors' thorough research, errors can creep in.
The publishers do not accept any liability for this. Whether you
want to praise, alert us to errors or give us a personal tip –
please don't hesitate to email or post:

MARCO POLO Travel Publishing Ltd
Pinewood, Chineham Business Park
Crockford Lane, Chineham
Basingstoke, Hampshire RG24 8AL
United Kingdom
Email: sales@marcopolouk.com

FSC
www.fsc.org
MIX
Paper from
responsible sources
FSC® C020056

10 REASONS
TO COME BACK AGAIN

1. Come rain or shine – London offers something for everyone **whatever the weather**.

2. The list of **free museums** is so long that one visit to London is not enough

3. A **boat trip along the Thames** always reveals different facets of the town

4. Not all hustle and bustle – London's **quiet corners** call out to be discovered.

5. You need time for all the **markets, outlandish shops** and **shopping temples**.

6. This town provides a **tasty menu for every budget**: eat elegantly or snack swiftly:

7. Theatre, concerts, cinema, sport, festivals – there are lots of **culture and leisure activities**.

8. Pub life or Champagne bar – **night owls** can hoot all night in London.

9. London's **skyline** changes at breathtaking pace. Come and see for yourself!

10. **Opposites do attract** – tradition und subculture live here in a perfect symbiosis.